DAILY LIFE IN

The Progressive Era

Recent Titles in
The Greenwood Press Daily Life Through History Series

Science and Technology in Modern European Life
Guillaume de Syon

Cooking in Europe, 1650–1850
Ivan P. Day

Victorian England, Second Edition
Sally Mitchell

The Ancient Greeks, Second Edition
Robert Garland

Chaucer's England, Second Edition
Jeffrey L. Forgeng and Will McLean

The Holocaust, Second Edition
Eve Nussbaum Soumerai and Carol D. Schulz

Civil War in America, Second Edition
Dorothy Denneen Volo and James M. Volo

Elizabethan England, Second Edition
Jeffrey L. Forgeng

The New Americans: Immigration since 1965
Christoph Strobel

The New Inuit
Pamela R. Stern

The Indian Wars
Clarissa W. Confer

The Reformation
James M. Anderson

The Aztecs, Second Edition
Davíd Carrasco and Scott Sessions

DAILY LIFE IN

The Progressive Era

STEVEN L. PIOTT

The Greenwood Press Daily Life Through History Series

Daily Life in the United States
Randall M. Miller, Series Editor

 GREENWOOD

AN IMPRINT OF ABC-CLIO, LLC
Santa Barbara, California • Denver, Colorado • Oxford, England

Library of Congress Cataloging-in-Publication Data

Piott, Steven L.
   Daily life in the progressive era / Steven L. Piott.
      p. cm. — (Daily life through history series. Daily life in the United States)
   Includes bibliographical references and index.
   ISBN 978-0-313-38184-3 (hardcopy : alk. paper) — ISBN 978-0-313-38185-0
(ebook) 1. United States—History—1865–1921. 2. United States—Social
conditions—1865–1918. 3. United States—Politics and government—
1865–1933. 4. Progressivism (United States politics) I. Title.
   E661.P63   2011
   973.8—dc22   2011013353

ISBN: 978-0-313-38184-3
EISBN: 978-0-313-38185-0

15 14 13 12 11   1 2 3 4 5

This book is also available on the World Wide Web as an eBook.
Visit www.abc-clio.com for details.

Greenwood
An Imprint of ABC-CLIO, LLC

ABC-CLIO, LLC
130 Cremona Drive, P.O. Box 1911
Santa Barbara, California 93116-1911

This book is printed on acid-free paper ∞

Manufactured in the United States of America

To Margaret Piott

Contents

Series Foreword

The books in the *Daily Life in the United States* series form a subset of Greenwood Press's acclaimed, ongoing *Daily Life Through History* series. They fit its basic framework and follow its format. This series focuses on the United States from the colonial period through the present day, with each book in the series devoted to a particular time period, place, or people. Collectively, the books promise the fullest description and analysis of "American" daily life in print. They do so, and will do so, by tracking closely the contours, character, and content of people's daily lives, always with an eye to the sources of people's interests, identities, and institutions. The books in the series assume the perspective and use the approaches of the new social history by looking at people "from the bottom up" as well as the top-down. Indian peoples and European colonists, blacks and whites, immigrants and the native-born, farmers and shopkeepers, factory owners and factory hands, movers and shakers, and those moved and shaken—all get their due. The books emphasize the habits, rhythms, and dynamics of daily life, from work to family matters, to religious practices, to socializing, to civic engagement, and more. The books show that the seemingly mundane—such as the ways any people hunt, gather, or grow food and then prepare and eat it—as much as the more profound reflections on life reveal how and why people ordered their world and gave meaning to their lives. The books treat the external factors shaping people's lives—war, migration, disease, drought, flood, pest infestations, fires, earthquakes, hurricanes, and tornados, and other natural and man-made disasters that disrupted and even shattered daily lives— but they understand that the everyday concerns and routines of life also powerfully define any people. The books therefore go inside homes, workplaces, schools, churches, meeting halls, stores, and other gathering places to find people on their own terms.

Capturing the daily life of Americans poses unique problems. Americans have been, and are, a people in motion, constantly changing as they move across the land, build new communities, invent new products and processes, and experiment with everything from making new recipes to making new governments. A people always in the process of becoming does not stand still for examination of their most private lives. Then, too, discovering the daily life of the diverse American peoples requires expertise in many disciplines, for few people have left full-bodied written accounts of their prosaic but necessary daily activities and habits, and many people have left no written record at all. Thus, the scholars writing the books in the series necessarily borrow from such fields and resources as archaeology, anthropology, art, folklore, language, music, and material culture. Getting hold of the daily life in the United States demands no less.

Each book at once provides a narrative history and analysis of daily life, set in the context of broad historical patterns. Each book includes illustrations, documents, a chronology, and a bibliography. Thereby, each book invites many uses as a resource, a touchstone for discussion, a reference, and an encouragement to further reading and research. The titles in the series also promise a long shelf life because the authors draw on the latest and best scholarship and because the books are included in Greenwood's Daily Life Online, which allows for enhanced searching, updated content, more illustrative material, teacher lesson plans, and other Web features. In sum, the *Daily Life in the United States* series seeks to bring the American people to life.

Randall M. Miller

Prologue

The intent of this book and of others in the *Daily Life Through History* series is to examine a historical period using the approach of the new social history that looks at people from the bottom up as well as from the top down. This particular volume is set in the Progressive Era, loosely defined as starting in the 1890s and coming to an end around 1920. The emphasis is on the habits and rhythms of daily life—living, working, playing, and interacting with one another in both rural and urban society and in white and black America. It is often the everyday actions of individuals—how they engaged themselves in their roles as farmers, workers, consumers, and citizens—as well as the more profound reflections they had on their lives at a given moment that reveal much about a period and its people. This volume is an attempt to show how people during the Progressive Era tried to give some order to their world and some meaning to their lives.

The period from the 1890s to 1920 was the time when modern America was really born. The world of small, family farms and sparsely populated settlements was giving way to a modern society of giant corporations, huge factories, and densely populated cities. Industrialization, urbanization, and external and internal migrations set society hurtling toward an uncertain future. The force of change seemed irresistible and affected virtually every aspect of

American life. The transformation of society toward the modern necessitated social and economic adjustments, and caused a great deal of personal trauma in the process.

Such was certainly the case for many of America's farmers. Farmers were caught in a dilemma. On the one hand, they were being enticed by the world of modern consumption and pushed toward an acceptance of urban standards of culture, taste, and style. Yet on the other hand, they remained ambivalent about the modern world. They worried about the corrupting influences of the city, and were leery of the economic and political bigness and organization that seemed to be so much a part of urban industrial life. These modernizing forces seemed to threaten the way of life they knew and wished to maintain. In more isolated regions of rural America, commercial development in the form of coal, timber, and textiles threatened old cultures. In the face of the emergence of company towns and regimented work routines, rural inhabitants resisted. They clung to preindustrial work habits, regarded the new jobs as a form of supplementary income, and refused to become rooted in what seemed like an alien environment. As the out-migration of younger people from the farms of the nation's heartland to the city continued to quicken its pace, and as agricultural productivity seemed to level off, various groups of urban reformers tried to impose their modern ideas on rural America in a largely unsuccessful attempt to make rural life more meaningful and farming more efficient and productive.

The tendency toward bigness, centralization, and integration in industrial America brought about not only changes in the ways factories operated at the top, but also in the way work was done at the bottom. The introduction of new technology accelerated the division of labor, diminished the importance of skill, and reduced the sense of autonomy and control that workers had over the production process. Job insecurity increased as a result. As the work process evolved in the direction of the assembly line, work became increasingly repetitive and dehumanizing. As scientific managers sought to overturn worker-controlled rules and systematize jobs for greater efficiency, workers resisted. They quit, they went on strike, and they organized in an attempt to use the collective power of the union to protect their interests. Eventually, various reform groups sought to win protections for workers in areas of wages, hours, health, and safety through legislation, and they initiated legal challenges to the doctrine of freedom of contract that had long blocked state interference in labor matters. The culmination of these efforts, achieved by the time of America's entry into World War I, was the enactment of federal legislation to restrict child labor, provide workmen's compensation, and set maximum hours for certain workers. Legally, the courts accepted the idea that the law should evolve in relation to social need and upheld labor demands long denied. By 1917 both the government and the courts had come to accept a degree of responsibility for human welfare.

The Progressive Era also witnessed a shift from the rather staid and traditional Victorian culture to a more vigorous mass culture, a reaction to both the enervating tendencies of modern life and the earlier period's emphasis on moralizing, self-control, and refinement. The new cultural emphasis was characterized by a shift in popular temperament toward a new hedonistic vitality. Where the earlier Victorian culture had celebrated a value system that emphasized hard work ("producerism"), self-sacrifice, and delayed gratification, the new, modern culture offered a different creed of immediate gratification and personal physical and psychological fulfillment through consumption. Stressing instant gratification, advertisers helped shift the Victorian emphasis on saving to an emphasis on spending as they constantly urged Americans to give in to the desire for consumption. Part of this new consumer culture involved new forms of recreational activity made possible by increased leisure time. This included the rise of urban spectator sports, the fascination with more vigorous forms of music such as ragtime and jazz, and the popularity of new forms of entertainment such as dance halls, motion pictures, and amusement parks. These new forms of recreation helped to define generational differences and allowed for a redrawing of cultural boundaries based on gender.

The rise of big business generated suspicions regarding concentrated economic and political power. When consumers confronted declining quality of municipal services, sharp price increases, or evidence that they were consuming unhealthful food or drugs, they increasingly suspected that corporate consolidation (trust formation) was to blame. In response, they supported the idea of municipal ownership, boycotted, and joined organizations that demanded that the federal government impose regulations. Voters developed similar suspicions. As society wrestled with the harsh realities that accompanied rapid urban and industrial growth, many felt increasingly ignored as participants in the political system. It seemed as though policymakers identified issues and established priorities in a political environment increasingly susceptible to the influence of

economic power. Issues that were of particular concern to workers, farmers, consumers, and taxpayers were ignored; elected representatives seemed no longer to represent their interests. Many
Americans looked to alter the existing situation and increasingly
suggested that expanding the parameters of popular democracy
was the way to do it. Some advocated granting the vote to women;
others favored enlarging the nominating process through the direct
primary or passing legislation to allow for the direct election of U.S.
senators; still others supported a more direct form of democracy
through the initiative, referendum, and recall. These economic and
political responses suggested that individuals, through their own
daily life experiences, were developing a new sense of citizen activism and sharpening their definition of the "public interest" in the
process.

Tensions based on class, ethnicity, and especially race intensified under the strain of transition to the modern and raised questions about equality, inclusion, status, and quality of life. Racism
increased during this period as culturally sanctioned attitudes of
white supremacy contributed to the further subjugation of nonwhites through social segregation, economic discrimination, and
mob violence. For the vast majority of black Americans, the Progressive Era meant disenfranchisement and intensified racial segregation in the South and the North. But African Americans did not
simply resign themselves to accept prejudice and discrimination.
They protested and, when those protests failed, relied on families,
churches, schools, community organizations, and music to foster group self-reliance and contest white supremacy. Some joined
W.E.B. Du Bois in the NAACP and demanded full equality; others
allied with Marcus Garvey and promoted black nationalism, black
capitalism, and black separatism. When faced with increased racial
violence in the form of lynchings and race riots immediately after
World War I, blacks fought back. Some found in that response the
expression of a new black spirit, perhaps connected to black participation in the military during the war. Some black intellectuals
began to speak of a new race consciousness and to identify a "New
Negro" type—bolder, more confident, more conscious of his rights,
and more determined to preserve them regardless of the cost.

It has been said that World War I was both a triumph and a tragedy for American society. The war stimulated patriotism and created a new sense of national purpose. The Wilson administration
used idealistic rhetoric to tap into a vibrant reform spirit to connect
the reform crusade at home to a war for progressive aims abroad.

As a result, the war became a great moral undertaking. But as the government launched campaigns to mobilize men, money, industry, and agriculture as well as various preparedness and propaganda campaigns, it generated a nationalistic spirit that it could not control. American society became more reactive and repressive. Steps were taken to suppress dissent and impose restrictions on speech and opinion. "Patriotism" and "Americanism" became sharply contested ideals. The social harmony that characterized America's entry into World War I came to an end in 1919 with runaway inflation, a wave of labor strikes, race riots, and the Red Scare. To many, it seemed as if America had "entered a frightening new terrain of diversity and change in which there lurked a thousand threats to the older orthodoxies."[1] It was a mood that would set a defensive tone for the 1920s.

NOTE

1. George Brown Tindall, *America: A Narrative History* (New York: W. W. Norton, 1984), 985.

Chronology

Pullman Strike in Chicago

Boll weevil crosses the Rio Grande into Texas

1895   Booker T. Washington gives "Atlanta Compromise" speech

1896   U.S. Supreme Court decides *Plessy v. Ferguson* and "separate but equal" principle

National Association of Colored Women founded

New York Journal creates the modern sports page

Eltweed Pomeroy organizes the National Direct Legislation League

1898   Spanish American War

Scott Joplin writes "Maple Leaf Rag"

South Dakota becomes the first state to adopt the initiative and referendum

Charlotte Perkins Gilman's *Women and Economics* published

1899   Thorstein Veblen's *The Theory of the Leisure Class* published

National Consumers' League founded

1900   Theodore Dreiser's *Sister Carrie* published

St. Louis Streetcar Strike

1901   Frank Norris's *The Octopus* published

Leon Czolgosz assassinates President William McKinley; Theodore Roosevelt becomes president

1902   Owen Wister's *The Virginian* published

Missouri Supreme Court conducts hearings on the Beef Trust

Harvey W. Wiley creates the "Poison Squad" to study food adulteration

1903   Wright Brothers make first powered flight in a heavier-than-air machine at Kitty Hawk, North Carolina

W.E.B. Du Bois's *The Souls of Black Folk* published

First World Series played (Boston Red Sox defeat Pittsburgh Pirates)

Jack London's *The Call of the Wild* published

S. S. McClure announces a new type of journalism (later known as muckraking)

Edwin S. Porter demonstrates the commercial potential of films with *The Great Train Robbery*

National Women's Trade Union League founded

1904   Sociologist Robert Hunter's *Poverty* published

Louisiana Purchase Exposition held in St. Louis

Theodore Roosevelt reelected president

1905   Niagara Movement formed

Thomas Dixon's *The Clansman* published

First nickelodeon opens for business

Samuel Hopkins Adams begins exposé on the patent medicine industry

1906   Upton Sinclair's *The Jungle* published

Pure Food and Drug Act enacted

Federal Meat Inspection Act enacted

Atlanta Race Riot

Brownsville, Texas, Race Riot

1907   Boy Scouts of America founded

President Roosevelt creates the Country Life Commission

1908   U.S. Supreme Court decides *Muller v. Oregon*

Henry Ford introduces the Model T

Springfield, Illinois, Race Riot

U.S. Supreme Court decides in Danbury Hatters Case that labor unions are subject to antitrust laws

Ash Can School of painters holds New York exhibition

William Howard Taft elected president

1909   National Association for the Advancement of Colored People organized

1910   Jack Johnson defeats Jim Jeffries in racially charged heavyweight boxing match

Los Angeles Times building bombed

1911   Triangle Shirtwaist Fire kills 146 workers

Statehood for Arizona vetoed by President Taft because of recall provision

Frederick W. Taylor's *The Principles of Scientific Management* published

McNamara Brothers Trial

1912   Lawrence, Massachusetts, Strike

Progressive (Bull Moose) Party formed

Woodrow Wilson elected president

1913   Income Tax (Sixteenth Amendment) enacted

Direct Election of Senators (Seventeenth Amendment) enacted

George Bellows's "Cliff Dwellers" appears

National American Woman Suffrage Association stages massive suffrage parade in Washington, D.C.

Alice Paul forms Congressional Union (later the National Woman's Party)

New York Armory Show of European modernism held

1914–1920   Great Migration

1914   Henry Ford introduces the assembly line

Marcus Garvey founds the Universal Negro Improvement Association

World War I begins in Europe

Clayton Antitrust Act enacted

1915   D. W. Griffith's *The Birth of a Nation* opens

Leo Frank lynched

Ku Klux Klan revived by William J. Simmons

Lusitania sunk by German U-boat; 128 Americans killed

1916   Woodrow Wilson reelected president; Keating-Owen (child labor) Act enacted

1917   U.S. enters World War I (April 6)

Selective Service Act enacted

First Liberty Loan drive launched

Committee on Public Information created

Espionage Act enacted

National Civil Liberties Bureau organized

Bolshevik Revolution in Russia

East St. Louis Race Riot

Houston Race Riot

David Graham Phillips's *Susan Lenox* published

Alice Paul's National Woman's Party begins to picket the White House demanding the vote for women

1918 Sedition Act enacted

Influenza pandemic

World War I ends (November 11)

1919 Seattle General Strike

Boston Police Strike

Chicago Race Riot

Great Steel Strike

Prohibition (Eighteenth Amendment) enacted

U.S. Senate rejects Treaty of Versailles

1919–1920 Red Scare

1920 Woman Suffrage (Nineteenth Amendment) enacted

League of Women Voters founded

"Black Sox" Scandal

Palmer Raids

Federal census reveals shift in population from farms to cities

1

Rural America

THE COMMERCIALIZATION OF AGRICULTURE

Rural America expanded dramatically during the last three decades of the nineteenth century. The number of farms, number of acres of farmland, and total value of farm property all doubled during the period. Farmers increasingly focused their attention on the cultivation of specialized cash crops for market, a process fueled by industrialization and urbanization that provided them with an expanding pool of consumers. Farmers on the Great Plains grew most of the country's wheat; those in the Midwest raised corn; southerners cultivated cotton, tobacco, and rice; and farmers in the far West grew grains, fruits, and vegetables. As farming became a business, success often depended on outside agents. Bankers and loan companies supplied capital to expand farm operations, and middlemen stored or marketed produce.

   In the two decades following the completion of the first transcontinental railway in 1869, the developing national railway network gave a tremendous boost to western settlement and drew the region's farmers into national and international markets. Settlers poured into Colorado and New Mexico, for example, in the 1870s on the heels of railroad expansion, and quickly transformed the region's economy and culture. Previously, the area's economy had been defined by Mexican farm families who followed both subsistence and communal farming and herding practices, and allowed the community to regulate shared common lands. Under the pressure of westward expansion and economic development, that system quickly yielded to a flood of private homesteaders who pursued commercial farming and cattle and sheep raising that was directly connected to the new rail system and to distant markets. By 1889 nearly 72,000 miles of track had been laid west of the Mississippi River linking farms to outside markets.

As farmers became increasingly market oriented, they eagerly used modern machinery to increase their production. Mechanical harvesters, binders, reapers, and other new machines performed more and more of the work. Working by hand, a lone farmer could cultivate about seven acres of wheat—roughly the amount he could reap during the 10 days or so when the grain was at its peak. Using an automatic binder to cut and tie the wheat into bundles, the same farmer could, by 1890, plant and harvest 135 acres or roughly 20 times his original output. The use of machines allowed the farmer to cultivate more land, but machinery was expensive, and many farmers had to borrow money to buy it. During the 1880s mortgage indebtedness grew two-and-a-half times faster than agricultural wealth. Although the small family farm remained the norm in the late nineteenth century, giant mechanized "bonanza" wheat farms had begun to appear in the Dakotas, parts of Kansas and Nebraska, and in California by the late 1870s, a phenomenon that provided the setting for Frank Norris's novel *The Octopus* (1901). By 1900 the average farm in the Dakotas measured 7,000 acres. Contractors and migratory crews served many of the larger ranches, and there was much use of seasonal labor in which ethnic minorities played a large role. Absentee landlords—often eastern investors or western speculators—owned many of these giant farms. Soon, grain elevators and giant grain silos became new landmarks of the shift to commercial farming and suggested the increasing control that financial capitalists and the new commodities exchanges were beginning to exercise. Such operations symbolized the tendency toward large-scale agriculture.

As farmers cultivated more land with the help of modern technology, they soon became victims of their own success. Farm productivity increased 40 percent between 1869 and 1899, and almost every crop registered gains in productivity. Yields for crops such as wheat were so large that the domestic market was unable to absorb them. Accompanying the expansion in productivity was a general decrease in farm prices. Corn, which had sold for 78 cents a bushel in 1867, had dropped to 23 cents by 1889. Wheat fell from

$2 a bushel in 1867 to only 70 cents in 1889. The first boom period
of settlement started around 1879 and lasted for roughly a decade,
as tens of thousands of families moved onto the Great Plains and
began farming. Paying no heed to the warnings of scientists such
as John Wesley Powell, whose famous *Report on the Lands of the
Arid Region of the United States* (1879) argued that the great variabil-
ity of rainfall from year to year made farming in the West a risky
business without adequate irrigation systems, restless westward-
looking farmers saw only a new Garden of Eden. Writer Hamlin
Garland remembered the excitement that possessed many of his
Iowa neighbors in 1881.

The movement of settlers toward Dakota had now become an exodus,
a stampede. Hardly anything else was talked about...Every man who
could sell out had gone west or was going.... Farmer after farmer joined
the march to Kansas, Nebraska, and Dakota. "We are wheat raisers," they
said, "and we intend to keep in the wheat belt."[1]

Some established claims under the Homestead Act of 1862, others
purchased land, and others rented because they lacked the necessary capital to purchase land and begin operations. In 1880 approximately one-fifth of farmers on the Great Plains and one-fourth of
farmers nationally were tenants or renters. By the end of the century, the national figure would increase to one-third.

By the late 1880s and early 1890s, the first boom on the Great
Plains had come to an end. Declining farm prices had reduced profits. The overabundant rainfall that had lured many farmers toward
the 100th meridian abruptly stopped. Terrible droughts followed.
Many farmers who had relied on easy credit to sustain their operations found that they had accumulated debts that they could not
repay. Thousands lost their farms to creditors. Some stayed on as
tenants, but many gave up and returned east. The population of
western Kansas fell by 50 percent between 1888 and 1892. A common slogan was "In God We Trusted: In Kansas We Busted." The
persistent problems of declining farm prices and mounting debts
were the primary factors pushing many hard-pressed farmers to
join the Farmers' Alliance and later the Populist Party as organized
forms of agrarian protest during this period.

In trying to capture the lives of the poor, weary figures who struggled with life on the prairie in the late 1880s and early 1890s, Garland wrote two collections of starkly realistic stories, *Main-Travelled
Roads* (1891) and *Prairie Folks* (1893). In each, he tried to describe
the overworked, hopeless farmers who the frontier has defeated.

Returning to South Dakota for a family reunion after having lived for several years in the East, Garland was shocked by the drabness, isolation, and drudgery of prairie farming. "I looked at the barren landscape," he said, "where every house had its individual message of sordid struggle and half-hidden despair. All the gilding of farm life melted away. The hard and bitter realities came back upon me in a flood." In describing one of the literary characters he created as a representation of the type of individual he had encountered while growing up on the plains, Garland noted that he lived in an unpainted, three-room cabin and "toiled on from year to year without any clearly defined idea of the future. His life was mainly regulated from without." The main business of such people, Garland bitterly noted, was "to work hard, live miserably, and beget children to take their places when they died." But as one author has noted, "Even though Garland's farmers lead dull, isolated, and barren lives of toil, they urge upon the reader a compelling form of courage—stoic, tenacious, redemptive in its perseverance."[2]

The boom-and-bust cycle of farming on the Great Plains and elsewhere signaled a change in American farming. As better crops and prices returned in the late 1890s, increases in agricultural productivity were being made with relatively fewer farmers. In several regions of the country, the small farm was giving way to more specialized operations. Rows of orchard trees, grapevines, and row crops "planted, cultivated, and irrigated with mechanical precision" were examples of the new pattern of farming that characterized much of California, as was the sugar beet industry in Colorado, wheat farming in Oregon, and hop raising in Washington.[3] Caught in the pinch of economic forces beyond their control, many smaller farmers continued to lose the battle with fluctuating commodity prices and farm incomes, and faced the ever-increasing burden of debt and the rising cost of credit. When agricultural commodity prices finally stabilized during the decade preceding World War I, a time that came to be known as the "golden age of agriculture," it was really a period of relative prosperity where the primary beneficiaries were those with large farms. The majority of America's farmers continued to struggle.

RURAL AMERICA AT THE TURN OF THE TWENTIETH CENTURY

The commercialization of agriculture not only affected how farmers produced and marketed their crops, it also changed how they lived. Farmers could now buy factory-made goods that were increasingly available in small-town stores or through mail-order houses such as Montgomery Ward or Sears, Roebuck and Company that tailored their offerings to farmers' tastes. They could purchase ready-made clothing, furniture, pianos, manufactured carpets, and literally thousands of other items. These mail-order firms, and the companies that advertised in newspapers, magazines, and farm periodicals, revealed to rural people a new world of consumption. The range and availability of these new goods was seductive. They suggested what rural people should possess. Farmers were given the opportunity to enrich their standard of living and enhance the family environment and neighborhood sociability that was such a central part of their lives. But the new consumption, vigorously promoted by urban advertisers and merchandisers, pushed the farmer toward an acceptance of urban standards of culture, taste, and style. It required the farmer to acknowledge a degree of deference to urban standards.

Despite the lure of the new consumer culture, rural conservatism tended to restrain the farmer from boldly embracing a new lifestyle. Farming was still a high-risk venture. Drought and insects could quickly destroy a crop, and commodity prices followed an unpredictable pattern. A run of bad luck could cause a farmer to lose his farm. As a result, farmers embraced new consumer opportunities tentatively. The U.S. Department of Agriculture (USDA) estimated that 60 percent of what the average farm family consumed was still being produced on the farm in 1900. Such statistics suggest that farmers were still ambivalent about the future at the turn of the twentieth century. Although they were materially better off than their predecessors, they still believed that they were at the mercy of an economic system over which they had little control. As historian David Danbom put it, "More and more they felt like strangers in their own country.... [T]hey saw the standards and values of their country defined increasingly by others, often at their expense. To live in the countryside in 1900 was to have the sense that the nation was passing you by, leaving you behind, ignoring you at best and derogating you at worst."[4] Danborn's comment suggests that many urban dwellers, who increasingly regarded themselves as sophisticated, urbane professionals, had, by the 1890s, developed a negative image of the previously noble, yeoman farmer.

Although a majority of Americans no longer lived on farms at the start of the twentieth century, the United States, in many ways, remained an agricultural nation. Perhaps two-fifths of the population still made a living from the land and three-fifths of the country's inhabitants were "rural" by census definition in 1900. Nearly 5 million whites and approximately 768,000 blacks, assisted by 4.4 million farm laborers, operated the nation's farms. Of that total number, only 69.4 percent of the white population and 26.9 percent of the black population owned the land on which they worked. Despite commercialization and technological innovation, American rural life in 1900 was much as it had always been. Although there were certainly differences based on region, race, ethnicity, income, and tenure status, the sharpest contrasts in 1900 were not those within agriculture, but, instead, those between rural-agricultural society and urban-industrial society. As one historian noted, "Industrial innovations in economic practices, social institutions, and political forms had little direct meaning for the farmer or for his way of life, and he was dubious of their merits. Living much as he always had, the farmer usually believed that way to be good and he hoped to continue it."[5] Another historian examining southern rural life echoed this same assessment: "[F]armers and their retainers rarely looked beyond the community, only occasionally showing interest in...the issues of the wider world. In many people's minds, the outside world seemed threatening, full of ideas that could jeopardize their way of life."[6]

At the start of the twentieth century, farming was still hard work. Farmers and their families worked from daybreak to sunset throughout the year to make a living. Most farms were general in nature, producing many of the products the family consumed as well as a cash crop for market. This meant that the farmer not only worked to maintain his cash crop, but also tended the vegetable garden and managed to find time to mind his poultry yards, dairy barn, orchard, woodlot, and smokehouse. Plowing, planting, cultivating, and harvesting were, depending on the primary crop, pretty much a year-round job. Winters were not as strenuous, but farmers still had to milk the cows, feed the stock, repair the tools and equipment, cut the firewood, clear new land, remove rocks, and pull up tree stumps. Few farmers enjoyed the benefits of machinery and equipment that might make their work more productive. In 1900 the average farm contained machinery valued at less than $131, but regional variations on this average were marked. On farms in Alabama the figure was only $39, in North Carolina $40, and in Georgia $44. In six states in the Southeast, the value of farm implements owned by sharecroppers and tenants fell in a range between $17 and $30. By comparison, figures were better in Kansas, Nebraska, and

Iowa, where the average investments in machinery and implements were $170, $205, and $253 respectively, but still surprisingly low. Hand tools and primitive equipment pulled by one mule or a horse were still the norm for many farmers, especially in the South.

SEPARATE FARMING CULTURES

Cotton

In studying rural life in the South, historian Pete Daniel has described a section characterized by separate cultures. In addition to the two primary cultures—white and black—there were also mountain people and low-country people, Louisiana Cajuns, and transplanted midwesterners. These separate cultures were linked to commodities such as cotton, tobacco, and rice that dictated their seasonal work routines. Most southerners were cotton farmers. In the late winter, they would break the land, run rows, and plant the cotton. After the plants sprouted, workers would pass through the fields, thinning them out and chopping weeds. Farmers continued to maintain the crop in this manner until midsummer, when field work ceased and the crop was "laid by." When the bolls filled out in late September or October, workers would once again move through the fields, this time with sacks to pick the cotton. This process continued throughout the fall as additional bolls appeared. Children were often kept out of school to help with the spring planting and the fall harvest. Most families, depending on size, could cultivate only 10 to 20 acres. Farm implements were primitive and most often consisted of plows and mules to pull them, mechanical seeders, hoes, cotton sacks, and a scale to weigh the crop. By the turn of the twentieth century, mule-driven gins to separate the seeds from the cotton on the farm had started to give way to commercial steam gins located in town. After the cotton was ginned to separate the seeds from the lint, the final product would be compressed into bales for transport. The farmer or his creditor would then sell the cotton to local buyers. The cotton seed fed a growing cotton-seed industry, which manufactured vegetable oil and related products.

Between 1890 and 1920, cotton farmers stood by helplessly as an insect, the boll weevil, left a path of devastation from Texas to Georgia and proved almost impossible to eradicate. The pest crossed the Rio Grande River into Texas in 1892 and began to destroy cotton bolls. By 1903 the invasion had spread across the southern half of Texas. Businessmen and farmers began to panic, and farmers began to leave the region. In areas where the crop-lien system was common, economic disruption was especially severe. Afraid that a crop could not be made, merchants refused to advance credit. Sharecroppers had no choice but to move as well. Alerted to the problem, the USDA assessed the situation and, understanding the emergency, advised the Texas legislature to halt cotton planting in the infested area for one year. When the legislature declined to take action, the USDA's entomologists began to advise farmers to pick up and destroy the infected buds that had fallen from the plants and served as nests for young weevils. But, as one black tenant farmer from Alabama later commented, it did no good.

Me and my children picked up squares sometimes by the bucketsful. They'd go out to the field with little sacks or just anything to hold them squares and when they'd come in they'd have enough squares to fill up two baskets.... I've gived my children many pennies and nickels for pickin up squares. But fact of the business, pickin up squares and burnin em—it weren't worth nothing. Boll weevil'd eat as much as he pleased.... You couldn't keep your fields clean—boll weevil schemin to eat your crop faster than you workin to get him out.... I was scared of him to an extent. I soon learnt he'd destroy a cotton crop. Yes, all God's dangers aint a white man.[7]

The entomologists also advised farmers to begin to apply insecticides. When attempts at killing the insect proved ineffective, experts shifted to practical solutions. They advised farmers to plant earlier in the hope that an early maturing crop could be produced before the weevil became most destructive, use a plow with a crossbar that would knock the infested buds from the plant during cultivation, and plow under or burn the cotton stalks immediately after picking. As the infestation continued to spread, some farmers and businessmen placed a bounty on the boll weevil of from 10 to 25 cents per 100.

When the initial responses failed to stop the eastward spread of the insect at the Mississippi River, the USDA began to instruct farmers on how to deal with the weevil. In 1902 the department hired Seaman A. Knapp, a farm expert who had been instrumental in developing the prairie rice culture in Louisiana, as Special Agent for the Promotion of Agriculture in the South. The following year, on a farm near Terrell, Texas, Knapp set up a demonstration farm to convince cotton growers that they could defeat the weevil if they used good cultivation practices. Knapp later worked in conjunction with black educator Booker T. Washington, head of the Tuskegee Institute in Alabama, to aid black farmers as well. When the weevil continued to move faster than the demonstrators who were trying to control it, Knapp instituted a broader county agent program in 1906. County funds would pay the salary of an agent who would teach the best farming practices. In educating the farmer, however, the extension agents stressed commercial farming with the most up-to-date machinery and methods. It was, in effect, the beginning of a top-down call for modernization that many farmers would receive during the Progressive Era. The advice helped the more educated and aggressive farmers survive, but it left marginal farmers in jeopardy, and many gradually began to give up. Cotton farmers continued to move from the infested areas, and cotton culture in general began to shift to the West. Others tried their luck at crops such as rice, peanuts, or vegetables, or tried raising hogs or cattle. Between 1910 and 1920, farmers, buoyed by rising cotton prices, increasingly turned back to cotton. They would cope with the weevil even though it meant less cotton would be produced. Ironically, the USDA, in focusing its attention on combating the boll weevil, probably missed an opportunity to encourage agricultural diversification in the South.

Tobacco

Southern farmers also produced tobacco. As in cotton culture, the entire family worked at cultivating a crop, but tobacco work was harder, dirtier, and more exacting than any other. The season began in the winter when growers sowed seeds in plant beds until the seedlings were ready to be transplanted in the fields. Farmers mixed the tobacco seed with sand or ashes and then raked and packed the ground. By the 1890s farmers had started placing cloth over the beds to keep out flea beetles. As the seeds germinated, growers cut wood to be used in the curing barns in the summer. As one Martin County, North Carolina, tobacco grower remembered, "They would get together and have a wood cutting. One neighbor would help out another neighbor and several families would join in to cut wood.... They would cut wood just about like the ladies would get together and have quilting bees." In the spring, tobacco farmers would harness the mules to break and harrow the land and plow the rows. Once the fields had been prepared, farmers planted the tobacco. As one farm woman recalled the process, "We took biscuit pans, wash pans, and all other pans on the plantation, and with a spoon we dug the plants up and placed them in pans, carrying them in small numbers to the field."[8] A worker would then use a foot-long sharpened stick to open the earth enough to drop in a plant, and then use his or her foot to press the soil around the plant. By 1910 many tobacco farmers had acquired mechanical planters that allowed workers to sit as they planted. After the plants had established root systems, workers would loosen the soil by plowing or hoeing (a process that had to be repeated three or four times before the plants finally matured). The entire family worked at plowing and chopping weeds, and later to maintain the plants by breaking off suckers (secondary growths that grew above the primary leaves and deprived them of nutrients) and flowery tops (which also sapped growth from the leaves) by hand. Tobacco growers also had to pick hornworms off their plants and guard against a number of possible diseases and pests such as wilt, angular leaf spot, wildfire, mosaic, black shank, blue mold, and frog eye.

At harvest time the entire family would begin the six-week process of bringing the tobacco to the barn. Workers would pull three or four ripe leaves from each stalk and then place armloads of the leaves onto a sled pulled by a mule. A "trucker" (usually a young boy) would then drive the sled to the barn, where women and young girls and boys would hand the tobacco bundle by bundle to the "stringer." The stringer would then tie the bundles to a stick. When a stick was filled, a stick boy would place it in a rack or stack it on the ground. It required about a dozen people—four pickers, a trucker, four to unload the sled, two stringers, and a stick boy—to fill a barn in one day. Workers would take a break in the morning and afternoon and have a soft drink or a MoonPie. At noon all the workers would come together for a large country dinner. Black and white workers ate separately. The crews would usually rest for an hour after dinner and then head back to the fields. At the end of the day, workers still had to return to the barn to hang perhaps 1,000 to 1,500 tobacco-filled sticks in the barn. A tobacco barn commonly measured 16 feet square by 20 feet high and contained four sets of tier poles. Most tobacco barns were made of logs daubed with clay or mortar and topped with a tin roof. A shed protected the furnace, and metal flues ran from the furnace along the barn floor to distribute heat. Curing the tobacco was a delicate process that required constant adjustment of the temperature to yield the desired golden leaf. At the end of the curing process, air was allowed to enter the barn to add moisture to the final product and prevent it from becoming too brittle. As the last step, each leaf was graded and then tied into "hands" (bundles of 25 to 30 leaves). The final crop was sold at auction.

Rice

In addition to cotton and tobacco, rice was cultivated by some southern farmers. During the 1880s a land-promotion scheme headed by railroads and real estate speculators drew thousands of midwestern farmers to southwestern Louisiana; they were looking to escape the problems of high interest rates, an unfavorable climate, and grasshopper plagues. Upon arriving in Louisiana, they encountered Cajuns who had previously populated the area. Louisiana Cajuns, descendants of French Canadians, had established their own separate culture with a French language. Cajuns tended to ignore the materialistic, market-driven world, choosing instead to live off the land by hunting, fishing, trapping, raising livestock, and growing small subsistence crops such as rice. They depended on rainfall to water their crops and, as with much of southern agriculture, they farmed with primitive implements. Feeling somewhat alienated at first from the Cajuns, these transplanted prairie farmers soon discovered that they too could successfully grow rice. These industrious midwesterners also brought with them more modernized notions of farming and quickly mechanized the entire process. They used mechanical reapers with binder attachments, tractors, and steam threshers to harvest their crops. Some rice farmers developed a system of irrigation canals to water their fields. Later, when a reservoir of underground water was discovered in the region, many rice farmers sank wells and installed pumping machinery to irrigate their fields. At harvest time a rice farmer would hire a crew to drive the binders and shock the rice. After the rice was allowed to dry in shocks, the crew loaded it onto wagons and hauled it to a thresher. For most of the season, one man and his family assisted by a hired hand could tend several hundred acres of rice.

Mountain People

One often overlooked aspect of southern culture was the mountain people, who differed from low-country people. Like Louisiana's Cajuns, mountain people were independent, self-sufficient, and more apt to adhere to a subsistence lifestyle and eschew outside economic forces. The relative seclusion of their mountain neighborhoods provided a sense of security and continuity that sustained a unique regional culture based on a strong attachment to the land and to family and kinship groups. Economic and social activities were largely self-contained, with individual households relying on themselves or their neighbors for both the necessities and enjoyments of life. Mountaineers commonly owned small farms in a valley and worked their farms with family members. That plot of land took on an almost sacred quality as it was passed from generation to generation. The cultivation of the land itself demanded little technology or capital. Mountain farmers probably owned a horse or a pair of mules to pull the plow, along with a group of wandering pigs or hogs, a flock of hens, some sheep that were allowed to graze on the rocky hillsides, and two or three milk cows. Corn was the staple crop on many highland farms, but oats and wheat were also cultivated to make flour, along with hay, sorghum, buckwheat, potatoes, and other crops. The wheat and heavy grains were cut with a cradle, but the hay was cut with a scythe and then raked and stacked. Every farm had a vegetable garden, a beehive, an apple orchard, and other fruit trees. Sheep provided wool that was carded, dyed, spun, and woven into cloth on the farm. Many mountain families also gathered medicinal herbs and roots such as ginseng, yellowroot, witch hazel, sassafras, galax goldenseal, and bloodroot from the forests. Most local merchants were willing to accept these plants in exchange for store commodities. The diversity of production on these mountain farms afforded complete support even for

A mountaineer's cabin and family of 15, in 1913. (Courtesy of the Library of Congress)

large mountain families, which were common in a region with one of the highest birth rates in the country.

The hilly terrain and subsistence nature of the region made good roads for commercial traffic unnecessary. Instead, mountaineers might walk for miles along rugged paths to a store or mill and then return the same day. Packing a "lazy man's load" of a bushel of corn on each shoulder to a mill perhaps 10 miles away was a weekly routine for many mountain people. For example, in Avery County, North Carolina, farmers raised cattle and corn but also maintained apple orchards. Every fall wagons loaded with apples would come down from the mountains to surrounding towns. The mountaineers would camp out near the towns for a few days and sell their apples. At night they would build fires, cook their meals, talk, and share stories. After selling their apple crop, they would likely shop for hardware items, shoes, or candy for the children. They would then head back to the mountains. This was the commercial world as they knew it. For the rest of the year, they would grow their food, tend their stock, and occasionally take a bag of corn to the mill to be ground into meal. Some might distill corn into liquor.

The nuclear family served as the primary social unit for mountain people. Religion helped bond the family and was often organized around kinship units, with single families dominating a neighborhood church. In some instances, a circuit rider would bring both the Gospel and news from other settlements once or twice a month. For the most part, the mountain church, as an extension of the family, served to reinforce the mores of the community and acted as an important means of social control. Education was also family centered. What formal education mountain youths did acquire usually occurred in the small community school, which was often taught by an aunt or uncle and attended primarily by neighbors and kin. Like rural people everywhere, men and women divided their labor. Men cleared the land, plowed, planted, and tended the crops, the farm stock, and the orchards. Women did the household chores, carded and spun wool and wove it into garments, knitted stockings, and made quilts and blankets. They also fed and milked the cows, slopped the hogs, fed the chickens, hoed the corn, tended the garden, and carried water from the spring. They washed the clothes in a big iron kettle in the side yard, made soap, and, occasionally, assisted in the fields. "The woman," wrote one author, "lived a life of physical labor and drudgery. Her faith in a reward in the next world for sufferings and work well done on earth is about all the encouragement or incentive which she has for living."[9]

Interaction with neighbors and kin reinforced the sense of community beyond the family. The harvesting of corn in the fall provided an opportunity for a corn shuck or a dance. The first frost brought men and older boys together for a hunting party. Women often gathered together for quilting bees and to lend assistance in times of births, illness, or death. Helping out was seen as a natural part of community life. Church worship, which occasionally included camp meetings and revivals, provided opportunity to visit and exchange gossip and news. "Singings" and church services were often all-day affairs and might include a "dinner on the grounds" following a morning service. Families often traveled distances of 10 miles or more to attend a church service and even farther for a revival or special meeting. One individual recalled such occasions as a time for excitement.

When they would have church near our house, I remember as high as thirty or forty people staying and eating and spending the weekend. Mom would take the feather beds off the beds and put them on the floor, and people slept just any place.... People did a lot of Sunday visiting with the neighbors. I remember almost every Sunday some family ate with us or we went and ate dinner with them.[10]

Mountain people often gathered to share the heavier work of planting, harvesting, clearing ground, raising cabins and barns, or constructing a schoolhouse or public building. These community "workings" provided occasions for social interaction as well as for getting the work done, and usually turned into major social events. One participant remembered the experience:

They sent out word in the neighborhood and everybody would come. They'd pitch in, and cleared up maybe two or three acres of ground for planting crops in one day. It was called "new ground"...and everybody pitched in and cut down the trees. They called it "grubbing." It was a lot easier and nicer to work with a group and get it done than to just linger along by yourself trying to clear three or four acres of ground.... All the family would come. The women did the cooking, and I'm telling you it was really cooking.[11]

Meetings of the circuit court in county-seat towns two or three times a year offered another opportunity for social interaction and entertainment. Families would pour into town to listen to the trials, shop at the local stores, bargain with an assortment of pack peddlers, and renew acquaintances. Election days were just as festive, as large crowds gathered to vote or listen to campaigning politicians. Local politicians were always available, shaking hands with the voters, talking to family leaders, and providing entertainment for those in attendance.

THE IMPACT OF COMMERCIAL DEVELOPMENT

Mountain people, however, could not stay isolated forever. The Appalachian Mountains possessed opportunities for commercial development, especially in the areas of timber and coal. The investors—speculators, industrialists, railroad men, and coal and timber barons—who began to enter the region around the turn of the century brought with them modernizing forces that would destroy the old culture. Most of the developmental capital came from the North, and most of the profits returned there. Soon, one could see a change taking place in the region, from small subsistence farms to lumber camps and mining towns. In the process, the mountaineer saw himself being transformed from a subsistence farmer into a millhand or miner.

The Timber Industry

The largest of the new employers in the region in the early twentieth century was the timber industry. Just as changing forms of land ownership pushed some mountain folk off the land and into the cities and towns, the promise of steady employment and cash income lured others into the mills and mines. Though a majority of the workers in the timber industry were employed directly in logging, others worked in small planing mills and pulp mills (wood pulp was used in the manufacture of rayon), or in small furniture factories. A by-product of the timber industry was tannin, a substance derived from tree bark and used in the manufacture of leather. The growth of the tanbark industry employed hundreds of mountain residents (nearly 1,200 in western North Carolina alone in 1916) and gave rise to a thriving leather industry in the region. Between 1900 and 1920, the number of individuals employed in lumber, furniture, leather, and rayon mills in western North Carolina increased more than tenfold.

The movement from agriculture to timber-related employment was accompanied by a migration from the farm to one of the numerous company towns that began to dot the region. Although some of the smaller timber-camp towns offered only temporary housing for male employees, the larger timber operations offered more substantial housing for entire families. The town of Sunburst in Haywood County, North Carolina, housed more than 2,000 at the height of the timber boom and had a commissary, boarding houses, and a church that also served as a school, a dance hall, and a skating rink. Housing in most of the timber towns reflected the temporary nature of the operations. Houses were small, of board-and-batten construction, and lacked any indoor plumbing or sanitation facilities. Residents of these company towns had little say in community affairs and were dependent on the company for maintaining public health and safety. When timber production declined at the end of World War I, residents became displaced, and most of the company towns disappeared. Some found wage employment elsewhere, perhaps in mining and smelting, but many returned to the farm. For many mountaineers who had been lured to the mills, the collapse of the timber industry was disillusioning. As one observer remembered, "When the sawmill had finished its work and folded up as suddenly as it had come, they saw the illusion of permanency by which they had been tricked; their fields overgrown, fences unrepaired, farm tools rusted, young men strangers to the plow and hoe, children demoralized." The decline of the industry had happened gradually, he recalled, "and when the people came to realize it, it was out of their control."[12]

Cotton Mills

Other mountain families were swept up in the textile boom that occurred in the region at the turn of the twentieth century. By 1904 the South had surpassed New England in the amount of cotton cloth being manufactured. As it became evident that closer access to the raw cotton, cheap water power, and lower taxes offered a regional advantage, New England investors began to transfer millions of dollars to the construction of cotton mills in Georgia, South Carolina, Alabama, and North Carolina. The greatest attraction, however, was the large, untapped source of cheap labor. In 1897 it was estimated that the cost of labor was 40 percent lower in the South than in New England and the average workday 24 percent longer. Between 1900 and 1920, thousands of mountaineers left their farms for the mills. This migration necessitated a radical break from the life they had known. Housing in the mill towns was poor, crowded, and unsanitary. Wages ranged from 35 to 60 cents a day. A typical workday was 11½ hours, and various members of the family (approximately 80% of the workers in most mills were women and children) worked from 65 to 72 hours a week.

Coal Mining

The other major industry to come to the Appalachian South and contribute mightily to altering the nature of mountain life was coal. The rising demand for coal after 1900 stimulated the rapid growth of the mountain coal industry. As demand increased, so did the number of mines. Between 1909 and 1919, the number of coal mines in the country increased by more than one-third, and the largest percentage of that rise came in the South. As coal operations began to spread in the mountains, the operators initially looked to the local population for workers. Later, as operations expanded, they would begin to recruit blacks from the South and immigrants from southern Europe. Many of the local farmers who entered the mines in the early days regarded the work as temporary and merely as a means to supplement farm incomes. Their work habits tended to be preindustrial—taking off work at certain times to attend to planting, harvesting, funerals, and family reunions, or to go hunting or fishing. Mountaineers often rejected the industrial work routines and schedules designed by mine managers if these conflicted with their traditional way of life. Occasionally, a miner might work only to make enough money to take care of his family for the rest of the month before quitting the mine for home. Early miners rarely settled at a mine for more than a year to two, often moving from colliery to colliery in search of higher wages or better living conditions. Gradually, mountaineers were required to adjust to the new industrial system. While local farmers slowly adapted to the time-oriented, routinized nature of the work, mine owners increasingly looked for additional sources of labor. Between 1900 and 1920, coal company agents were sent into the South and to Europe to recruit miners to the mountain coal fields. As a consequence, the racial and ethnic composition of the mountains began to change. Faced with constant labor shortages, operators eventually tried to secure a more permanent, family-based work force by providing schools, clubs, theaters, and churches.

Work in the coal mines was arduous. The workday started before daylight and often did not end until after dark. Miners, carrying their lunch pails and water bottles, and wearing their oil lamps, would descend into the mines around 6:00 A.M. At the coal face, a miner and his helper/loader would set to work undercutting the coal seam. The miner usually did this by lying on his side and swinging a short-handled pick into the coal seam. After taking two or three hours to finish his cut, the miner then drilled holes in the coal, loaded black powder into the holes, and fired them to bring down the undercut coal. After the dust had settled, the men would push empty mining cars into the room being worked to load the coal, making sure to pick out the pieces of rock and slate so as not to be docked for loading dirty coal. The loaded cars would then have to be pushed to the room entrance to be hauled away. The miner would place a brass check bearing his payroll number near the bottom of the cart. The "check man" at the mine tipple would remove the check and credit the tonnage to the miner. After the car was removed from the workplace, the miner still had to remove the waste rock and debris from the room and then lay steel track from the main entry to the new facing. Miners were also usually required to set their own timber props to support the roof from collapsing. These safety procedures were usually done on the miner's time, because he was paid only by the ton of coal loaded. If the mine drained poorly, a miner's clothes often got wet with the first

A young coupling-boy, who appears to be between 12 and 14 years old, at the tipple of a Proctor Coal Company mine near Jellico, Tennessee, in 1910. (Courtesy of the Library of Congress)

undercutting, and he would have to work the rest of the day in damp clothes. At the end of his shift (usually around sundown), the dust-blackened miner would trudge home to get a few hours' rest before beginning the work cycle all over again. An average pick miner earned about $2 a day at the turn of the century. An exceptionally hard worker might earn $3.

Conditions in the company towns in the mining areas were bleak. Houses were often little more than shanties, tossed up against the hillsides or backed up to the railroad tracks with no attention to appearance, comfort, or community plan. Houses nearest the tipple received a daily shower of coal dust. A study done by the U.S. Coal Commission in the early 1920s found that one-third of company-owned houses in the southern coal fields were still finished in the cheapest manner with weatherboard and clapboard as the outside finish. Less than one-third were plastered inside, and less than one-tenth had shingled or slated roofs. Instead, wood sheathing covered the interior walls and composition paper covered the roof. Only about 14 percent of the company houses in West Virginia, Kentucky, and Virginia had indoor running water. Hydrants placed along the street and supplied from a tank high up in the valley furnished water in most mining communities. Less than 3 percent of the houses surveyed had a shower, bathtub, or flush toilet. Only 2 percent of the company communities had a sewer system, and outside privies, which often emptied directly into the creek, were the standard means of sewage disposal. Over 70 percent of the miners' homes, however, had electric lights. Hung from the ceiling in the center of the room, these single, bare bulbs were one of the few amenities of life in the coal camps.

According to the Coal Commission Report, the opportunities for recreation and amusement in these coal communities were meager. A few of the larger coal companies provided activity centers with movie theaters, bowling alleys, pool tables, and soda fountains (all available for a small fee), but the average mining town lacked those facilities. Most mining communities fielded a baseball team, and most miners owned a hunting rifle, but baseball and hunting were seasonal activities, and for most of the year there was little to do for recreation. Almost every camp and town, however, did have a saloon. In the heady days before World War I, when coal was king and wages were high, the saloon was most often the focal point of the male community. Whiskey sold for 10 cents a drink or $1 a bottle. On payday, professional gamblers from the nearest city would come into the region with their games of chance. At the hub of the community was the company store. This building would commonly house the commissary, barber shop, and post office. Convenient for shopping and a place to meet and chat with neighbors and friends, the company store was often the center of economic and social activity in the community. Commissaries offered a variety of merchandise, from foodstuffs to home furnishings. All of these items could be purchased on credit or with company scrip. Prices in these stores varied, but they were always considerably higher than in independent stores in the area.

This last point was indicative of a larger theme of life in the coal towns. The power of the mine operator was nearly complete, extending over nearly every aspect of village life. He commonly divided the community into an "immigrant town," a "colored town," and an "American town," and monitored the social barriers dividing each group. He granted residents little voice in the management of public affairs, restricted access to the company town by outside merchants, policed morality, and wielded a heavy hand against any conduct or activity that threatened to hinder the production of coal. His relationship to the miner has been described as that of master to servant rather than landlord to tenant. With that power he could limit personal and social liberty and leave residents powerless to control their own lives.

THE HARDSHIP OF FARM LIFE

Life in rural America in general was especially hard for the farmer's wife and children. The farm wife did the cleaning, washing, and cooking, but without most of the modern household conveniences increasingly being adopted by the modern, middle-class, urban housewife. Tending the vegetable garden, feeding the poultry and managing the farm's egg production, and churning the butter often found a place on her list of duties. At crucial times of the year, she might also be called to work in the fields. By most accounts, farm women endured their daily drudgery without complaint. Work was understood as a way of rural life, and without the effort of every family member, the family and the farm might not survive. "I doubt if it ever occurred to our parents," recalled one observer, "that their twelve-to-fourteen-hour days, seven-day weeks, fifty-two-week years might be considered drudgery. They had always worked; they assumed that work was a condition of life."[13]

Farm children helped out as well. Tasks were assigned to farm children as young as five. Children worked in the home or barn.

An 11-year-old boy cultivating peas in Lawton, Oklahoma. His father says he can pick 200 pounds of cotton a day. (Courtesy of the Library of Congress)

Young children milked, brought in wood, fed the chickens, weeded the garden, and herded cows. Between the ages of 8 and 12, some gender divisions began to occur. Girls learned home tasks such as baking, caring for children, cleaning, filling oil lamps, and sewing. Children also began to perform more labor-intensive tasks. They could plant and dig potatoes, set tobacco, pick berries, and harvest vegetables. At age 12 or 13, young boys began to take on full-time crop work and operate farm machinery. Plowing in the spring was usually a young boy's first adult responsibility. At about the same age, young girls learned new skills such as canning and churning. Older boys might shock wheat, stack hay, cut thistles, and husk corn. Child labor on the farm was much like an apprenticeship, but, like child labor in the cities, it robbed children of their childhoods and often stunted them physically and intellectually. Author Mari Sandoz, who was born in rural Nebraska in the 1890s, remembered her early days on the farm. "[A]ll of us knew children who put in twelve-, fourteen-hour days from March to November. We knew seven-, eight-year-old boys who drove four-horse teams to the harrow, who shocked grain behind the binder all day in heat and dust and rattlesnakes, who cultivated, hoed and weeded corn, and finally husked it out before they could go to school in November."[14] In some poor or large farm families, older children between the ages of 14 and 16 might work for wages on a neighbor's farm and then give most of the money they made to their parents. The primacy of the work ethic in rural society colored the way many rural people viewed some of the by-products of modernization. The increased leisure time that had begun to characterize much of modern America tended to be met with suspicion by people who believed that if work was a virtue, then play must be a vice. One rural economist in North Carolina noted in 1925 that the "farm people of the South are suspicious of what we call play and recreation." If children were having too much fun, he commented, "their fathers and mothers are apt to think that they are in a state of mortal sin."[15]

CLASSES OF FARMERS IN THE SOUTH

Throughout the agricultural regions of the United States, there were different types of farms and different classes of farmers. Farms might differ in size, productivity, the quality of the soil, crops and livestock raised, tenure, and the overall standard of living they provided. This was especially true in the rural South. At the top of the social scale were a relatively small number of large farmers and planters. In 1900 there were roughly 40,000 to 50,000 farmers in this category (approximately 2% to 3% of all farmers in the South), who owned from a few hundred to several thousand acres of land. At the opposite end of the spectrum were the sharecroppers and poorer tenant farmers who farmed between 20 and 50 acres. In 1900 almost two-thirds of southern farmers fell into this category. Between these two extremes were approximately 750,000 farmers who worked 100 to 200 acres of land that they either owned or rented.

Large Farmers and Planters

Most large planters maintained a good standard of living. They had the income to send their children to schools and subscribe to farm magazines. They rode to town in buggies pulled by handsome teams of horses, dressed in the latest fashions, and maintained active social lives. Most of the work on the plantation was done by servants and laborers who worked for meager wages. A common wage for a field hand might be only $8 to $12 a month. Managers usually supervised most of the production operations. Smaller planters who engaged a small number of tenants spent more of their time as managers and usually lived more modestly. Although farmers in this category still had to contend with weather, commodity prices, credit, and dealings with tenants and sharecroppers, and although debts often harried many of them, they still produced enough income to live well and perhaps even expand their land holdings.

Tenant Farmers

Only about one-half of all southern farmers owned their own farms in 1900, and the prospects of becoming an owner were becoming more difficult. Between 1880 and 1910, the percentage of all types of tenancy in the South increased from 36 to 49 percent. This was well above the national rate of farm tenancy, which was 37 percent in 1910. In states such as Mississippi and Alabama in the Deep South, tenancy rates exceeded 60 percent. In a study of 878 sharecroppers and tenant farmers in the Mississippi-Yazoo Delta done by the USDA in 1913, investigators found that those who farmed fewer than 15 acres of cotton earned only $239 a year, those with 15 to 19 acres averaged $332, and those with 20 to 24 acres averaged $387. Tenants who worked more than 24 acres of cotton had an average income of $622. Unlike new farmers in the North, who commonly rented land for several years before buying, southern tenant farmers paid cash or a portion of their crop to use land and were usually unable to purchase land of their own.

Always in search of greater economic stability, tenant farmers moved frequently. In some localities as many as one-half of the tenants changed farms every year or two in search of a more generous landlord, a better parcel of land, or a situation that offered more livable housing. Most tenants did not move far, usually staying within the county, but frequent moves required social adjustments—new neighbors, a new social network, new schools, and new churches— and perhaps made social life less satisfying. Some tenants chose to try something new, such as working in a textile mill. Frank and Sally Martin worked at sharecropping until 1914, when, as Frank later recounted, they "made fourteen bales of cotton, thirty-one barrels of corn and three hundred bushels of potatoes besides a sight of peas. It was one of the best crops I ever knowed ... and we came out about the poorest we ever done."[16] So they packed up and moved to a mill town. Southern textile mills employed more than 97,000 workers by 1900. Many rural families moved back and forth from farming to mill work, taking jobs in the off season or trying a mill job for a few years before giving farming another try.

Sharecroppers

A step below a tenant farmer, a sharecropper lived an even more precarious existence. To start with, the typical sharecropper owned almost nothing. The landowner would supply a mule, tools, seed, fertilizer, and a dwelling. He also determined the cash crop he wanted grown (usually cotton) and commonly took one-half of the cash value of the harvested crop. The landowner or, in many cases, the furnishing merchant would also provide food and other necessary items on credit at wildly inflated rates of interest. The amount owed would also be deducted from the sharecropper's share after harvest. As a result, few sharecroppers saw any cash under what was known as the crop-lien system, which tied any credit extended to the requirement to grow a particular crop, almost invariably cotton. Not surprisingly, many sharecroppers found themselves trapped in a cycle of debt peonage whereby they were obligated to the debts incurred in previous years and bound to the land they worked.

Living Conditions

The homes of tenants and sharecroppers were usually unpainted, one- or two-room cabins or shacks. Made of logs or rough lumber with a fireplace, the houses usually sat on posts about a foot above the ground. Spaces between the logs or boards let in the cold winds, and the roofs often leaked when it rained. A popular joke was that farmers were both astronomers and agronomists: they could study the stars through the roofs of their leaky shacks and examine the soil through the gaps between the boards on the floor. Occupants sometimes covered the walls with pages from old newspapers to minimize the outside chill. Many cabins lacked glass windows. Renters usually left the wooden shutters open to provide ventilation and light, but the openings also let in flies, mosquitoes, and other insects. When a black women living in a shack near Tuskegee, Alabama, was asked if snakes crawled in through the cracks in the floor, she responded, "Oh, yes, they gets in sometimes, but I just bresh 'em out."[17]

Conditions in a sharecropper's or tenant's cabin were primitive. Families often cooked, ate, and slept in a single room. Most cabins had a porch where families could sit in the evening, and occasionally there might be an outbuilding or lean-to where cooking could be done. It was not uncommon for three or four children to sleep in one bed. These poor farm families had little or no furniture. There was usually a pine table, two or three chairs, and sometimes a cupboard that might hold an assortment of dishes and pans. In some instances, dishes were simply placed on board shelves nailed to the walls. If a cabin had a second room, it usually served as a separate bedroom. It might contain one or two beds with rope supports that held a mattress, which might be filled with corn shucks. A trunk or a chest might sit in the room to hold clothing and bedding. Cooking was done over a fireplace, and iron pots and skillets were the primary cooking utensils. A simple clock, a family Bible, and a few pictures on the walls provided the only adornments. Some families planted flower beds to give their drab cabins a little cheer, but in many instances, cotton had been planted to within a few feet of the cabin door. The family water supply usually came from a well, a spring, or a stream. To obtain water, one either lowered a bucket or used a hand pump. For most families, an unsanitary outdoor privy served as the common toilet. Often located too close to the well, it could easily contaminate the family's drinking water. Poor farm families might also maintain one or two outbuildings in which to keep a few farm animals. Although a renter probably kept a mule that belonged to the landlord, most sharecroppers and many tenants owned very few cows, hogs, or chickens.

Middle-Class Farmers

Middle-class farmers fared a little better. Many owned frame houses with five or six rooms. Their farms also had more outbuildings to keep livestock and poultry. Fences and the general upkeep of the farm tended to be better. Heat for the farmhouse might still come from a fireplace, but cooking was probably done on a stove. The interiors of middle-class farmhouses had better furnishings and more amenities. Dishes were more likely to be kept in cupboards, beds had better mattresses, and chairs and tables were of better quality. There might even be a piano or organ as a sign of luxury.

Rural Diets

Part of the early twentieth-century rural stereotype was that rural living was physically superior to urban living. Yet, as the years progressed, urban observers increasingly maintained that rural standards of diet and sanitation were often below those of urban America, and that rural health was inferior to urban health. Rural diets were criticized; and farmers were accused of eating too much fried food and starches, and too little fresh produce and milk. Pork, potatoes, gravy, buttered bread, and coffee seemed to comprise the basic rural diet. Most poor farmers lived on a limited and unhealthy diet that changed little between 1870 and 1920. Standard fare at each meal for much of the year might consist of salt pork, cornmeal, and molasses or syrup. In literally thousands of poor farmhouses, farm wives mixed cornmeal with water and cooked it in a skillet or on a griddle over an open fire in a fireplace. Corn was also eaten as grits and hominy. Salt pork (mostly fat) was sliced thin and fried. Syrup would be mixed with the grease to make "sap," which was poured over corn bread. Some farmers were able to vary this monotonous and unhealthy diet with collard and turnip greens, which provided leafy vegetables for at least part of the year, and sweet potatoes. Farm families that maintained gardens might also have beans, okra, peas, and cabbage to eat during the summer months. Many farmers had no milk cows, and eggs were scarce because of the small number of chickens. Thus, the common diet for many was nutritionally unbalanced—high in fat and carbohydrates, and low in minerals, protein, and vitamins.

Health Standards

Substandard housing, unbalanced diets, unsanitary living conditions, and often impure water supplies all contributed to poor health among farmers, especially in the South. Adults and their children were often subject to dysentery, malaria, typhoid, hookworms, and pellagra. Children contracted hookworm, a parasite that sapped a person's strength, by going barefoot in unsanitary places. Pellagra, a niacin deficiency, resulted from diets that lacked milk, eggs, vegetables, fruits, lean meat, and other foods rich in vitamins and proteins. Pellagra victims usually lost weight and had little energy or vitality. Professional medical attention was hard to come by. Rural childbearing practices remained relatively primitive, and most women still gave birth at home with the aid of only a midwife. Poor farmers seldom had enough money even to call one of the few doctors who might be in the area. As a result, farm families relied on patent medicines and home remedies such as castor oil, calomel, paregoric, salts, quinine, and herbal tea. But rural health, dietary, and sanitation practices had not regressed; they had simply not changed. In urban America, change seemed to promote further change and innovation, but not in rural America. Many farmers still lived unaffected by the industrial age.

Rural Isolation

Another aspect of rural life that complicated its relationship with an emerging modern order was rural isolation. Millions of individuals lived their entire lives without ever being exposed to the influences of growing urbanization. As late as 1900, one could travel for hundreds of miles through much of rural America and never encounter a place of 8,000 or more people—an urban center as defined in the census. A large part of the rural South was not fully integrated into the rest of American society. Poor roads accounted for part of the problem. By 1910 fewer than 18,000 of the 500,000 miles of road in 10 southern states had been improved with gravel surfaces. Isolation encouraged individualism and self-reliance, reinforced the family-centered nature of rural life, and intensified psychological pressures, especially on farm women. Though men often went to town to sell and purchase commodities, and children went to school, social contacts for farm women were limited. In 1923 a Federal Children's Bureau investigator encountered a woman who lived only three miles from town but had not seen another woman in a year. One rural sociologist remembered an instance in which he met one farm woman who was so totally preoccupied with her duties that she had not ventured beyond the confines of the family farm in more than three years. "It is remarkable," he said, "that she and thousands like her are able to withstand the strain and keep from succumbing to an overwhelming depression."[18] Southern farm women worked longer and harder than other family members and had the fewest opportunities to enjoy social life. The large majority of lower- and middle-class farm women (those who could not afford any household help) were buried in tasks that wore them out before their time. In addition to rearing children, farm wives cooked, kept house, washed clothes, sewed, and usually maintained a garden. Southern farm women often worked in the fields either hoeing or picking cotton. As a result, social activities were limited to visiting neighbors or occasional trips to town or church.

The isolation of the rural family, and the equally isolated nature of the rural community as a whole, had broader consequences. Isolation strengthened the hold of traditions and superstitions and made rural people even more resistant to change. For example, the ancient practice of moon farming—where planting, harvesting, and slaughtering were based on phases of the moon—was still followed by many. Most farmers paid more attention to almanacs than to notions of scientific farming. As one observer noted, "The conditions of agriculture so far as the application of science to the tillage of the soil is concerned is conservative. The methods of traditional farming are modified only by the effect of the railroads and of the blind, economic forces which have influenced the farmer against his will."[19] Isolation also affected the political nature of farmers in that it intensified localism. At the turn of the twentieth century, both the state and federal governments had relatively little direct impact on farmers, and farmers had yet to form an interest group powerful enough to act in their behalf in the distant world of national politics. As a result, farmers were primarily concerned about local issues such as school policy and taxation. Localism served as yet one more buffer between rural inhabitants and the changes taking place in the society beyond them.

Rural Schools

Of major importance to the rural community was the country or rural school. Unlike its idyllic place in American folklore, the little red schoolhouse in reality was cramped, poorly lighted, inadequately ventilated and heated, unsanitary by urban standards, and stunted by the poverty and traditionalism of rural America. In 1910 it was estimated that 6.7 million students (roughly 37.6% of the nation's public school pupils) attended one of the nation's 212,380 one-room schools. Each of those schools usually had only one teacher, who attempted to instruct about 30 students scattered over eight grades. At the turn of the century, there were 42,000 one-room schools in Indiana with fewer than 20 students. Many rural schools were even smaller. Investigators estimated that one-fourth of the schools in rural Iowa had 10 or fewer students. Although overcrowding was a problem in many schools in impoverished areas, especially in the South, in other areas it was not uncommon to find that all the students were from three or four families. Simple frame shacks or log houses often served as schoolhouses in the rural South. A common board structure might measure 14 by 20 feet, with a door at one end and three bare windows on each side. Students hung their coats on pegs or nails on the walls, and sat on straight board seats.

Inadequate funding constantly plagued rural education. Most schools were poorly equipped, and many schools lacked desks of any kind. The U.S. commissioner of education reported in 1899 that the average annual expenditure per pupil was $3.59 in Alabama, $7.30 in Georgia, and $7.70 in Louisiana, compared to $18.99 for the nation as a whole. Rural schools were often staffed with inadequately trained teachers who were often not too far ahead of their pupils. Having a firm grasp of economic reality, many communities simply disregarded certification standards and allowed teachers to teach with temporary certificates. Rural districts simply could not compete with urban pay scales or offer the independence that city schools and city life provided to qualified teachers.

Students gained rudimentary instruction in reading, writing, spelling, arithmetic, history, geography, and civics. Subjects were taught primarily through the recitation method. As one rural resident on the northern plains remembered the experience,

Study and recitation proceeded simultaneously. While a Sodergreen or a Wennerholm was stumbling through the capitals of the...states...the youngest Olson sat with eyes shut, stuck in the multiplication table.... The scrape of pencils on slates told of others working out more complicated problems, or trying to diagram sentences. It was good training in concentration.[20]

Most of the students probably learned the basics, but few were pushed beyond that. The rhythms of rural life—planting season and

A group of children at a district school near Corsicana, Texas, in 1913. Only 40 percent of the students are in attendance because the cotton is still being picked. School terms were often shortened to accommodate the harvest. This is an above-average school, with only 2 of the 10 families represented being "renters." (Courtesy of the Library of Congress)

harvest—often interrupted the school year and reduced attendance. Many rural schools in the South met for only three or four months a year. Compulsory school attendance laws were not enacted in southern states until after 1905 and then not rigidly enforced. In 1910 the average urban school year was 184 days, but the average rural school year was 46 days shorter. Average daily attendance in urban schools was 79.3 percent, and the comparable figure for rural schools was 67.6 percent. Few students managed to complete the eighth grade, and even fewer attended the almost nonexistent country high schools.

Although open to criticism, the rural common school had many positive features from the vantage point of local residents. First, it was locally rooted, and in regions of some settlement, few students lived farther than two or three miles from the school. Second, although the rural curriculum would have seemed limited to urban educators, the local school also did what most rural parents wanted it to do-supplement and reinforce the lessons learned in the context of the rural home and family. Finally, country schools also served as social centers for rural inhabitants, and the spelling bees, school plays, and community suppers held there were important to rural life.

Rural Churches

One other institution that held an important place in rural life was the church. Religion could provide solace for many a disheartened farm family. By the 1890s hundreds of churches could be found in the rural countryside, especially in the South. Most southerners were fundamentalists; they accepted the Bible literally and attended Baptist and Methodist churches. Southerners believed that sin was knowable and would be punished by a just God. They also believed that there was a better life in the hereafter for the poor and oppressed. A central feature of small towns, the country church was both a social and spiritual institution. Churches in the South were racially segregated. Black congregations tended to affiliate with the Colored Methodist Episcopal Church, the African Methodist Episcopal Church, the National Baptist Convention, and other denominations. Church membership among southern farm people increased substantially during the last decade of the nineteenth century and the first two decades of the twentieth century. During that period the number of churches in North Carolina grew from 6,824 to 9,135 and membership grew from 685,660 to 1,080,723. Sunday school also became an increasingly important part of Sunday services. As church membership increased in the region, the old primitive log churches began to give way to frame, and occasionally brick, buildings.

Rural churches often had a hard time attracting and keeping ministers. Most southern preachers devoted only part of their time to church work. Many worked as farmers. Preachers generally lacked formal education and tended to preach a simple faith unencumbered by complex theology. People who attended Sunday services could expect to hear an old-fashioned gospel of personal salvation and morality. The average size of most southern congregations was small, usually fewer than 100 members, and members supported their church by free-will offerings. A black pastor in Mississippi in 1916 might expect to earn a salary of only $270 a year, but that was still a better income than that earned by most sharecroppers; and it came with a degree of respect for an acknowledged leader in the community, and often with gifts of food and other products from grateful congregants.

An important part of religious life in the rural South was revival meetings. Often called "protracted meetings," such gatherings could last for a week or more. Commonly held in the late summer just before cotton picking began, the open-air or tent meetings would attract farm families from miles around. Usually led by a well-known evangelist and assisted by local preachers, these meetings were highly emotional. Describing a revival meeting in Marengo County, Alabama, in 1910, one observer stated that preachers "pounded the pulpit, lashed the air and ranted about sins."[21] Among the list of sins that people were exhorted to forsake were dancing, card playing, swearing, drinking, gossiping, and "petting," and there were mourners' benches for repentant sinners. The revival meetings served both spiritual and social functions. Families would share food and eat together after church. These occasions offered farmers the opportunity to visit with neighbors and friends and exchange personal news.

Although revival meetings were important to many rural communities, there were other ways for rural people to socialize. Farmers often joined fraternal orders such as the Masons, the Woodmen of the World, and the Odd Fellows. There were also picnics, county fairs, Grange meetings, and political rallies to attend. For many farm people, just going to town was a special social experience.

AGRARIAN EXODUS

It has been suggested that the American farmer entered the twentieth century both attracted and repulsed by the changes taking place in society. One thing that worried many rural inhabitants was the departure of many of their offspring to the cities. The percentage of Americans who worked in agriculture declined from almost 40 percent in 1890 to just over 30 percent in 1920. The increasing difficulty of obtaining good, cheap land, and the promise of opportunities and material advancement in urban-industrial America contributed to what many saw as a growing agrarian exodus. Some worried that those most likely to leave would be the more ambitious and better educated, including the better-trained teachers, doctors, and lawyers. Many feared that if this happened, then the quality of both rural people and rural services would be lowered, and the community would sink into moral decline. One sociologist envisioned the bleak result:

The roads are neglected, which means less social intercourse and a smaller turnout to school and church and public events. School buildings and grounds deteriorate, and the false idea takes root that it pays to hire the cheaper teacher. The church gets into a rut, fails to start up the social and recreative activities which bind the young people to it, and presently ceases to be a force. Frivolity engrosses the young because no one organizes singing schools, literary societies, or debating clubs. Presently a generation has grown up that has missed the uplifting and refining influence of these communal institutions.[22]

Although many parents agreed that material opportunities were greater in the mills, factories, and cities, and that there was no place on the farm for all of their children, they still wanted their children to stay with them. They worried about the corrupting influences of the city should their children choose to leave. As one historian put it, "[T]hey distrusted the urban mob, with its strange immigrants, curious values, and exotic religions, and they were leery about the economic and political bigness and organization that seemed to be so much a part of modern urban and industrial life."[23]

PROSPERITY?

The first two decades of the twentieth century offered farmers a rare taste of prosperity. During this period, real farm income (gross income adjusted for inflation) increased by 40 percent, and the value of the average farm more than tripled. Much of this was due to an imbalance in supply and demand. During the period of 1870 to 1900, the amount of cultivated land doubled, and the production of major agricultural staples advanced along with the increase. By 1900, however, most of the good land was already being put to productive use. Over the next 20 years, acreage being farmed increased by only 12 percent. Compounding the problem of weakened expansion was poor productivity. Between 1900 and 1910, agricultural productivity barely increased, and it advanced at a rate of less than 1 percent per year during the first two decades of the twentieth century. With the general population increasing by 40 percent between 1900 and 1920, farm prices began to rise faster than the general price level. And what was happening in the United States was also occurring in much of the rest of the world. As a result, prosperity encouraged farmers to participate more actively in the market and to place increased emphasis on commercial products over those produced on the farm. The trend would continue throughout the Progressive Era. In 1920 the USDA estimated that the average farm family produced only 40 percent of what it consumed, down 20 percent from 1900.

Until the heady days of World War I, however, the level at which farmers reinvested their profits was minimal. Few farmers expanded, and most were reluctant to mechanize, purchase pure-bred stock, or upgrade their operations. Naturally conservative, most farmers remembered the economic downturns of the previous period and were reluctant to abandon caution for new spending habits. This is not to say that they did not spend money. They often taxed themselves to upgrade their schools, hire more adequately trained teachers, or purchase educational supplies. They bought items to make their homes more comfortable—kitchen devices, new carpets, drapes, and furniture. Many installed a new hand pump (usually connected to a cistern) in the kitchen to eliminate the onerous task of carrying buckets of water from a spring or well to the house. Others built privies and began screening windows and doors to keep out insects. One very popular improvement was the telephone (service provided by hundreds of small companies), which diminished rural isolation.

The Impact of the Automobile

The most popular material acquisition for rural people, however, was the automobile. Where there had been only a few thousand cars in the entire country in 1900, there were almost 2½ million in the rural countryside alone in 1920. By that date over 30 percent of farmers owned at least one car. The Model T Ford was the vehicle of choice for most farmers. It was inexpensive and relatively easy to repair. Its light weight, tight turning radius, and high center of gravity made it ideal for narrow, rutted, and often muddy rural roads. It also made farm work easier. If a piece of farm machinery broke, a repair part could be obtained quickly in town. Trucks, which became an increasingly common feature of farm life during and after World War I, made the marketing of farm produce easier. The automobile also enhanced leisure activities. The Sunday drive quickly became a staple for rural families, and the new mode of transportation allowed families to visit friends, broaden their social activities, and perhaps explore beyond the limits of the local village or town. The automobile also allowed young people to alter courtship rituals and escape the prying eyes of parents and neighbors. The new mobility intensified the discussion of new political issues in the countryside, such as funding for road improvements and campaigns for the consolidation of schools and churches. It also created divisions within the community. Merchants complained that customers stopped patronizing their businesses to shop in larger towns. Ministers argued that Sunday drives reduced church attendance. And the automobile created a new personal problem in that it placed an added burden on family finances. In Lee County, South Carolina, in 1920, for example, it took one-third of the value of the cotton crop just to service and fuel the car. A family's financial commitment to the automobile could limit the ability to enhance life in other areas.

Many contemporary observers debated the question of whether the automobile would hasten or hinder the migration of rural inhabitants to the towns and cities. To some, what was needed was a means of introducing the conveniences of modern, urban life into the rural environment without upsetting the benefits they believed derived from living in the country. Henry Ford thought that the automobile (along with good roads to enable the farmer to travel to market, and a moving picture theater in the community where a farm family might enjoy an evening of entertainment) could check the decided drift away from the farm. Offering a similar opinion, one rural observer in Maryland in 1916 suggested that, as a result of the automobile, young people would no longer yearn to get away "simply because they have discovered that they can go when they like, and their easy touch with the outside has rubbed off the glamour." Perhaps a more accurate assessment, though, came from yet another observer in 1919, who stated that the automobile "has saved the farm," but "not in the way you might think. It didn't keep the boy and girl on the farm, but it provided the farmer with means for getting people from the town to take their places."[24]

A Buick roadster waits for a horse-drawn wagon to pass on a narrow country road, ca. 1912. (Courtesy of the Library of Congress)

These visible signs of rural prosperity were misleading. Although a rural family might aspire to middle-class urban standards, that goal remained largely beyond their grasp. A farm family might be able to afford to install a pump in the house, but it was probably unlikely to have indoor plumbing or a water heater. Because access to a central power station was usually unavailable, few rural families had electricity. And lack of electricity denied them a wide range of amenities that made urban living easier. The cold reality was that urban living standards remained higher, urban institutions were judged to be superior, and urban life was considered to be much richer. To underscore this point, young people living in rural environments maintained their active desire to leave the countryside for the city.

THE COUNTRY LIFE MOVEMENT

During the Progressive Era, many of the problems and developments associated with rural life began to capture the attention of various groups of urbanites—educators, social scientists, philanthropists, politicians, and religious leaders—who became the leaders of what became known as the Country Life movement. What appeared to concern them most was the apparent desire of young people to leave the countryside for the city. Fearful that this process of out-migration was selecting the smartest, most ambitious, and most promising young people, these socially oriented Country Lifers worried that rural America would become an intellectually blighted area, with unfortunate consequences for the nation as a whole. They tended to see the process as being motivated, like most migrations, by both pull and push factors. They understood the seductive qualities of the city—its cultural opportunities, intellectual stimulation, recreational and social options, and modern lifestyle—that lured young people, but they also perceived that rural life was dull, stultifying, and lacking in the social and cultural resources that might satisfy the young. If rural life was not enlivened and made to seem more meaningful, then the countryside would become a land occupied by the ignorant and indolent.

Adding impetus to the social argument was a group of other more economically oriented Country Lifers—bureaucrats, businessmen, and agricultural scientists—who were concerned that the prospect of a future of diminished agricultural productivity would create other problems. The United States had been a country of cheap food. Because food was inexpensive, it was argued, wages could be held in check, and the price of American farm exports could remain competitive. But if population growth continued to outstrip food production, food prices would rise. Labor unrest would follow as workers demanded higher wages, and American industrial exports could become less competitive. Farmers, increasingly victimized by low productive efficiency, could also be squeezed out of world markets by more efficient competitors.

These reformers received a boost in 1907 when President Theodore Roosevelt created the Country Life Commission to study rural problems and recommend solutions. The commission was chaired by Liberty Hyde Bailey, a Cornell University horticulturist who had been an advocate of revitalizing rural institutions as a way to slow the exodus of young people to the city. Supporting his efforts on the commission were Kenyon L. Butterfield, president of the Massachusetts Agriculture College and a noted rural sociologist; Walter Hines Page, editor of *World's Work* magazine and an authority on education, sanitary conditions, and farming in the South; Gifford Pinchot, a conservationist and expert on economic efficiency; Henry Wallace, editor of *Wallace's Farmer* and an influential agricultural spokesman in the Midwest; Charles S. Barrett, president of the Farmers' Cooperative and Educational Union of America; and William A. Beard, editor of the *Great West Magazine* and chairman of both the Sacramento Valley Improvement Association and the National Irrigation Society. In a real sense, the creation of the commission and the experts who staffed it lent legitimacy to the concerns of the Country Life reformers. The commission traveled widely, gathered testimony from hundreds of witnesses, and collected surveys from thousands of respondents. When the commission issued its report in 1909, it delineated an array of social and economic problems and concluded that "better farming, better living, and better business" were needed if rural America was to keep pace with a modernizing urban society.[25] In general, the commission called on rural people to beautify their homes and add modern conveniences, suggested that the rural church be redirected and that rural schools be reformed, and encouraged farmers to become more efficient producers and better businessmen.

The Rural Church as a Vehicle for Modernization

Some Country Lifers hoped that the rural church could be regenerated in ways that would allow it to become a vehicle for agricultural modernization. Their model was the Social Gospel movement, which was currently being accepted by many urban churches as a way to make them more relevant to urban-industrial problems. Simply stated, Social Gospelers believed that churches should take an active role in bringing about social and economic reform. Country Lifers viewed the country church as clinging to a narrow emphasis on doctrine and an old-fashioned orthodoxy that made no attempt to link religion to the social problems of the time. Its ministers were poorly paid, its membership in decline, and its buildings in various states of disrepair. All were symptoms of a failure to adapt to the modern age. A revitalized church, however, could provide the leadership that was necessary to bring about economic and social change in a seemingly stagnant society. Some advocates of country church reform went so far as to suggest that ministers be given agricultural courses during their seminary training so that they might be better informed about the rural world in which they were to work. These enthusiasts envisioned ministers spreading information on scientific agriculture, holding institutes and demonstrations, organizing marketing cooperatives, and encouraging their congregations to farm more effectively.

Not everyone even in the Country Life movement agreed. Warren Wilson, superintendent of the Department of Church and Country Life of the Presbyterian Church, remarked with a bit of humor that "the modern minister is to serve not vegetables, but men."[26] He went on to state that because a minister worked with human beings, he should be a specialist in social science rather than soil sciences or animal husbandry. Many rural ministers thought the new gospel would undermine the rural church's unique social role and perhaps its divine mission as well. "The main work of the church must not be simply to furnish enjoyment and pleasure, good roads and methods," cautioned one Wisconsin minister in 1911. "I am willing to speak a good word for those things, but the thing we want is the moral and religious basis for the development of the heart and the soul of life and the church must do that ..." Another minister scoffed at the suggestion that the "chief concern [of the church] is to make roads as 'a way of salvation,' 'to raise fat pigs for the glory of God,' to 'clean up dirty privies,' to turn the house of worship into a dance-hall and the preacher of the Gospel of Jesus Christ into the director of the dance."[27] In the end, reformers naïvely hoped for too much. The country church had never been an agency for rural change. Unlike education, which held a public function and might be modified by insistent governmental bodies, the church was essentially a self-controlled, private institution where change would have to come voluntarily. Stymied, reformers would have to look elsewhere for help.

The Rural School as an Agency for Change

The area on which most Country Lifers focused their attention was education. Finding existing rural schools deficient, they hoped to substantially change them by altering the curriculum to make it richer and more relevant to rural life. They regarded the current curriculum, emphasizing reading, math, history, and civics, as too narrow. Instead, they recommended that subjects such as music, art, and physical education be added to enrich the curriculum and make rural education more interesting. The assumption seemed to be that a richer assortment of course offerings would stimulate intelligent young people and keep them in the countryside. At the same time, Country Lifers hoped to add more practical courses in vocational agriculture, industrial arts, and home economics (domestic science). Such courses would, they believed, enhance appreciation for farming and homemaking as honorable professions, and the progressive practices learned by students would be carried home to influence their parents as well. Bailey also favored the addition of nature study to the core curriculum to help young people understand and appreciate life in the country.

Closely tied to the proposed changes in curriculum were suggestions aimed at school reorganization. The key to this idea was school consolidation that would unify several one-room school districts. Consolidated districts would have broader tax bases, which would facilitate the hiring of better-qualified teachers who specialized in specific subject areas. Unlike the ungraded, one-room rural school, consolidated schools would be divided into grades based on age and skill levels. And consolidated schools would diminish the influence of local interests that had previously sought to direct the education process.

Not surprisingly, rural people showed little enthusiasm for the suggested changes. Many rural people were naturally defensive when their existing educational system was criticized by urban outsiders. Many failed to admit that there was a crisis in rural education. Schools were doing what they always did, and that was what parents wanted. The existing curriculum was considered to be adequate. Art and music were regarded as frills. Vocational agriculture and home economics were already being taught on the farm, and any suggestion that this was being done imperfectly was an affront. "Education means ability to read, write, spell, and figure" to rural people, remarked one Wisconsin school official, and, by implication, not instruction in how to plow, plant, cook, or sew.[28] The idea of school consolidation frightened many parents. One fear was cost: farmers believed that school consolidation would raise taxes. Many opposed the transportation of their children to school and worried where the school would be located. They were also concerned that because the new school would be more remote, local control would be lost and their influence diminished. It would also involve their children in contact with children from other neighborhoods, who might have different religious beliefs, ethnic backgrounds, and value systems. And because the one-room school was a social institution that served many social functions and united the community, they were reluctant to see time-tested social benefits sacrificed for the possibility of educational advances. Such antipathy did not halt school reform. During the Progressive Era, states would begin to establish curriculum requirements and set minimum standards for teacher certification that would push rural education along the course suggested by Country Lifers, but rural resistance did mean that educational changes would come more slowly.

The Push for Progressive Farming

Other Country Lifers focused on the problem of sluggish agricultural productivity and directed their attention to a different type of education—the dissemination of agricultural knowledge. The USDA, the land-grant colleges, and the various state experiment stations had been conducting agricultural research for some time prior to 1900. They had identified area-specific crop varieties; developed ways to increase animal production; and established principles of crop rotation, fertilization, and cultivation that had both enhanced agricultural productivity and conserved topsoil. There were some indications of success, even in the South. In 1909 a USDA representative reported the results of an experiment with 509 farmers in Alabama who produced an average of 33¼ bushels of corn per acre on their experimental plots, compared to the state average of only 13½ bushels. Three years before that experiment, researchers from the Louisiana Agricultural Experiment Station and the USDA worked with tenants on the Rosalie Plantation of William Polk in Moreland, Louisiana, and convinced each tenant to set aside two acres on which they planted potatoes, sweet corn, cabbage, and watermelons. The overall results of the experiment, which were published as a USDA Farmers' Bulletin, were favorable, and the farmers' income increased. The researchers concluded that it was possible to establish a system of crop diversification on plantations. But there was a catch. The landlord had to be supportive, and the tenants had to receive instruction on how to care for the new and different crops. Without hands-on assistance, it would be up to the farmer to write for various experiment station bulletins. That required the ability to write, to read, and to understand, and assumed a desire on the part of farmers to at least consider new methods. The high rate of illiteracy among southern farmers, white and black, precluded that option. Although scientific information was readily available, most farmers were not utilizing the information at hand.

Convinced that farmers would change their inefficient practices only if they could be shown that different methods of production would pay on their farms, agricultural experts, assisted by the railroads, various farm machine companies, and other businesses, renewed their emphasis on demonstration plots or farms. These demonstration farms would not be operated or worked by USDA personnel; rather, the agents would only provide advice and instruction to farmers who agreed to participate in the program. Agents would go into farm communities and select in each a cooperating farmer who would agree to provide roughly 10 acres of land for demonstration purposes. The success of these efforts would then be shown to other farmers in the area. By 1912 there were approximately 100,000 farmers cooperating with the program as demonstrators. Railroads supported these efforts by distributing information and providing farm speakers with free or reduced transportation rates. They also sponsored seed, crop, and milk trains to promote improved methods, and displayed the products of improved farm practices. Some railroads set up demonstration farms of their own. Boys' and girls' clubs were organized in many communities with the idea that if young people could be convinced of the advantages of diversification and better methods, change would come with the next generation of farmers. There were also corn clubs and pig clubs that encouraged efforts to increase efficiency and productivity. Congress agreed to support the general program and in 1914 appropriated federal funds to hire county farm agents and home agents (female agents who would work with rural women) if states and counties contributed one-third of the cost of maintaining the agents.

Despite more than 20 years of effort to get farmers to diversify, adopt scientific methods, and become more efficient, relatively little was achieved. The rural landscape, especially in the South, looked little different than it had a generation earlier. The agricultural census of 1910 revealed how little had been accomplished. In the South between 1899 and 1909, the number of farmers growing cotton had actually grown from 1.4 to 1.7 million. Total land devoted to cotton cultivation had increased by roughly 6 million acres. In 1899 cereal crops had been raised on 35 percent of the improved land in Alabama, but 10 years later comprised only 29 percent of the total. Instead of turning to other crops and livestock and reducing their cotton plantings, southern farmers were becoming more dependent on cotton. Attempts to get farmers to plant grass and legumes to improve soil quality met similar results. Hay and forage did increase after 1900, but in the southeastern cotton states, only between 2 and 4 percent of the improved cropland was in hay and forage in 1910. Southern farmers did increase the number of livestock, but only three-fourths of the farmers in the south Atlantic and east south central states owned any milk cows in 1910. Farmers in North Carolina, Alabama, Tennessee, and Texas actually had fewer hogs in 1910 than they did in 1900. Farmers in the South were not reducing cotton to move into forage crops, livestock, or cereals as preached by the advocates of diversification. Producers were also not acquiring farm units of more economic size. In fact, the amount of cultivated acreage per farm family in the South was declining. In 1880 the average rural family supported itself on 140 acres of land; by 1920 it was trying to get by on slightly more than 52 acres. In Louisiana, Mississippi, Alabama, Georgia, and the Carolinas the average farm size was only about 37 improved acres. Many tenants and sharecroppers farmed only 20 to 30 acres, insufficient for them to produce enough to provide adequately for their family.

There were many reasons for the failure of progressive farming to take hold. In the South, planters were reluctant to let their sharecroppers and tenants grow any commercial crop other than cotton. Cotton remained the most valuable cash crop. It was also the principal basis for credit. Money was advanced to growers on the crop, and it was the only collateral accepted by most furnishing merchants and landowners. To obtain a loan to buy cows or hogs would have been unthinkable. To support livestock on hay, a farmer would have to plow, plant, and fertilize the soil at considerable cost. Where cattle were left to find their own food, they often died. Pigs and chickens were subject to disease. If the animals died, the lender would be left with a worthless note. To develop a diversified farm, farmers needed more land than they had. The 20-to-50-acre plots that were common in the cotton belt were just too small to provide pasture and feed crops for cattle, or provide land for corn or other cereals in addition to cotton. Diversification also assumed that there would be adequate markets for perishable crops such as fruits and vegetables. Though profits could be made from "truck farming," this involved a great deal of risk. In the end, perhaps the biggest hurdle for any southern farmer looking to modernize was the lack of capital to bring about change. To buy farm machinery, shift from a one-mule to a two-mule operation, or move into livestock production required an investment beyond farmers' means.

Although the idea of agricultural extension may have captivated the imagination of reformers and policymakers, it was not embraced by all farmers. Few farmers had asked for the program (still regarded as a form of "book farming"), and they proudly resented the implication that they did not know how to farm. Others simply resented advice delivered from a livery rig or offered in a patronizing manner. In addition, many farmers suspected that what agents really wanted was for them to grow more food, which would drive down farm prices. In many areas, chambers of commerce and commercial clubs were the most vigorous supporters of the program, which added to the distrust felt by many farmers. Many farm women objected to the gender divisions built into the program. Home agents focused on improving domestic skills such as cooking and canning, how to better make one's own clothing, and child rearing, while farm agents worked exclusively with men. For women who also played significant roles in farm production, this was an affront. It was also not uncommon for agents to fail to produce desired results among suspicious farmers. Such failures could ruin a county program. Extension endured because it was still the best way to disseminate information, but it never became the panacea that Country Lifers had sought to cure the problem of stagnant productivity.

It has been argued that what was most significant about the Country Life movement was what it symbolized concerning the shifting position of rural America in a modernizing nation. Prior to 1900 "rural" had been considered to be the norm and "urban" had been regarded as the strange or unusual. The typical American was a farmer, and he stood as the symbol of virtue and the enduring strength of the republic. But by the early twentieth century, farmers had become the "peculiar" ones and the objects of concern. Urban reformers now suggested innovations for their institutions and solutions to their problems. As one historian concluded, "The farmer had been transformed from paragon to problem, and rural America from backbone to backwater. Whatever its intensions and accomplishments, the Country Life Movement represented the diminished status and growing peripheralization of rural America."[29]

THE IMPACT OF WORLD WAR I ON RURAL AMERICA

The interest that policymakers and reformers had taken in rural America actually increased in 1917 when the United States entered World War I. The government was apprehensive that rural America would have trouble meeting the demand for foodstuffs that would accompany the war. In response, it placed farm and home extension agents in every agricultural county and gave the USDA emergency authority to allocate scarce seed and fertilizer, issue "work or fight" orders to threaten transients with the draft if they did not help with work on the farms, and organize townspeople to help with harvests. In the South, farm agents tried to dissuade black sharecroppers and laborers from leaving the region in search of better paying jobs in northern cities. The intention was to assist the most productive farmers and enable efficient production. At the same time, the newly created U.S. Food Administration encouraged food production and saving. Farmers were asked to produce as much as they could, and consumers were asked to reduce the consumption of certain foods and urged to use substitutes for certain items. Food Administration propaganda also affected fashions and styles. For example, shorter skirts were encouraged to save cotton, and a new emphasis on slimness encouraged the acceptance of the slim female figure in place of the more full-figured one as the new American ideal.

The war also placed added stress on existing community problems. Churches lost ministers to the military or to better-paying urban posts. Schools were disrupted as teachers sought better opportunities and were not always replaced. Regular school terms, which had been lengthened as a part of general education reforms, were temporarily shortened in the interest of winning the war. The enlistment of hundreds of thousands of rural men in the army heightened the existing concern over rural depopulation, because many believed that they would not return to the farm even if they survived the war in the trenches. A popular song of the day, "How Ya Gonna Keep 'Em Down on the Farm (After They've Seen Paree)" expressed this very theme. That worry was further exacerbated by the fact that their undrafted neighbors were already leaving the countryside in large numbers for jobs in defense-related industries, encouraged to do so by labor agents who recruited aggressively in rural districts. It was ironic that this spike in rural-to-urban migration was taking place at a time of unprecedented agricultural prosperity. The period from 1916 to 1920 witnessed a dramatic surge in agricultural prices at the end of a period when farmers had generally done well economically. Farm incomes rose along with farm prices and actually exceeded average urban incomes for one of the few times in American history. It was easy to draw the conclusion that physical and social disadvantages endemic to rural life—not incomes—were the primary factors driving inhabitants to the cities.

There is evidence to suggest that those who remained "down on the farm" tried to modernize and overcome the shortcomings of rural life. They spent some of their higher incomes to enrich the lives of their families materially, accepted higher taxes to improve schools and roads, and reinvested some of their wartime profits in upgrading the operation of their farms. Gasoline-powered tractors became more numerous, and even though fewer than 4 percent of farmers owned them at the end of the war, most concurred that they were the wave of the future. Other farmers improved the quality of their livestock, purchased land even at inflated prices, and convinced themselves that the current boom would not be followed by a severe downturn. They were wrong. Commodity prices fell sharply in 1920 and remained down throughout the next decade. Those who had borrowed heavily, as well as those who were unable to mechanize and achieve economies of scale, had difficulty surviving. The number of farms and farmers continued to decline. The future seemed to belong to the large, highly mechanized, and well-capitalized farmer. As one historian concluded, "The farmer was no longer the average American, and it was becoming clear that the average American could no longer hope to be a farmer."[30]

NOTES

1. Rodman W. Paul, *The Far West and the Great Plains in Transition, 1859–1900* (New York: Harper and Row, 1988), 232.

2. David E. Shi, *Facing Facts: Realism in American Thought and Culture, 1850–1920* (New York: Oxford University Press, 1995), 204–206.

3. Thomas J. Schlereth, *Victorian America: Transformations in Everyday Life* (New York: HarperCollins, 1991), 43.

4. David B. Danbom, *Born in the Country: A History of Rural America* (Baltimore: Johns Hopkins University Press, 2006), 134.

5. David B. Danbom, *The Resisted Revolution: Urban America and the Industrialization of Agriculture, 1900–1930* (Ames: Iowa State University Press, 1979), 4.

6. Pete Daniel, *Standing at the Crossroads: Southern Life since 1900* (New York: Hill and Wang, 1986), 4.

7. Theodore Rosengarten, *All God's Dangers: The Life of Nate Shaw* (New York: Avon Books, 1974), 234–235.

8. Pete Daniel, *Breaking the Land: The Transformation of Cotton, Tobacco, and Rice Cultures since 1880* (Urbana: University of Illinois Press, 1985), 25, 26.

9. Ronald D. Eller, *Miners, Millhands, and Mountaineers: Industrialization of the Appalachian South, 1880–1930* (Knoxville: University of Tennessee Press, 1982), 32.

10. Ibid., 34.

11. Ibid., 35.

12. Ibid., 123.

13. Danbom, *Resisted Revolution*, 6.

14. Steven J. Diner, *A Very Different Age: Americans of the Progressive Era* (New York: Hill and Wang, 1998), 104.

15. Daniel, *Standing at the Crossroads*, 8.

16. Diner, *Very Different Age*, 112.

17. Gilbert C. Fite, *Cotton Fields No More: Southern Agriculture, 1865–1980* (Lexington: University Press of Kentucky, 1984), 35.

18. Danbom, *Resisted Revolution*, 10.

19. Ibid., 11.

20. Ibid., 14.

21. Fite, *Cotton Fields No More*, 44.

22. Michael L. Berger, *The Devil Wagon in God's Country: The Automobile and Social Change in Rural America, 1893–1929* (Hamden, CT: Archon Books, 1979), 81.

23. Danbom, *Resisted Revolution*, 19–20.

24. Berger, *Devil Wagon*, 82.

25. Danbom, *Born in the Country*, 170.

26. William L. Bowers, *The Country Life Movement in America, 1900–1920* (Port Washington, NY: Kennikat Press, 1974), 84.

27. Danbom, *Resisted Revolution*, 82.

28. Ibid., 77.

29. Danbom, *Born in the Country*, 175.

30. Ibid., 187.

2

Workers

As American capitalism emerged from the depression of the 1890s, businessmen had reason to be optimistic that a new, prosperous era was about to begin. Despite the severity of the recent economic collapse, the United States emerged from the crisis as the world's preeminent industrial power. In a sense, the depression only temporarily slowed a process that was already well underway. Rapid industrial expansion had been fueled by a number of factors: population growth, an expanding domestic market, extensive supplies of mineral and fossil fuels, a flood of new inventions, and the pro-economic growth policies of state and federal governments. The latter included land grants to railroads, protective tariffs, favorable tax laws, and a general absence of regulation of economic activities. By the start of the twentieth century, the United States led the world in the production of iron, steel, and coal. By 1920 it would be the world's largest producer of raw materials and food. After the Spanish American War in 1898, American control of Cuba, the Philippines, Puerto Rico, Guam, and the Hawaiian Islands offered new opportunities for investment and the development of new foreign markets. As presidents Theodore Roosevelt, William Howard Taft, and Woodrow Wilson increasingly pursued an interventionist foreign policy in Latin America, new markets opened there as well. U.S. exports to Latin America more than doubled between 1900 and 1914.

Reflected in the dramatic increase in industrial productivity were the changes in scale and organization that accompanied it. Only a handful of factories had employed more than 500 workers in 1870, but in 1900 there were 443 that employed more than 1,000 workers. By 1915 companies such as Armour's Chicago meat-packing plant (6,000 workers), the United States Steel works in Homestead, Pennsylvania (9,000 workers), and Henry Ford's automobile plant in Highland Park, Michigan (16,000 workers) were becoming the new norm. Increasingly dwarfed by their workplace, American workers were becoming members of armies of employees working under the same factory roof. The tendency toward bigness, centralization, and integration of operation generated the need for a new, white-collar managerial class. Characterized by engineers, accountants, personnel managers, and efficiency experts, these middle managers changed the ways in which factories operated. As corporations increasingly divided their activities into various departments (production, finance, shipping, receiving, purchasing, and marketing), the new managerial class used the latest techniques to increase productivity, control costs, and extend their supervision of the workforce. At this same moment in time, the process of economic consolidation began to accelerate. Between 1898 and 1903, some 276 corporate combinations occurred. According to financial expert and editor John Moody, almost 450 "trusts" had been formed. By 1909 1 percent of the industrial corporations in the country were producing 44 percent of the nation's manufactured goods. The process of industrial consolidation signaled cause for concern. Small businessmen became increasingly anxious about their ability to compete with the larger corporations, and consumers worried about the increase in prices that might result from any destruction of competition.

THE CHANGING NATURE OF WORK

Industrial productivity fueled the demand for industrial workers. Factory owners increasingly hired unskilled and semiskilled workers (a category that increasingly included women, new immigrants, migrants, blacks, and Mexicans) to do work previously done by skilled craftsmen. The introduction of new technology hastened the de-skilling process, and the perfection of techniques that would commonly be known as "scientific management" further divided skilled tasks to maximize the employment of lesser-skilled and lower-paid workers. The changes created problems for both groups. Skilled workers faced a diminishing sense of autonomy and a heightened sense of job insecurity, whereas unskilled and semiskilled operatives confronted a work process that was becoming increasingly repetitive, frenetic, and dehumanizing. As the U.S. Industrial Commission noted in its 1902 report, "[I]n nearly all occupations an increasing strain and intensity of labor is required by modern methods of production."[1]

Meat Packing

The inevitable result of modernization in a number of industries was the assembly line. Aspects of this process had been developed in the late nineteenth century in the manufacture of firearms, tool-and-die making, grain milling, bicycle manufacturing, and meat packing, to name a few. In the meat-packing plants of Chicago, the process was actually one of "disassembly." Upton Sinclair offered a vivid description of both the production line method and the nature of work being done in those plants in his famous novel *The Jungle* (1906).

[In the pork plant there] was a long, narrow room, with a gallery along it for visitors. At the head there was a great iron wheel, about twenty feet in circumference, with rings here and there along its edge. Upon both sides of this wheel there was a narrow space, into which came the hogs at the end of their journey;...[The wheel] began slowly to revolve, and then the men upon each side of it sprang to work. They had chains which they fastened about the leg of the nearest hog, and the other end of the chain they hooked into one of the rings upon the wheel. So, as the wheel turned, a hog was suddenly jerked off his feet and borne aloft.... [A]t the top of the wheel he was shunted off upon a trolley, and went sailing down the room.... [O]ne by one [the men upon the floor] hooked up the hogs, and one by one with a swift stroke they slit their throats. There was a long line of hogs...until at last each started again, and vanished with a splash into a huge vat of boiling water. It was all so very businesslike.... It was pork-making by machinery, pork-making by applied mathematics.... The carcass hog was scooped out of the vat by machinery, and then it fell to the second floor, passing on the way through a wonderful machine with numerous scrapers, which adjusted themselves to the size and shape of the animal, and sent it out at the other end with nearly all of its bristles removed. It was then again strung up by machinery, and sent upon another trolley ride; this time passing between two lines of men, who sat upon a raised platform, each doing a certain single thing to the carcass as it came to him.... Looking down this room, one saw, creeping slowly, a line of dangling hogs a hundred yards in length; and for every yard there was a man, working as if a demon were after him.

[In the beef plant] where every hour they turned four or five hundred cattle into meat... all this work was done on one floor, and instead of there being one line of carcasses which moved to the workmen, there were fifteen or twenty lines, and the men moved from one to another of these. This made a scene of intense activity, a picture of human power wonderful to watch.... They worked with furious intensity, literally upon the run—at a pace with which there is nothing to be compared except a football game. It was all highly specialized labor, each man having his task to do; generally this would consist of only two or three specific cuts, and he would pass down the line of fifteen or twenty carcasses, making these cuts upon each.... There were men to cut it, and men to split it, and men to gut it and scrape it clean inside. There were some with hoses which threw jets of boiling water upon it, and others who removed the feet and added the final touches. In the end, as with the hogs, the finished beef was run into the chilling room, to hang its appointed time.[2]

THE WORKING-CLASS COMMUNITY

The Physical Environment

Most of those who worked in the Chicago plants lived in a neighborhood surrounding the adjacent stockyards. James R. Barrett has offered a rich portrait of life in this community known as Packingtown in his book *Work and Community in the Jungle*. The industrial impact on the living environment could be readily seen in the pollution and extreme overcrowding. Fertilizer dust, smoke, and other noxious elements filled the air around a community of some 40,000 people. The advantage of living in the community was that it was close to the meat-packing plants, and workers could walk to their jobs—an important factor for the numerous "casual laborers" looking to find work by appearing before the factory gates on a daily basis. With the exception of two streets, Packingtown's roads were dirt. By comparison, the roads in the middle-class community of Hyde Park, located a mile or two to the east, were almost all paved. The working-class community also had fewer sewage facilities than its neighbors. With an average family income in 1900 of less than one-fifth that of its more upscale neighbor, Hyde Park, Packingtown had more than 14 times the number of families on relief. Although conditions in Packingtown may have been extreme in certain aspects, the economic realities faced by the workers who lived there were very similar to those faced by millions of workers in industrial America between 1900 and 1920.

Illness, Injury, and Death

For those living near the meat-packing plants and working in their damp cutting rooms, there was not only the constant threat of irregular employment and the ever-present burden of meager wages, but also the haunting specter of illness and death. Although the population of Packingtown was less than twice that of Hyde Park in 1900, its death rates from consumption, bronchitis, diphtheria, and other contagious diseases ranged from two-and-a-half to five times those of the middle-class neighborhood on its eastern border. The rates for tuberculosis and infant mortality were also inordinately high. In 1909, one of every three infants died before the age of two. Excluded from such "health" statistics was the number of occupational injuries that occurred as part of the mass-production process. Swift and Company reported 3,500 injuries during the first six months of 1910. Armour's Chicago plant averaged 23 accidents a day in 1917. Each job had its dangers—the dampness and cold of the pickling rooms, the sharp blade of the butcher's knife, the noxious dust of the fertilizer plant, the frenetic movements of a startled steer on the killing floor. Problems intrinsic to the nature of the work were compounded by the speed at which the work was done. Of the 284 households studied by the U.S. Commission of Labor in 1905, 12 percent of the heads of families had periods of unemployment averaging 12½ weeks as a result of injury or illness related to their job.

Housing

The housing of those who lived in Packingtown presented yet another social problem that had to be endured. Almost 93 percent of the buildings in Packingtown were of the wood-frame variety, built before housing reforms were enacted in 1902. In a word, they were firetraps. The typical tenement in the community was a dilapidated, two-story structure partitioned into four or more apartments. Each apartment connected with four ill-lit and poorly ventilated rooms shared by members of the nuclear family and their boarders. An average household included 6.7 people. Poorer families were forced to take in more boarders. As much as boarding exacerbated crowding, it was essential to economic survival. The system provided cheap lodging for single workers (helping to subsidize low wages) and an important supplement to a family's income. Boarders comprised almost one-third of Packingtown's population in 1909. The average cost for a room and board was about $10.25 per month (slightly lower for women). This was approximately one-fourth the average monthly wage for men and about one-third the average monthly wage for women.

In compiling statistics for a census of the area done in 1905, investigators gathered enough data to show that these overcrowded frame tenements were also people's homes. Many displayed photographs of relatives from the old country, and pictures of the Madonna and Christ and numerous patron saints served as common adornments. Some families managed to acquire rugs and draperies; others planted flowers. Early twentieth-century photographs of Packingtown show adults sitting on the stoops (porches), and photographs of cluttered alleys and flooded roads often show groups of children at play. One interesting aside that seems inconsistent in the midst of all the poverty was the unusually high rate of home ownership (22.5% of the families surveyed in 1905). Although explanations vary, home ownership offered working-class families a hedge against catastrophe. As workers passed beyond middle age, wages declined and the probability of illness or injury increased. Most workers in the early twentieth century could not count on a pension or workmen's compensation. As a result, home ownership held out the hope that there would be an opportunity for a sustained income from rent and boarding as they struggled to survive in their older years.

Family Finances

Packingtown's physical environment offers one indication of living standards; family finances offer another. Wages for most workers in the community were very low. The "common labor" rate, earned by at least two-thirds of those who worked in the plants, varied from 15 to 20 cents an hour between 1900 and 1917. Hourly wage earnings, however, are misleading because of the prevalence of irregular employment. Thousands of workers in the meat and pork plants were laid off two or three months a year. During slack periods, skilled workers were often forced to accept jobs as common laborers at reduced wages. Thousands of workers milled around the factory gates looking for work. Many were called to work when the assembly line was about to start and sent home as soon as it was stopped for that day. A reliable study conducted by investigators from the University of Chicago Settlement House in 1911 estimated that the average weekly wage for laboring husbands was $9.67, but the estimate of the minimum weekly expenses needed to support a family of five was $15.40 (average family size in Packingtown was 5.33). Thirty percent of the families studied showed budget deficits. Obviously, survival depended on additional income.

To supplement yearly income, husbands looked for alternative employment during slack periods. Wives, as mentioned, took in boarders and sometimes did work for pay at home. Children left school early for factory work. To make ends meet, some families scavenged for coal or wood to sell or use as fuel. About 27 percent of families in Packingtown depended on the earnings of children under the age of 16. Young boys worked as messengers and errand boys as well as machine tenders. Joining them were their sisters. As production lines became increasingly characterized by division of labor and as mechanization continued to diminish the degree of skill required for many operations, women became acceptable and desired as workers. Most of the women who worked in the plants were young and single. They worked from financial necessity, but in some instances they were actually the family's primary breadwinners. A 1906 U.S. Bureau of Labor Statistics report noted that 55 percent of young women workers came from families in which the father's earnings were compromised due to injury, disease, or chronic unemployment, or as a result of desertion, divorce, or death. These young girls worked in the packing plants making labels, filling cans, trimming meat, and making sausage casings. By 1920 women represented 12.6 percent of Chicago's packinghouse workers.

Female Workers

The work performed by women in the meat- and pork-packing plants differed from that of men in a number of ways. If women replaced men, they did so in the most poorly paid positions while men kept the "better" jobs. In sausage making, for instance, women twisted, linked, and tied, but men operated the stuffing machines and received a much higher rate of pay. Advancement for women was almost impossible, and most women employees never progressed beyond unskilled work. Pay systems differed as well. Very few men worked for piece rates (where payment was made for each item completed, rather than as a set wage for the hour or day), but women commonly did. As a result, these women not only earned less than men, they also earned less than women in other Chicago industries. Of the young women interviewed in 1912, 90 percent earned $4 or less per week. Women also had far less job security than did men, and were affected much more by seasonal layoffs. One interesting note is that despite evidence of considerable job dissatisfaction and high rates of turnover among young women, they still chose factory work over domestic work because it offered them more freedom and independence.

280 Making link sausages—machines stuff 10 ft. per second, Swift & Co's. Packing House, Chicago, U.S.A. Copyright 1905 by H. C. White

Workers making link sausages at Swift and Company's packing house, Chicago, ca. 1905. (Courtesy of the Library of Congress)

SOCIAL INSTITUTIONS

The Saloon

One of the central social institutions in Packingtown was the working-class saloon. Although denigrated by a number of contemporary social scientists as an indication of the degenerate character of the neighborhood and its inhabitants, the saloon provided a variety of often overlooked social functions. Because saloons offered one of the few halls in the community, they became common sites to hold weddings and dances as well as places for fraternal clubs, ethnic associations, and union locals to meet. Workers who gathered in the saloons at lunchtime or after work could exchange employment information and share grievances. Saloons also cashed checks and served hot meals for the price of a beer. Many saloon keepers were actually retired workmen. In many instances, the man behind the bar might have been a skilled Irish butcher who had traded in his workman's overalls for a bartender's apron.

The Settlement House

If the saloon performed a variety of social functions for men (women were excluded) in Packingtown, the University of Chicago Settlement House served somewhat the same function for women. Organized in 1894 and located in the heart of Packingtown, the settlement was operated by Mary McDowell and her middle-class associates, and worked hard over the years to become an integral part of the community. It offered its meeting space to ethnic groups, ran a day nursery, organized clubs for both youth and working-class adults, took working-class children to parks and summer camps, set up a playground and a gymnasium, and raised funds for a municipal bathhouse and a public library. The settlement also became active in public health issues in the area of sanitation, and McDowell helped to establish the Illinois Women's Trade Union League in 1903 to improve working conditions for women by encouraging the formation of trade unions.

THE AUTOMOTIVE ASSEMBLY LINE

As much as the production line in the meat-packing plants had been refined for efficiency, it was the introduction of the chain-driven assembly line at Henry Ford's automotive plant at Highland Park, Michigan, in 1913–1914 that really perfected the assembly process. By initially placing 29 workers at a waist-high sliding table surface, Ford's production engineers designed a process by which each worker was required to perform one particular part in the process of building a magneto. After one worker had completed his simple task, he would slide the unit down the table to the next worker, and so on. One worker had been able to assemble 35 magnetos in one day, but now a group of workers performing repetitive tasks could produce 1,188 in one shift. After making some minor adjustments—raising the workbench several inches to reduce back strain, installing a chain to continuously pull the units at a set speed, and reducing the number of workers from 29 to 14—the line increased its production to 1,335 magnetos in a single eight-hour shift. The same technique was used to reduce engine assembly time (cut by 40%) and the assembly of the automotive chassis. Using time-and-motion studies, Ford's engineers placed the parts and the men needed to assemble them at different intervals along a moving, 250-foot production line. By 1914, after the length of the line, the divisions of labor along the line, the number of workers, and the speed of the line had been refined, Ford was turning out 1,212 chassis on three automated lines in an eight-hour period.

Scientific Management

"Systematic" or "scientific" management as reflected in Henry Ford's famous assembly line were ideas advanced by a number of individuals, of whom Frederick Winslow Taylor was most prominent. Taylor had pioneered in experiments to improve plant efficiency while employed by the Midvale Steel Company in the 1880s. He wanted to understand the intricacies involved in the work process, and he concluded that the most efficient method of operation was to separate the thinking from the doing of a job. Taylorism, as the new method of operation came to be known, involved four basic concepts: (1) each distinct work operation would be timed with a stopwatch and analyzed to determine its "time" rate; (2) centralized planning would then direct the production process through its various stages, regulated by synchronized time clocks in the factory; (3) specific instructions would be given to foreman and workers, describing in detail what work should be done and how long it should take to complete it; and (4) wage rates would be pegged to a worker's performance (how well he followed instructions and adhered to the established time constraints). Such changes imposed a new managerial logic in the factory and consciously set out to replace older, established patterns of worker control based on custom and experience. As Taylor envisioned the process, managers would assume "the burden of gathering together all of the traditional knowledge which in the past has been possessed by the workmen and then of classifying, tabulating, and reducing this knowledge to rules, laws, and formulae." To increase efficiency, workers would have to give up control of the shop floor to management. "Faster work can be assured," said Taylor, "only through *enforced* standardization of methods, *enforced* adoption of the best implements and working conditions, and *enforced* cooperation.... And the duty of enforcing...rests with the *management* alone."[3] Simply put, scientific management changed the way many workers performed their everyday jobs in the factory.

Worker Control

Many workers regarded the implementation of scientific management as an attempt to eliminate the control that they historically exercised over the production process. Skilled craftsmen possessed what historian David Montgomery called "functional autonomy," which rested on their superior knowledge, passed from generation to generation, and the self-directing manner in which they performed their tasks. According to Montgomery, "Iron molders, glass blowers, coopers, paper machine tenders, locomotive engineers, mule spinners, boiler makers, pipe fitters, typographers, jiggermen in potteries, coal miners, iron rollers, puddlers and heaters, the operators of...stitching machines in shoe factories, and...machinists and fitters in metal works exercised broad discretion in the direction of their own work and that of their helpers." On most jobs, workers commonly engaged in a "stint," an output quota fixed by the workers themselves. In other words, workers thought they knew what entailed a proper day's work as well as the proper way to do it. As one efficiency consultant acknowledged, "There is in every workroom a fashion, a habit of work."[4] Thomas Bell, in his compelling novel *Out of This Furnace* (1941), a story about three generations of an immigrant Slovak family in the steel mills of Braddock, Pennsylvania, touches on this point in describing how the appearance of the general superintendent in the factory disrupted the rhythm— the relationship—between worker and his job.

With his appearance the furnace and the men became separate. It was now his furnace and they its servants, and his; for its well-being they were responsible now not to the furnace and to themselves, their pride in knowing how to handle her, but to him. He took it away from them. They ceased to be men of skill and knowledge, ironmakers, and were degraded to the status of employees who did what they were told for a wage, whose feelings didn't matter, not even their feelings for the tools, the machines, they worked with, or for the work they did.[5]

Worker Resistance

As scientific managers sought to uproot these established, worker-controlled rules and systematize the job for greater efficiency, workers resisted. They regarded stopwatch supervision as demeaning and found assembly-line work monotonous. When managers designed specific tasks and set the rhythm of that work to the time clock, workers regarded the loss of their traditional control over the work process as a loss of freedom. When told to leave their old tool boxes at home and use the newly designed tools instead, they complained that pride in their work as craftsmen was being undermined. When managers dictated the pace of work, they cried "Speedup!" Although the number of labor strikes had decreased during the depression of the 1890s, with the return of prosperity in 1898, "both strikes and union organizing quickly resumed their upward spiral, [the debate over] work rules again seized the center of the stage, and sympathetic strikes became increasingly numerous and bitterly fought."[6] Workers also resisted the new processes in another way: they quit. To be certain that 15,000 workers could be kept on the lines every day, Henry Ford had to hire 53,000 people every year. To bring about some stability of his workforce (and to blunt union organizing), the company reduced the workday to eight hours in 1914 and implemented a bonus system that increased a laborer's wage to $5 per day (more than double the pay of most industrial workers).

WAGE LABOR

America's workers were finding out that material conditions were not keeping pace with the country's growing national wealth. The depression of the 1890s had eroded living standards. Testimony before the U.S. Industrial Commission in 1900 suggested that wages were 10 percent below what they had been in 1893. Some economists calculated that only 16 percent of workers earned more than $15 a week in 1900 and that average annual earnings were in the neighborhood of $480. That same year a government investigation of conditions in the anthracite coal regions revealed that miners averaged only $240 a year in earnings, or roughly $4.60 a week. Such figures applied only to those workers who were fully employed. The U.S. Census of 1900 reported that nearly 6½ million workers were unemployed during some part of the year, and that nearly 2 million (especially those in seasonally affected trades) were without work from one-third to one-half of the year. Overall, wages for most skilled workers did advance in the years following the depression of the 1890s, but for some skilled workers and the vast majority of the unskilled, wages advanced only slightly or remained stagnant. The introduction of labor-saving technology and the burgeoning number of new immigrants actually contributed to a labor surplus. As a result, most workers had to confront the fear of job insecurity.

Industrial Work

At the turn of the twentieth century, more than 5 million women worked for wages (one-fourth held jobs in manufacturing) and together constituted roughly one-fifth of the workforce. They swelled the labor supply in industries such as clothing, textiles, and food production. They supplied the majority of the workforce in cotton mills, garment factories, canning plants, and commercial laundries. They tended to be young, single, and either first- or second-generation immigrants. Single women outnumbered married women in the workforce by about seven to one, but more than one-third of married women were forced to work because of the difficulty of supporting a family on one income. Typically unskilled or semiskilled, they earned about one-half the pay of men in industrial work. The average weekly wage for women in 1905 was $5.25. Of 473 women interviewed that year, 28 percent earned less than $300 a year, 53 percent earned between $300 and $500, and only 7 percent earned more than $600. One woman who earned $6 a week summed up her circumstance: "I didn't live. I simply existed.... It took me months and months to save up money to buy a dress or a suit or a pair of shoes."[7] Many women worked at routinized but demanding factory jobs under male supervisors. Gender discrimination compounded the hardship of factory work for women. Employers paid women less than men even if they did the same work. In the clothing industry, women earned 68.5 percent of the pay given to men. In the packing plants, women earned $1.25 a day for doing the same work that a man did who earned $1.75 a day.

Domestic Work

Approximately 2 million women worked for subsistence wages or less in some sort of domestic service. Work that may have been done by "help" or "hired girls" on a temporary basis in the late nineteenth century had been transformed by the 1890s into domestic labor of a more permanent sort. Most domestic servants were expected to be at work before the employing family arose in the morning and stay on the job until after the family retired at night. They were allowed little time off (usually one evening or afternoon a week, and a full Sunday every two weeks), which meant that many domestic workers constantly looked forward to a better job that would give them more time for themselves. Domestic servants received pay that was often a combination of room and board and wages. Although the type of work varied little over the years, the type of worker varied. In 1900 60.5 percent of Irish-born, wage-earning women were domestics. But this was to change. Only 18.9 percent of their children followed in their footsteps. By 1915 domestic workers were increasingly African American. As blacks migrated from the South to the North, and as employment agents traveled the South offering transportation and a guaranteed job, black women moved into the field of domestic labor. According to the memoir of one black woman who worked as a domestic nurse in a southern city, where she estimated that more than two-thirds of the African American women living there worked as "menial servants of one kind or another," the work was exceptionally arduous.

I frequently work from fourteen to sixteen hours a day. I am compelled by my contract, which is oral only, to sleep in the house. I am allowed to go home to my own children...only...every other Sunday afternoon.... I don't know what it is to go to church; I don't know what it is to go to a lecture or entertainment or anything of the kind; I live a treadmill life.... You might as well say that I'm on duty all the time—from sunrise to sunrise, every day in the week. I am the slave, body and soul, of this family. And what do I get for this work—this lifetime bondage? The pitiful sum of ten dollars a month![8]

Whereas black women comprised roughly one-fourth of domestic workers in 1900, they would form nearly one-half of the servant population by 1930. As a reflection of socioeconomic conditions during the Progressive Era, although 33 percent of married black women worked in 1920, only 6 percent of native white married women and 7 percent of married white immigrant women did.

Retail Sales Work

Women also moved into retail selling jobs, which commanded more status and money than did factory work. Whereas "saleswomen" were too few in number to be counted as a separate category in the 1870 census, they numbered more than 142,000 in 1900. By 1920, largely due to the rapid growth in the number of department stores, the number doubled. Being a saleswoman, however, was not without its problems. Wages were low. A 1909 federal study of women wage earners showed that women who worked in a Chicago store had almost an even chance of earning a living wage of $8, yet a similar saleswoman in New York City had only a one-in-four chance. Saleswomen also earned less than their male counterparts. They averaged 42 to 63 percent less in pay than salesmen, and earned only 70 to 90 percent of what a man earned when he worked in the same store department. Part-time saleswomen earned on average 10 percent less than women who worked full-time.

The problem of low wages was compounded when one factored in fines for procedural errors and tardiness. Some department stores implemented incentive plans—offering bonuses on sales above a set quota—that resembled piecework schemes in many sweatshops and factories. Saleswomen had to endure the common practice of unpaid overtime. Long hours were also a problem. Although their hours averaged fewer than those of women who worked in manufacturing, saleswomen still had to stand for nine hours a day (making seats available for saleswomen became a major issue for early twentieth-century reformers). As part of their work environment, saleswomen had to deal with arbitrary treatment from store managers and floorwalkers. They also had to adjust to condescension from upper- and middle-class customers and to a litany of work rules (separate employee entrances and elevators, time clocks, spy systems and the inspection of employee packages, and dress codes) that they often found degrading or demeaning.

On the positive side, women who worked in retailing enjoyed steady, full-time work with fewer seasonal layoffs than other workers experienced, opportunity for career advancement (perhaps to one day become a buyer), white-collar prestige (although not as much as in clerical work, which required more education), the chance to exercise initiative and autonomy on the job, and the opportunity to develop a sense of pride in one's skill as a salesperson. Sales work required being attuned to middle-class tastes.

Personnel managers used training programs to eliminate any signs of working-class dress, speech, and mannerisms, while trying to inform new employees about middle-class lifestyles so that they might better interact with customers. An interesting dynamic soon developed between store managers who issued directives— dos-and-don'ts booklets of store regulations and instructions on interacting with customers—and shop girls who wanted to control their work. Many employees simply ignored instructions that they considered unreasonable. Saleswomen, much in common with those in other occupations, developed a work culture that revolved around the idea of the stint. Much like the skilled craftsmen in a factory, they had a clear comprehension of the amount of sales (a "good book") that constituted a good day's work. New workers quickly learned not to deviate too far from that standard. To fall below the mark invited the ire of management. To sell too far above the norm, or to be a "hog" or a "grabber" by competing too energetically for customers, risked alienation from co-workers.

Office Work

As corporate and governmental bureaucracies grew in size and complexity, and as the distribution sector of the economy expanded in the late nineteenth and early twentieth century, office staffs changed as well. By 1900 women comprised more than one-third of all clerical workers (as well as one-third of all federal employees). Over the next twenty years, that number would increase to more than one-half. With limited access to the professions aside from teaching and nursing, educated women turned to office work. Many enrolled in courses in the rapidly growing number of business schools or took business courses that were being offered in the new high schools. And clerical work paid better. Clerical workers could count on earning about 25 percent more than retail sales workers. A high school graduate who turned to teaching in an urban public school might earn $450 a year, but her counterpart who took a job in an office might earn $660. Although women clerical workers could expect some upward mobility, few became executives. A woman might become the supervisor of a firm's typing staff or the head of its bookkeeping department, but advancement beyond that was exceedingly rare. As in industrial work, a gendered hierarchy of pay and power existed in the office as well. Clerical workers were viewed as process workers in specialized departments—accounting, purchasing, credit, personnel, marketing, filing—with little authority and increasingly tied to their machine (the typewriter). As Thomas J. Schlereth has noted, "Perhaps the most potent sign of the clerical worker's parallel with the plant worker was the time clock's appearance in business offices by 1910."[9]

The "Spirit of Personal Independence"

It has been suggested that the working woman—both immigrant and native, working class and professional—who emerged in increasing numbers in the late nineteenth and early twentieth century was motivated not only by economic need, but by the spirit of female emancipation. Although there were many limitations to that freedom, such as wage discrimination and exclusion from many jobs and unions, working women still developed a sense of independence. Charlotte Perkins Gilman argued in her influential book *Women and Economics* (1898) that the growing number of women who were seeking careers offered strong evidence that they possessed a "spirit of personal independence."

One of its most noticeable features is the demand in women not only for their own money, but for their own work for the sake of personal expression. Those who object to women's working on the ground that they should not compete with men or be forced to struggle for existence look only at work as a means of earning money. They should remember that human labor is an exercise of faculty, without which we would cease to be human.[10]

It was this new, collective feeling that signaled a transformation of economic life and also a shift in gender relations within the old patriarchal family. "With the larger socialization of the woman of to-day, the…desire for…more organized methods of work for larger ends, she feels more and more heavily the intensely personal limits of the more primitive home duties." As Gilman saw it, the path to full emancipation for women would come through gainful employment outside the home and the economic independence derived from it.[11]

Wages

Compounding economic problems for the working class were the prices of essential commodities. Food costs increased 16 percent between 1896 and 1903, energy costs (coal and coal oil) jumped

40 percent, and rents rose 20 percent. In 1914 the cost of living was 39 percent higher than it had been in the 1890s. Historian Philip Foner has argued that from 1900 to 1914, a living wage was the exception rather than the rule for one-half to two-thirds of American wage workers, and that three-fourths of adult male wage earners did not earn enough to provide their families with a minimum level of health and decency. In August of 1902, the *Baltimore Sun* printed an excerpt from a study done for the Maryland Board of Statistics. The investigator reported that only 2 of 20 typical Baltimore working men's families owned their own homes, only 2 of the men were able to save anything from their earnings, and only 12 had total incomes that exceeded $300. A standard rate for common labor in Pittsburgh's steel mills in 1910 was 16.5 cents an hour. Two-thirds of the immigrant workers in that city made less than $12.50 per week, and one-third earned less than $10, which was well below the minimum ($15) deemed necessary by the Pittsburgh Associated Charities to support a family of five. Thomas Bell, in his novel *Out of This Furnace*, makes reference to the same cold reality:

[F]acing them was the inescapable fact that even with work good and the wage cut restored they couldn't live on what he made; or rather, they could just keep alive. A full week of seven days, eighty-four hours—ninety-six in the weeks he worked the long turn—brought him about thirteen dollars. Two people, if they were thrifty, their wants simple, could manage on that. Two people with debts and growing children could not.[12]

In 1904 sociologist Robert Hunter argued, in his pathbreaking study *Poverty*, that 6 million individuals, or approximately one-fifth of the population of the industrial states, lived in poverty, with inadequate food, clothing, and shelter. Some have argued that because Hunter set his poverty line at $460 a year for a family of five, his estimate of the extent of poverty was actually too conservative. Others argued that $600 was a more accurate minimum necessary for a family of five, and $800 in some more expensive areas. Using an average of $700 for a family of five, John Whiteclay Chambers II has suggested that there may well have been somewhere between 30 and 50 million people (roughly 40% of all wage earners and clerical workers in the United States) living in poverty during the first decade of the twentieth century, and that figure does not include those living in rural poverty—sharecroppers, tenant farmers, and migrant workers.

Hours

Compounding the problem of low wages was the burden of long hours. Men commonly worked 12 to 14 hours a day. In the steel industry, workers toiled 12 hours a day, 7 days a week. They were given every other Sunday off, but only after doing a "long turn" of 24 hours on the previous Sunday. Carmen on the transit systems worked 7 days a week with no time off. Women routinely worked long hours at night and during the day in book binderies, laundries, paper box factories, and garment workshops. Florence Kelley, the first female factory inspector in Illinois, noted that it was not rare to see girls who worked long hours in Chicago's laundries faint at their work after toiling 16- to 20-hour days in hot, damp, poorly ventilated working environments. Thousands of young women worked in the garment district of New York City. They commonly worked 56-hour, 6-day weeks for a wage of roughly $6 a week. Many women were required to rent their own sewing machines and to pay for the electricity they used. Pay deductions were routinely taken for mistakes. Female workers in New York canneries often put in 15- to 17-hour days for 10 cents an hour. One investigator testified that the floors in these establishments were "covered with water," the rooms "hot and full of steam," the noise of the machinery "deafening," and the experience "more than I could stand."[13] In addition to working 70 hours a week, most women also had to do their own housework—cooking, washing, cleaning, and child care.

Workplace Hazards

The endless routine of work was very often made precarious because of the hazardous nature of many of the industrial jobs that workers performed. Workplace injuries loomed over the life of every worker, especially in mechanical industries, where equipment commonly lacked safety guards and where safety procedures were all but nonexistent. A 1904 study of nearly 20 million workers in trades and occupations classed as dangerous revealed that over 15,000 died because of conditions in manufacturing. During 1907, 4,534 railroad workers died in collisions, derailments, falls, and shop accidents. One compiler of such statistics estimated in 1913 that 25,000 workers were killed each year in industrial accidents and another 700,000 were maimed or disabled. Hat and cap makers died from pulmonary and respiratory disease at a rate of 643 per 1,000, cigar and tobacco workers at a rate of 457, and marble and stone workers at a rate of 398. Other high-risk occupations included quarrymen, masons, carpenters, garment workers, iron workers, painters, dryers, enamellers, and miners. Asthma took a toll in dust-filled potteries, lead poisoning recorded high mortality rates in glass factories, and arsenic poisoning did likewise in the lithographic printing trades; and mortality rates from a wide variety of diseases claimed the lives of thousands of workers cramped together in sweatshops.

The reasons cited for the high accident rates are numerous: the absence of safety devices; the refusal of corporations to follow state codes or the recommendations of factory inspectors; the failure of enforcement procedures; the speedup of work on the job; the reluctance of workers to complain of dangerous conditions, fearing that they would be discharged or blacklisted; and worker negligence and fatigue. Making the human cost of an industrial accident even more appalling was the absence of workmen's compensation in the early twentieth century and the rule of common law, which held an employer liable only if an accident resulted directly from his negligence. An injured workman or his family could receive compensation only if the employer could be shown to be solely to blame. Courts generally took the view that a workman knew the risks when he accepted the job, and that he had voluntarily accepted those risks.

The Triangle Shirtwaist Fire

A tragic example of deplorable working conditions, the lack of safety standards and codes, and the greed of some businessmen was the Triangle Shirtwaist Fire that occurred on March 25, 1911. The Triangle Waist Company occupied the top 3 floors of the 10-story Asch Building on the Lower East Side of New York City near Washington Square. Owned by Max Blanck and Isaac Harris, the company produced women's blouses. Made of lightweight cotton or linen, the shirtwaist, or high-necked blouse, had become a standard mode of dress for women of all classes at the turn of the century. By allowing more freedom of movement than the confining Victorian dresses, these blouses suggested a more public role for women and were commonly worn with simple A-line skirts to work, to the market, or to church. The company employed many Jewish and Italian men and women who worked at cutting and sewing garments. The owners preferred to hire immigrant women, who would work for less pay than men and, it was believed, were less susceptible to union organizers. The women worked long hours in a cramped, unhealthy environment, for low wages. They were required to buy their own needles and thread, fined for talking, singing, and taking too many breaks, and verbally abused by supervisors. As one employee recalled the disciplined working environment, "[I]f you were two or three minutes longer than foremen or foreladies thought you should be, it was deducted from your pay. If you came five minutes late in the morning because the freight elevator didn't come down to take you up in time, you were sent home for half a day without pay."[14] As one historian noted about these workers, "They particularly objected to the lack of respect they were shown—marginalized as young immigrant women and daily 'searched like thieves' before they left the factory."[15]

When the fire broke out, there were over 500 women working on the 8th, 9th, and 10th floors. It was believed that the fire was started when a male cutter tossed a match into a scrap box of waste fabric. The fire spread quickly, fueled by oily rags, paper patterns, cuttings, and finished garments hanging above the cutting tables. The workers tried to extinguish the fire, but could get no water (the owners had rejected the fire department's recommendation to install sprinklers). Responding to the fire was difficult. The factory floors were crowded. On the 9th floor alone there were 310 workers and 288 sewing machines. The number of fire escapes was inadequate. There was only one fire escape at the rear of the building; it was too small and too flimsy to accommodate the number of employees, and iron shutters on the outside of the building obstructed access to the outside platform. Although many managed to get onto the fire escape, their combined weight caused the fire escape to tear away from the building. Supervisors routinely locked doors (which opened to the inside rather than outside) to prevent workers from taking breaks, leaving work early, and stealing garments, or, it has been said, to deter union organizers from mingling with the workers. Many workers were crushed against the doors as they tried to leave the burning building, and 30 died trying to slide down the cables to the elevator. The fire department rushed to the scene, but its ladders could reach only to the 6th floor and its hoses only to the 7th. Faced with the choice of suffocating or burning to death, many women chose to leap (some clasping hands with co-workers as they did so) from the windows to the street 100 feet below. Safety nets proved useless in trying to break the fall. In all, 146 women perished in the fire. Civil suits brought against the company owners were finally settled in March of 1914. At that time, cash payments of $75 were awarded to the families of each employee who died in the fire.

The fire dramatized the plight of working men and women as nothing else could have done. The investigations that followed underscored both the exploitation in the industry and the excesses of unregulated industrial capitalism. After the disaster, the Joint Board of Sanitary Control in the cloak, suit, and shirt industry examined conditions in 1,200 factories. Its report listed 14 factories with no fire escapes, 1,173 with doors that opened inward, 23 with doors that were locked during the day, 60 with hallways less than 36 inches wide, 58 with dark stairways, and 78 with obstructed fire escapes. As a result of the disaster, the New York state legislature passed a series of comprehensive laws regulating industrial work that became models for other states.

Living Conditions

Living conditions for workers reflected not only earning power, but also the effects of urban population growth. Improvements in urban transportation during the 1890s allowed wealthier urban residents to move to the edge of the city in "streetcar suburbs," while the poor remained trapped in the urban center. Rising land values encouraged property owners to intensify land use while rising property values contributed to urban congestion and crowding. In cities such as Baltimore and Philadelphia, where single-family home ownership remained rooted in the culture, developers constructed block after block of row houses. In cities such as Newark and Boston, the trend was toward four-story apartment buildings. In New York City, however, high rents forced many low-income families into small, cramped, badly illuminated, poorly ventilated apartments or tenements of six or seven stories. One historian noted that on a single block in New York's East Side, 39 tenements provided housing space for 2,871 persons. There was not a single bath in the entire block, and only 40 of the apartments had hot water. The tenements in New York's Lower East Side had one of the highest mortality rates in the world. Thousands died from a variety of common diseases such as typhoid, diphtheria, and tuberculosis. These conditions could be duplicated in any major urban-industrial center.

Above the poor and lowest-paid workers was a broad and divergent middle class. The middle class included most native white

Americans and descendants of earlier immigrants from western and central Europe. Members of this social class might include skilled workers, shopkeepers, small entrepreneurs, and small manufacturers, as well as professionals—teachers, lawyers, and doctors. They were joined by others that some have chosen to call the new middle class—primarily white-collar employees in shops and offices in the growing urban commercial districts. The homes of this class ranged from row houses in the city to single-family dwellings in the suburbs.

Upward Mobility

Despite the differences in wealth and the social stratification of society, white America remained a highly fluid society. Upward mobility for whites, both immigrant and native born, was not uncommon. One historian has noted that among Italians and eastern European Jews who lived in Manhattan between 1905 and 1915, 32 percent moved from blue-collar to white-collar occupations. Although industrialization increased the distance between the rich and poor, it also created a wide range of new occupations that facilitated the expansion of the middle class. Ironically, as Chambers has noted, the expansion of the middle class served to reinforce the belief among many in society that the individual, rather than one's social or economic environment, was responsible for his or her own social position. "The persistence of this belief," said Chambers, "contributed to the fact that the United States was the last advanced industrial nation to begin constructing a system of social welfare for its people—beginning with voluntary organizations and some state and local governments in the Progressive Era—and that it built such a system more slowly and more grudgingly than any comparable nation."[16]

Sweatshops

Fueled by the growing demand for inexpensive, ready-made clothing, many poor, inner-city immigrant women worked in sweatshops. Under this system, a contractor might convert a second-story loft or basement into a workshop, fill it with tables and sewing machines, and then hire women to work in this ill-ventilated, cramped environment turning cloth into finished garments. The contractor or "sweater" provided the raw material to be "sweated," and paid piecework rates to his assembled workers. Driven to work fast and pressured not to make mistakes that would cause work to be rejected, even young workers would be worn out by the exhausting work after just a few years. For many of the lower class, a dingy tenement apartment doubled as both home and workplace. Known as "homework," "tenement work," or "finishing work," the labor performed in an already crowded tenement flat was merely an extension of the sweatshop system with a twist. In this case, all members of the family were forced into service.

By comparison, homework was perhaps even more exploitative than sweatshop labor. Contractors paid lower piecework rates for homework and saved money by not having to pay for a rented space, heating, or lighting. Homework also reduced the number of machines that an employer had to buy and maintain. Workers rolled cigars, sewed clothing (knee pants known as knickerbockers and the blouses known as shirtwaists were commonly stitched items), performed hand finishing on garments (making buttonholes and attaching pockets to shirts or collars and cuffs to coats), did fancy embroidery work, assembled toys, sorted and packaged items, or made jewelry or artificial flowers. Younger children helped by pulling out basting threads; older ones sewed on buttons, made labels, or stripped tobacco for cigar making. Young boys did odd jobs, or they served as couriers carrying raw materials or finished products back and forth from the supplier or contractor. In 1910 it was estimated that there were 250,000 home workers in New York City alone. As typical home workers, an entire family might earn $5 a week.

Child Labor

One investigator estimated that to get by in 1900, approximately 64 percent of working-class families relied on income other than that brought in by the male head of the household. Although homework was one way to supplement a family's income and use the labor of children, there were other ways. Children worked in sweatshops, factories, cotton mills, coal mines, and shrimp canneries. They hawked newspapers on busy city streets; peddled fruits, flowers, and candy; shined shoes; made deliveries; and ran errands. According to the U.S. Census of 1900, 1,750,000 children between the ages of 10 and 15 (almost 20% of that age group) were part of the paid workforce. This number would rise to roughly 1,990,000 in 1910 and then drop to approximately 1,061,000 by 1920 (primarily the result of enforced child labor legislation and compulsory school attendance laws). In 1912 the National Child Labor Committee visited 181 families and found 251 children under the age of 16 at work. Girls, sometimes as young as 12, tended dangerous spinning machines in textile mills. "Bobbin boys," who were often no more than 10, hauled boxes of heavy spindles back and forth from the spinning to the weaving rooms of the same textile factories. "Breaker boys" as young as 8 commonly worked in anthracite coal mines separating slate rock from coal. Such jobs stole their youth, aged them permanently, and often damaged them physically.

Children who worked the street trades commonly suffered from chronic respiratory infections, tuberculosis, and exposure to cold (Jacob Riis's photographs of newspaper boys huddled together atop street grates above the press rooms to get warm readily come to mind). Street work brought many children into contact with criminals and prostitutes, and contributed to juvenile delinquency. Many children worked at night, especially in glass factories (earning 75 to 95 cents a day) where furnaces were kept running nonstop. Boys worked in the furnace rooms, where they squatted near blazing furnaces, constantly exposed to intense heat and bright light. In these same factories, girls decorated glassware or packed finished items for shipment. One observer has captured the essence of the type of work done by children in such factories.

A 6-year-old newspaper boy working the streets of Los Angeles, 1915. (Courtesy of the Library of Congress)

By the side of each mould sat a "take-out boy," who, with tongs, took the half-finished bottles—not yet provided with necks—out of the moulds. Then other boys, called "snapper-ups," took these bodies of bottles in their tongs and put the small ends into gas-heated moulds till they were red-hot. Then the boys took them out with almost incredible quickness and passed them to other men, "finishers," who shaped the necks of the bottles into their final form. Then the "carrying-in boys," sometimes called "carrier pigeons," took the red-hot bottles from the benches, three or four at a time, upon big asbestos shovels to the annealing oven, where they are gradually cooled off to insure even contraction and to prevent breaking in consequence of too rapid cooling. The work of these "carrying-in boys," several of whom were less than twelve years old, was by far the hardest of all. They were kept on a slow run all the time from the benches to the annealing oven and back again.[17]

A critical observer of child laborers was Lewis Hine, who gained fame as a photo realist. Quitting his teaching job in 1908 to work as a staff photographer for the National Child Labor Committee, Hine spent 11 years traveling the country documenting children at work. Beginning in the anthracite coal fields of Pennsylvania, he photographed boys hauling wagon loads of coal and some who had been maimed in mining accidents. Children told Hine of their experiences working 12 to 14 hours a day, six days a week, related their fears of being injured or killed in a mining accident, and complained about the foul air they breathed every day. The following account expands upon the points made by Hine.

[During a strike in Kensington, Pennsylvania, in the spring of 1900.] Every day little children came into Union Headquarters, some with their hands off, some with the thumb missing, some with their fingers off at the knuckle. They were stooped little things, round-shouldered and skinny. Many of them were not over ten years of age, although the state law prohibited their working before they were twelve years of age.

The law was poorly enforced and the mothers of these children often swore falsely as to their children's age ... it was a question of starvation or perjury.... the fathers had been killed or maimed at the mines.

From November until May a breaker boy always wears a cap and tippet, and overcoat if he possesses one, but because he has to rely largely upon the sense of touch, he cannot cover his finger-tips with mittens or gloves; from the chafing of the coal his fingers sometimes bleed, and his nails are worn down to the quick. The hours of toil for slate-pickers are supposed to be from seven in the morning until noon, and from one to six in the afternoon; but when the colliery is running on "full capacity orders," the noon recess is reduced to half an hour, and the goodnight whistle does not blow until half past six. For his eleven hours' work the breaker boy gets no more pay than for ten.

The coal so closely resembles slate that it can be detected only by the closest scrutiny, and the childish faces are compelled to bend so low over the chutes that prematurely round shoulders and narrow chests are the inevitable result. In front of the chutes is an open space reserved for the "breaker boss," who watches the boys as intently as they watch the coal.

The boss is armed with a stick, with which he occasionally raps on the head and shoulders a boy who betrays lack of zeal.[18]

The stories of children working in glass factories and coal mines could be duplicated in an endless list of similar endeavors. In the sugar-beet fields of Nebraska and Colorado, children worked at the hazardous task of topping beets with a 16-inch knife. Children as young as seven worked 12-hour days as members of migrant families following the crops as hired laborers. Other children worked 10- to 12-hour days in textile mills in New England and the South, tending fast-moving machinery as they threaded bobbins, spun thread, or made buttonholes. Still others worked in shellfish canneries along the coast of the Gulf of Mexico, shucking oysters and

Child labor in a textile mill; some boys were so small that they had to climb up on the spinning frame to mend the broken threads and replace the empty bobbins, 1909. (Courtesy of the Library of Congress)

peeling shrimp. Many of the young workers were the children of Polish immigrants. Cannery workers were paid by the pot of seafood shelled rather than by the hour and, in an attempt to earn a living wage, often started work as early as 4:00 A.M. The illiteracy rate among these children was very high. Only 1 in 10 attended school, and many of those only intermittently. These shellfish canneries also posed a health risk. Shrimp secrete a corrosive acid that causes the skin of the workers to peel and crack. In order to toughen their hands, the workers dipped them in alum, a harsh mineral salt. Newspaperman George Creel estimated that "at least two million children were being fed annually into the steel hoppers of the modern industrial machine...all mangled in mind, body, and soul, and aborted into a maturity robbed of power and promise."[19]

THE CONFLICT BETWEEN LABOR AND CAPITAL

One consequence of rapid industrialization, and its harsh consequences for many workers, was increased confrontation between labor and management. Wage cuts and layoffs had traditionally triggered resistance by workers. Industrial violence often resulted from workers' attempts to organize unions and management's attempts to destroy them. Twice as many strikes occurred in the first decade of the twentieth century as occurred as in the last decade of the nineteenth century. Although only a minority of workers joined unions during the Progressive Era, organized labor, led by the American Federation of Labor (AFL), made great strides. From fewer than 450,000 in 1897, union membership jumped to over 2 million by 1904. To obtain higher wages, shorter hours, and improved working conditions, the skilled craft unions of the AFL engaged in hundreds of strikes and boycotts between 1900 and 1910.

The sharp increase in craft unionism and labor militancy convinced some employers to seek a peaceful solution to labor problems. Looking to promote a more cooperative approach to industrial relations, a number of corporate leaders met in 1898 to form the National Civic Federation (NCF). Labor leaders such as James O'Connell of the Machinists Union, John Mitchell of the United Mine Workers, and Samuel Gompers of the AFL were also asked to join. The organization accepted the premise that labor and capital had a mutual interest in economic stability and that industrial conflict could be settled without resort to crippling strikes. The goal of NCF was to seek to arrive at negotiated labor agreements on an industry-wide basis. But the mood of cooperation was not to last. Skilled workers never abandoned the fear that employers were planning to weaken their control over the workplace, and employers never stopped being alarmed at the growing power of organized labor.

Co-option—"Welfare Capitalism"

While labor and capital drifted toward renewed confrontation in the workplace, a small number of employers offered one ingenious program aimed at conciliation. Known as welfare capitalism, the idea was essentially an attempt to co-opt the growth of trade unionism through kindness. If employers could diffuse labor animosity through concessions, then perhaps strikes could be averted. Production could then proceed uninterrupted, and closer labor-management cooperation could be encouraged. That might allow programs for industrial efficiency to be more easily implemented, which would lead to greater production per worker and greater profits. If a new bond between labor and management could be established, labor turnover might be reduced as well. To win employee allegiance (and a promise not to join a union), corporations set up profit-sharing schemes; paid bonuses in company stock; created pension and retirement programs that rewarded workers who stayed with the company; provided group insurance policies that were voided if a worker switched jobs; and offered various health, safety, and recreational programs. The system was premised on the notion that workers would eschew the advantages of genuine collective bargaining and meaningful employee representation ("company unions" would be allowed, but they would be totally controlled by the corporate sponsor), and identify with their employer and not their union, if the company was doing more for their welfare.

Confrontation—the "Open Shop" Campaign

By 1903, however, many employers had come to the conclusion that the proper plan of operation was to destroy unions and block any further gains by labor. Instead of accepting labor's right to exist, or trying to co-opt the union movement through concessions, many employers counterattacked. Many formed employer associations and championed the "open shop" (the idea that employers could prohibit unions in their factories). After 1903, the National Association of Manufacturers took control of the anti-union movement. Attacking the "closed shop" (the idea that employers could not prohibit unions in their factories) as un-American, and defending an individual's legal right to enter into a contract with his employer, the association mailed millions of anti-labor pamphlets to schools, churches, and newspapers in a concerted effort to influence public opinion. They maintained non-union shops; resorted to the use of lockouts to thwart attempts at unionization; employed labor spies; hired professional strikebreakers and exploited black and immigrant workers to break strikes; used the "yellow-dog" contract (which required employees to pledge that they would not join a union); blacklisted union activists; and gave financial assistance to struck companies. The impact was immediate. Labor saw existing agreements in the machinery and metal trades broken, and lost strikes in the steel and meat-packing industries. After roughly seven years of growth, membership in the AFL decreased by almost 200,000 members in 1905. For the next four years, union growth remained stagnant.

Labor Violence

In the structural iron industry, the breakdown in union-management cooperation led to open warfare, with workers resorting to violence and dynamite. The climax of this protracted struggle came in October 1910, when an explosion destroyed the printing plant of the *Los Angeles Times*, killing 20 employees. The owner of the newspaper, Harrison Gray Otis, was well known as a staunch foe of organized labor and ran a non-union plant. The two men accused of the bombing, J. J. McNamara and his brother James, were officers in the International Association of Bridge and Structural Iron Workers. The union had been locked in a long-running battle with the National Erectors' Association (NEA). By 1910 the NEA had virtually eliminated the hiring of union workers in the plants of its members. In the process the NEA had forced down wages, lengthened the workday, and set whatever working conditions it wished. Convinced that it had little chance to change conditions by peaceful means, the union began a campaign of dynamiting. Between 1906 and 1911, union leaders condoned some 110 explosions, which were intended to frighten employers into granting union demands rather than do extensive damage to the targeted plants. The McNamara brothers were eventually arrested and placed on trial for murder. One of the reporters covering the trial was noted muckraking journalist Lincoln Steffens. Steffens believed that the two brothers were guilty, but thought there was a larger issue to be considered.

The public, he thought, needed to know the reasons behind the use of dynamite, the injustices suffered by labor, and the causes of the intense animosity between capital and labor. To that end, he offered to be a mediator.

Steffens proposed to save the McNamara brothers from the death penalty by making a bargain with the anti-labor establishment. The brothers would plead guilty, their sentences would be reduced, and a conference between the leaders of capital and labor would be held to see if class warfare could be replaced with some form of industrial harmony. Steffens hoped that if both sides accepted his proposal, he could convince a frightened public that they (society) were complicit in the process that exploited labor and drove it to revolution. For a time, it seemed that his plan might work. The defense attorney, the accused, and the leading business leaders all agreed. Unfortunately for Steffens, the public and the churches did not. Instead of forgiveness, the public wanted revenge. In the end, the judge, who Steffens accused of giving in to public opinion, reneged on the deal, handed down harsh prison sentences, and publicly condemned the crime. Another opportunity for dialogue and possible accommodation had been missed.

Immediately after the trial, one Chicago labor leader tried to put the proceedings in some perspective: "If a man says to me that the McNamaras should be condemned, my reply is: all right.... but we will also condemn the National Erectors Association. Before the union began to use dynamite their men lived on starvation wages, some of them on less than $400 a year, with families!...put on the searchlights and we are willing that our sins should be compared with the sins of the employers."[20] Labor activist Kelley remarked that working men like the McNamara brothers committed violent acts "as a cornered rat bites, not according to reasoned theories, but in the wrath and despair of baffled effort and vain struggles."[21] Those sentiments were echoed by Eugene V. Debs, former leader of the American Railway Union in the famous Pullman Strike and current leader of the American Socialist Party.

If you want to judge [the McNamaras] you must first serve a month as a structural ironworker on a skyscraper, risking your life every minute to feed your wife and babies, then be discharged and blacklisted for joining a union.... It is easy enough for a gentleman of education and refinement to sit at his typewriter and point out the crimes of the workers. But let him be one of them himself, related in hard poverty, denied education, thrown into the brute struggle for existence from childhood, oppressed, exploited, forced to strike, clubbed by the police, jailed while his family is evicted, and his wife and children are hungry, and he will hesitate to condemn these as criminals who fought against the crimes of which they are the victims of such savage methods as have been forced upon them by their masters.[22]

Strikes

During the years between 1905 and 1917, less-skilled, primarily immigrant workers staged epic strikes of their own. One such strike occurred in 1912 in Lawrence, Massachusetts, a center of the textile industry. The strike was fought over a pay cut of 30 cents a week or, as one historian noted, about the cost of five loaves of bread. But working-class families in Lawrence lived so close to the bare minimum that 30 cents could well have meant the difference between survival and starvation. Employed in the huge woolen mills were 32,000 men, women, and children comprising 25 different nationalities. They worked six days a week and earned an average of 16 cents per hour. When the Massachusetts legislature passed a law in January 1912 that limited the workweek for women and children to 54 hours (they had been working 56), employers of the mills reduced the weekly pay of those who had been working longer hours. One-half of the workers in the mills were young women between the ages of 14 and 18, and many were suffering from malnutrition and overwork. Already angered by the long hours, and aroused by a strike of weavers at the mill the previous year to protest a speedup and pay cut, 20,000 textile workers decided to strike. In their list of demands, the workers called for a 15 percent pay increase based on a 54-hour work week, double pay for overtime work, and the abolition of all bonus systems (the basis of the recent speedup).

Aided by organizers from the Industrial Workers of the World (IWW), the workers organized commissaries and soup kitchens, set up strike and relief committees for each nationality group, established picket lines to deter scabs from entering the mills, and regularly marched through town in organized protest. When mill owners and government officials declared martial law, mobilized the National Guard, and banned all public meetings, strikers began sending their children to families in New York City for their own safety. The sight of pale, ill-nourished, and poorly clothed children marching up Fifth Avenue from Grand Central Station led to an outpouring of sympathy for the strikers. When local authorities tried to stop the exodus by instructing club-wielding police to use force to drive parents and their children from the Lawrence train station, it produced headlines across the country. In March, after the strike had lasted for eight weeks, the mill owners agreed to a settlement that raised pay rates on a sliding scale (the lowest-paid workers, who earned 9.5 cents an hour, were to get the largest increase) and granted time-and-a-quarter for overtime pay. It has been said that a quarter of a million textile workers in New England received pay increases as a result of the Lawrence strike. One popular banner carried by the Lawrence strikers read, "We want bread and roses, too." It was an indication that the strike was not only about wages, but also about having the opportunity to enjoy the finer things in life.

Similar strikes involved semiskilled clothing workers concentrated in cities such as New York and Chicago. The garment industry (which had doubled in size between 1900 and 1910) operated on a two-tier system. On one level were hundreds of small shops, each employing fewer than 20 girls, and each competing with the others to reduce labor costs and sell more cheaply. The second level was comprised of a number of larger factories, each employing between 200 and 300 workers. The workforce in the garment industry was composed primarily of Jewish and Italian women, many of whom possessed skills acquired in European workshops. The work was seasonal, the hours long (56 hours a week in addition to overtime), and layoffs common. Wages varied widely depending on whether workers were paid on a time or piecework basis and whether the workers were skilled. Workers were charged for the machines they used; charges included electricity, needles, and thread. Workers were docked pay if they reported to work late, and charged for a whole length of cloth for even minor mistakes. Over one-third of the workers in the shirtwaist industry, for example, were "learners" or apprentices, young women who earned from $2.50 to $4 a week. About one-half of the workers were more experienced and earned roughly $9 a week. Skilled male workers (primarily cutters and pressers) comprised the remaining 15 percent of the workers and earned from $15 to $23 a week.

In the fall of 1909, a number of women in small shops in New York City began to walk out over a series of issues involving pay, the outsourcing of work, and layoffs. After a labor rally at Cooper Union, shirtwaist workers called a general strike. Within the next two days, 20,000 workers had struck. The main issue in the strike quickly became union recognition, but the strikers also demanded an end to the existing subcontracting system, payment every week instead of every two weeks, a 52-hour workweek, a limit on the amount of overtime work, an end to the practice of charging workers for electricity and materials, and safety improvements (adequate fire escapes and open doors). The conflict persisted until February 1910, when the International Ladies' Garment Workers Union (ILGWU) and employers reached a partial settlement. Although the workers failed to gain recognition of the union, they did achieve shorter hours, a promise of improved working conditions, and an agreement to arbitrate future disagreements.

Only months after the shirtwaist strike, 60,000 New York City cloakmakers (mostly men) began a strike of their own that ultimately led to the unionization of the garment industry. These strikes were followed by those of men's clothing workers in Chicago against the Hart, Shaffner, and Marx Company in October 1910 and fur workers in June 1912. The Chicago strike ended in an agreement that created the "preferential shop," in which union members would be given preference in hiring over non-union workers if their skills were comparable, and a company promise to submit all future grievances to a board of arbitration. The board, which was composed of members from the company, the union, and mutually acceptable public figures, had the power to render binding decisions. The strike and ensuing agreement paved the way for the establishment of the Amalgamated Clothing Workers in 1914. In women's clothing, a more conventional collective bargaining system ultimately replaced the earlier arbitration agreement in 1916.

Gender Bias

It might be noted that most craft unions affiliated with the AFL excluded women, immigrants, and the unskilled from its membership. Most women were barred from even potential membership because they were denied entry into skilled occupations. When women did venture into the factories, their presence was deemed to be temporary. This assumption was used to justify wages well below those paid to men even when the jobs were comparable. When women worked alongside men, they were treated with contempt if not open hostility. Gompers, head of the AFL, often explained his union's position in bread-and-butter terms. Craft unions, to Gompers, fought to achieve the "family wage," which enabled male workers to support their families as responsible husbands, fathers, men, and citizens. However much the demand for a family wage might have legitimized Gompers's position, it served to devalue the work done by women and limit, to some extent, their participation in the labor movement.

In a context where women had not yet won the right to vote, they were also disenfranchised in the wage-earning economy and in the labor movement. As a result, many garment workers, among others, gravitated to more radical organizational alternatives such as the Socialist Party (which had 41,000 dues-paying members in more than 3,000 local branches by 1908) or the IWW, which was committed to organizing the most impoverished workers and showed no bias in organizing skilled and unskilled, men and women, immigrants, blacks, and Mexican workers. Women workers in the garment industry were also aided by the Women's Trade Union League (WTUL), a coalition of trade unionists, social reformers, and a number of wealthy supporters organized in 1903. The league sought to improve the everyday lives of women workers by organizing them into unions, teaching them leadership skills, and lobbying for legislation that would shorten hours and improve working conditions. The WTUL ultimately played a major role in convincing the U.S. Bureau of Labor to conduct a study of the conditions under which women and children worked, and its efforts helped in the creation of the Women's Bureau in the Department of Labor.

The Role of the Courts

In labor's battle with capital, the courts proved to be valuable allies of the latter. The courts often granted injunctions to halt strikes, rendered judicial decisions restricting workers' rights, and nullified one of labor's most effective weapons, the boycott. Unions had been successful in asking their members and other union sympathizers to refrain from purchasing products that did not bear the union label, or were made by companies that refused to recognize unions or were engaged in strikes with them. In 1902 the United Hatters of North America Union called for a national boycott of items made by D. E. Loewe and Company of Danbury, Connecticut, to support a strike by a local union. The company took the matter to court, charged the union with engaging in a conspiracy in restraint of trade in violation of the Sherman Antitrust Act, and sued for triple damages from the individual members of the local union who had participated in the strike. After a 14-year legal battle, a federal court ruled in favor of the company and levied $252,000 in fines. The bank accounts of the 197 union members were seized and foreclosure proceedings begun against their homes. Although the fines were eventually paid through contributions from the national union and the AFL, the decision shocked organized labor. The decision brought secondary boycotts under the purview of the Sherman Antitrust Act, appeared to place organized labor at a decided tactical disadvantage in contests with employers, and made individual union members personally liable for damages that could take away their homes and wipe out their life savings.

As the Danbury Hatters Case made its torturous way through the courts, the AFL became involved in an even more significant legal suit. In 1906 the AFL placed the Buck's Stove and Range Company of St. Louis, Missouri, on its "We Don't Patronize" list in the *American Federationist* in support of metal polishers who were striking in opposition to an increase in the hours they worked. J. W. Van Cleave, president of the company and head of the National Association of Manufacturers, asked for and received a court injunction prohibiting the union from placing his firm on the boycott list and from in any way calling attention to the strike either orally or in writing. When union president Gompers claimed that the sweeping court order was an unconstitutional limitation of his right of free speech and refused to comply with the injunction, he was found in contempt and sentenced to a year in prison. Although the case was eventually dismissed and Gompers's prison sentence aborted, the verdict seemed to show that organized labor had very few weapons at its disposal in its ongoing battle with big business. As one labor historian has noted, "The formerly accepted theory that possible injury to property rights through strikes or boycotts was only incidental to their legitimate purpose of seeking to improve working conditions was being denied under conditions which seemed to threaten the very existence of unions."[23] The two verdicts were the two most important factors forcing labor leaders such as Gompers to qualify the principle of voluntarism (the idea that the union would not have to seek the helping hand of government because it could protect its members through the collective power of the union) and consider political action to beat back the legal constraints being imposed upon labor through the courts. In 1906 the AFL took direct political action and drew up a Bill of Grievances, which it submitted to President Theodore Roosevelt and to Congress. Among its demands were those calling for an exemption of labor unions from the Sherman Act and relief from the use of court injunctions in labor disputes.

Protective Labor Legislation

At the start of the twentieth century, there was a general lack of legislative protection for workers in the areas of work hours, wages, and working conditions, or in compensation for injuries incurred on the job. The primary reason for the legislative impasse was not so much a lack of public support as the collusion of business interests and their representatives in the state legislatures and in Congress who sought to block the intervention of government in the workplace and the enactment of expensive safeguards for workers. Complicating the push for the adoption of protective labor legislation was the aforementioned position of the AFL. Gompers feared that legislation drawn up by third parties (legislators) could actually harm the labor movement. Preferring "pure and simple unionism" and collective bargaining between unions and employers as the proper method to solve economic problems, Gompers and the AFL opposed the effort to obtain shorter hours, higher wages, and workmen's compensation. In fact, the AFL's political involvement after 1906 was largely restricted to concerns considered to be beyond its control—curtailing the use of labor injunctions, exempting labor from antitrust laws, restricting immigration, and curtailing the practice of employing imported contract laborers.

The push for protective labor legislation during the Progressive Era was in many ways a combination of a growing sense of social responsibility and a deepening of humanitarian feeling for the plight of the working class on the part of various social reform groups such as the American Association of Labor Legislation, the General Federation of Women's Clubs, the National Women's Trade Union League, the National Consumers' League, the National Child Labor Committee, and a legion of settlement house workers. It actually had less to do with a general concern for labor's rights—union recognition and collective bargaining—and more to do with a concern for the negative consequences of industrialization and the economic hardship being endured by all workers, women and children in particular. One area of concern was child labor and the need for laws that placed restrictions on the age at which children might be employed in manufacturing operations as well as on the hours they could work, and under what conditions. By 1912 as many as 38 states had adopted some form of child labor legislation. Another issue that attracted the attention of reformers was the need for some form of workmen's compensation laws that would provide compulsory benefits for industrial accidents. Although these laws were often inadequate and not always effectively enforced, they did bring about acceptance of the principle that employers had a responsibility for the health and safety of the workers in their factories and mines. By 1915 at least 35 states had enacted workman's compensation statutes. After the Triangle Shirtwaist Fire, many states enacted factory safety statutes as well.

Another topic that drew the attention of social reformers was a limit to the hours that women worked, and, ironically, it was a landmark court case that turned the tide. Prior to 1908 challenges to existing working conditions had made little progress in the courts. The stumbling block for reformers was the Fourteenth Amendment to the Constitution, which prohibited a state from depriving a citizen of "life, liberty, or property without due process of law." The Supreme Court had defined *liberty* in the due process clause as the freedom of contract and had found the principle violated when the state interfered with the employer-employee relationship. The legal assumption was that an individual had the right to sell his own labor and, as an individual, to negotiate a fair contract with his employer. As a result, the only way a state could limit the hours of work was to demonstrate that such limitation was necessary under its police power to protect the health or safety of the general public. To make its point, the Supreme Court had, in *Lochner v. New York* (1905), overturned a 10-hour law for bakers. Because counsel had not proven that such a law was necessary to protect the health of the workers, the Court found it to be an infringement of the freedom of contract.

Muller v. Oregon

The issue appeared again in 1907 when reformers learned that an Oregon maximum-hour law for women was to be challenged before the Supreme Court. The Oregon law prohibited the employment of women in factories, mechanical establishments, and laundries for more than 10 hours a day. In September of 1905, the supervisor of the Grand Laundry in Portland violated the law by requiring one of his female employees to work more than 10 hours. Curt Muller, the owner of the laundry, was found guilty of a misdemeanor and fined $10. Muller, however, appealed on the grounds that the right of freedom of contract under the due process clause of the Fourteenth Amendment had been abridged. By 1908, when the case finally reached the Supreme Court as *Muller v. Oregon,* that line of reasoning was open to challenge. In the early nineteenth century, before the rise of large factories and giant corporations, working conditions were considered to be part of a contract between employers and individual workers, and power relationships were considered to be equal. But during the early twentieth century, as giant corporations increasingly resisted recognizing unions as the representatives of workers as a group, and continued to base their position on the tenuous logic of individual rights and freedom of contract, it was obvious to many that the power relationship between one worker and a corporation had become unequal, and that some sort of state intervention was necessary.

In contesting Muller's claim, the state of Oregon hired attorney Louis Brandeis. His defense was innovative. He started with a short legal argument or brief (two pages of abstract logic and prior legal precedents), which was common practice at that time, but he supported his argument with 100 pages of economic and sociological statistics (actually gathered by the National Consumers League) to show the negative effects of long hours on women and the possible benefits that might result if those hours were reduced. Agreeing that the right to purchase or sell one's labor was protected by the Constitution, Brandeis argued that such freedom might be subject to such reasonable restraints as a state might impose in exercising its police power. The question, as Brandeis saw it, was whether a woman's anatomical and physiological differences and lack of strength when compared to men required that her hours be restricted. Brandeis presented data from hundreds of reports of factory inspectors, physicians, boards of health, trade unions, economists, social workers, experts in hygiene, and special industrial commissions to prove that long hours of work were dangerous to the health, safety, and morals of women. In a unanimous decision, the Supreme Court ruled against the contention of Muller's lawyers that the freedom of women workers to bargain with their employers was violated by the Oregon statute, and affirmed the state's 10-hour law.

The decision in *Muller v. Oregon* revitalized the topic of protective labor legislation. Over the next eight years, 41 states enacted maximum-hour laws for women. The decision also opened the door for future restrictions on hours for men and on working conditions, and stimulated the debate over minimum wage laws as well. But *Muller v. Oregon* was important for workers on other levels. In accepting what became known as the Brandeis brief, the Supreme Court allowed a new form of legal argument—sociological jurisprudence—and set a precedent for the submission of factual data to establish the need for social legislation. The case also seemed to confirm the view that the meaning given to the law must evolve in relation to human need.

Most reformers during the Progressive Era were thrilled with the *Muller v. Oregon* decision. They thought that workers, especially women, had a right to a workday and a work environment that did not threaten their health, safety, or morals, and that the government (state and federal) needed to assume greater responsibility for guaranteeing those rights. Not everyone then or since, however, has agreed with that assessment. A number of critics argued that the decision in *Muller v. Oregon* actually did women an injustice and slowed the advance toward gender equality. They argued that the language of both Brandeis's brief and the Supreme Court's decision actually degraded women by regarding the differences between female and male workers as evidence that women were inferior. The decision seemed to entrench the principle of female difference in constitutional law—that women, as a class, should be treated differently, and that the resulting "protective" classification actually perpetuated their dependency and subordination. Organizations such as the Women's League of Equal Opportunity and the Equal Rights Association argued that protective labor laws should be abolished because they disadvantaged women economically as well. Maximum-hour laws could deny women employment (after the *Muller v. Oregon* decision, Muller fired his women workers and hired men), overtime pay, and promotion. Other restrictions, such as those that imposed bans on night work, or excluded women from certain hazardous occupations, or placed limits on the weights that women could lift, might have a similar negative impact.

The general conclusion was that gender-specific protective laws denied women complete equality. Such statutes defined women as weak and dependent, made them wards of the state, and prevented them from competing with men for better-paying jobs and advancement. It should be noted, however, that those who championed the idea of maximum-hour laws for women and other labor protections did so in an incredibly hostile environment. As they saw it, they faced powerful adversaries—greedy, insensitive employers; a recalcitrant labor movement (AFL); and an archaic legal doctrine of freedom of contract that seemed to block social change at every turn. It was those formidable obstacles that narrowed their options and molded their strategies.

Federal Action

During the second decade of the twentieth century, progress in the area of protective labor legislation reached the federal level. In 1910 Congress approved an eight-hour law for workers on public contracts and established the Industrial Relations Commission to study the underlying causes behind the surge in labor unrest. In 1914 Congress enacted the Clayton Antitrust Act, which appeared to strengthen earlier antitrust legislation and provide a long-sought exemption for labor under its provisions. The act specifically declared that "the labor of a human being is not a commodity or article of commerce," and stated that nothing in the antitrust laws should be interpreted so as to regard unions as illegal combinations or conspiracies in restraint of trade. It also outlawed the use of injunctions in disputes between employers and employees "unless necessary to prevent irreparable injury to property, or property right...for which injury there is no adequate remedy at law." Organized labor interpreted the law as a guarantee of workers' right to organize, bargain collectively with their employers, strike, boycott, and picket. In the following years, though, labor's interpretation proved far too optimistic. Exceptions to the law were found in the supposed exemptions of unions from antitrust prosecution, and provisions in the area of injunctions were interpreted so as to deny organized labor any real relief. As one labor historian has noted, the principle that labor was not a commodity remained in the law, but in practice, it had no direct effect in the relations of employers and employees.

During President Woodrow Wilson's second term in office, Congress passed a series of progressive measures to protect workers. The Keating-Owen Child Labor Act of 1916 set a national minimum age of 14 in industries that produced nonagricultural goods for interstate commerce or export, and placed limitations on the length of the workweek and restrictions on night work for children. The LaFollette Seamen's Act provided federally guaranteed rights to merchant seamen and greatly improved their living and working conditions. The Adamson Act mandated an eight-hour day for all railroad workers, with time-and-a-half for overtime. The Kern-McGillicuddy Act authorized workmen's compensation for federal employees. Although the federal child labor law was overturned in 1918, and the laws guaranteeing an eight-hour day and workmen's compensation applied only to a narrow group of workers, the actions were important precedents in expanding the scope of federal responsibility for human welfare and pointed the way to more extensive labor legislation passed during the New Deal.

NOTES

1. David Brody, *Workers in Industrial America: Essays on the Twentieth-Century Labor Struggle* (New York: Oxford University Press, 1993), 7.

2. Upton Sinclair, *The Jungle* (New York: New American Library, 1960), 38–44.

3. Brody, *Workers in Industrial America*, 12.

4. David Montgomery, "Workers' Control of Machine Production in the Nineteenth Century," *Labor History* 17 (1976): 487–488, 490.

5. Thomas Bell, *Out of This Furnace: A Novel of Immigrant Labor in America* (Pittsburgh: University of Pittsburgh Press, 1976), 166.

6. Montgomery, "Workers' Control of Machine Production," 506.

7. Philip S. Foner, *History of the Labor Movement in the United States*, Vol. III (New York: International Publishers, 1964), 18.

8. Robert D. Marcus and David Burner, eds., *America Firsthand: From Reconstruction to the Present*, Vol. II (New York: St. Martin's Press, 1995), 116.

9. Thomas J. Schlereth, *Victorian America: Transformations in Everyday Life, 1876–1915* (New York: HarperCollins, 1991), 68.

10. Charlotte Perkins Gilman, *Women and Economics* (New York: Harper and Row, 1966), 152, 157.

11. Ibid., 156.

12. Bell, *Out of This Furnace*, 150.

13. Foner, *History of the Labor Movement*, Vol. III, 20.

14. Carol Brown, *America through the Eyes of Its People: A Collection of Primary Sources* (New York: HarperCollins, 1993), 150.

15. Jo Ann E. Argersinger, *The Triangle Fire: A Brief History with Documents* (Boston: Bedford/St. Martin's, 2009), 11.

16. John Whiteclay Chambers II, *The Tyranny of Change: America in the Progressive Era, 1890–1920* (New York: St. Martin's Press, 1992), 89–90.

17. Catherine Reef, *Working in America* (New York: Facts on File, 2000), 194.

18. Ibid., 192.

19. Page Smith, *America Enters the World: A People's History of the Progressive Era and World War I* (New York: Penguin Books, 1985), 263.

20. Ronald L. Filippelli, *Labor in the USA: A History* (New York: Alfred A. Knopf, 1984), 120.

21. Smith, *America Enters the World*, 258.

22. Foner, *History of the Labor Movement*, Vol. V, 27.

23. Melvin Dubofsky and Foster Rhea Dulles, *Labor in America: A History* (Wheeling, IL: Harlan Davidson, 2004), 185.

3

Popular Culture

One of the main themes in popular culture during the decades between 1890 and 1920 was the transition from a rather staid and traditional Victorian culture to a more activist and modern mass culture. There seemed to be a growing reaction to both the enervating tendencies of modern life and the emphasis on the moralizing, self-control, and refinement that characterized the earlier period. One point shared by most social commentators during the 1890s was that society was suffering from a malaise that they commonly diagnosed as over-civilization. The argument strongly suggested that the social dependency that accompanied urbanization was producing a new generation of "pathetic, pampered, physically and morally enfeebled ninety-seven pound weaklings—a poor successor to the stalwart Americans who had fought the Civil War, battled Indians, and tamed the continent."[1]

A NEW CELEBRATION OF VIGOR

The shift to a more activist mood found expression in a robust nationalism (often coupled with a virulent nativism); a new fascination with nature and the wilderness; a vigorous popular music; a more realistic literature and art; and a boom in sports (for both participants and spectators), recreation, and outdoor activities such as hiking, camping, and automobile touring ("motoring"). The new celebration of vigor even found expression in the national fascination with bicycling, which became a new exercise and sporting craze in the 1890s. Sales of bicycles jumped from 1 million in 1893 to 10 million in 1900. Cyclists formed clubs, staged popular races, and even organized their own national association. Frances Willard, head of the Woman's Christian Temperance Union, took up bicycling in her fifties as a form of exercise and embraced the fad with enthusiasm. Her book *A Wheel within a Wheel* (1895) was a best seller and undoubtedly encouraged many women to cast off gender stereotypes and take up the fad.

Adult–Supervised Recreation

The shift in the popular temperament toward a new vigor and vitality could also be seen in the growth of adult-supervised recreational programs for youth. The motivation for this new interest was part of a larger dynamic. Middle- and upper-class adults were increasingly concerned that the new urban-industrial society had compromised old ways of child rearing, especially weakening the family as the primary nurturing institution. The city seemed to emphasize the triumph of the values of the marketplace, the erosion of traditional social restraints, and the creation of an infinite number of possible perversions for young people that served to diminish the importance of the church and the family and to undermine a sense of community. Games and sports, directed by adults, could counter the harmful effects of urban life and offer a safe haven for young people after school. Many reformers thought that team games and sports could reduce tensions among children of different ethnic and religious backgrounds, who, as teammates, would discover a mutual identity and work toward a common goal. Reformers also believed that recreation, if properly supervised by trained adults, could be a means of social control. It would be a way to assimilate and acculturate the children of immigrants, instilling values such as hard work, fair play, and democracy.

The adult-supervised playground idea quickly took hold. In 1903 voters in the Chicago South Park district approved a $5 million bond issue to construct 10 parks. Each park had a field house and a gymnasium for both boys and girls. The Chicago authorities also hired a professional physical educator as director of the program, and furnished each park with two year-round instructors to supervise play activities that ranged from the creation of organized athletic leagues to community folk dances. Inspired by the Chicago example, and motivated by the same anxieties generated by the modern cities, middle- and upper-income taxpayers demonstrated a strong enthusiasm for supervised recreational programs. Between 1900 and 1911, municipal enthusiasts constructed more than 1,500 municipal playgrounds in 200 cities and employed more than 4,000 "play directors" to supervise the programs.

Spectator Sports

The rise of commercialized spectator sports suggested a new respect for virility, strength, and energy and presented its own challenge to the more genteel Victorian spirit. Although boxing, which began to soften its brutish image after Gentleman Jim Corbett defeated John L. Sullivan with padded gloves rather than bare knuckles in 1892, and horse racing had both gained in popularity, they were still hampered by rather severe legal and social restrictions. Football, although still stigmatized for its brutality, remained an amateur sport. It had, however, become a craze on college campuses. A number of major universities had begun to construct large stadiums in response to the sport's growing popularity and to promote their own institutional status. Track and field, basketball, and wrestling became increasingly popular collegiate sports as well.

Baseball

By far the most popular sport during the early twentieth century was baseball. Although favored as a sport before the Civil War and regarded as America's pastime by the 1870s and 1880s, baseball's unsurpassed popularity occurred during the Progressive Era, when the game seemed to capture the country's imagination. The rapid expansion of the sport soon saw the establishment of professional teams in nearly every major city. Although attendance figures for the period prior to 1910 are only rough (and probably inflated) estimates, total big-league attendance reached 1.8 million in 1901 and grew to 7.2 million by 1909. By 1920 more than 9 million fans would attend games. Minor league attendance grew at an even faster rate, and the number of minor leagues expanded from 13 in 1900 to 46 in 1912. Spectators came primarily from the upper-lower to lower-middle class and tended to have western European or old-immigrant backgrounds. Many were white-collar workers with the occupational flexibility to attend afternoon games and the financial ability to afford the $0.50 admission fee (a bleacher seat cost another dime and a grandstand seat another quarter).

In response to the unruly crowd behavior that was common at nineteenth-century ballparks, steps were taken in the early twentieth century to civilize crowd behavior. As the dimensions of the modern ballparks increased, spectators were moved farther away from both players and umpires. Owners also began to promote the attendance of women, and initiated Ladies' Days on which women were admitted for free or a nominal fee. The growing feminine interest in baseball was recounted in a popular song of 1908, "Take Me Out to the Ball Game," in which a girl tells her date that she would prefer an afternoon at the ballpark eating peanuts and Cracker Jack and rooting for the home team over attending the theater or some other entertainment. The growing popularity of the sport encouraged owners to construct expensive new parks that would soon seat over 40,000 spectators. Between 1909 and 1916, 10 new major-league ballparks were constructed at an average cost of $500,000. The World Series, begun in 1903, culminated the season and became a spectacle of national interest exceeded only by presidential elections.

The Pittsburg(h) Pirates baseball team, 1907. (Courtesy of the Library of Congress)

The growth and expansion of the sport had little to do with innovations to the game and more to do with economic prosperity, urban growth, and improvements in transportation and communication. Cities provided the necessary market for baseball to thrive economically. An improved standard of living (especially for the middle class) and a reduction in the average hours of the workweek (roughly 56 hours in 1900, 52 in 1914, and 49 in 1920) provided many with the discretionary income and leisure time to take in a game. Improvements in transportation—streetcars, elevated railways, and subways—enabled fans to attend games from any part of the city. Serving to hype interest were any number of inexpensive newspapers, popular magazines, sporting weeklies, and specialized monthly periodicals such as *Baseball Magazine* (1908). The various publications provided fans with schedules, game reports, the latest information on pennant races, baseball gossip, and feature stories about various technical aspects of the game.

In addition to economic, social, and technological factors, baseball's popularity benefited from a well-planned and vigorous public relations campaign conducted by baseball owners and sportswriters eager to promote the sport. According to Steven A. Riess, sportswriters convinced the public that participation in the sport (either as a player or vicarious spectator) contributed to both individual self-improvement and national betterment. Baseball was not as many Victorians had viewed it, a waste of time, but an acceptable, enjoyable, and useful leisure activity. In fact, baseball was portrayed as an important part of American life. It was a valuable promoter of social integration that brought social classes and communities together as it instilled civic pride. It was a safety valve, providing a release for those working long hours at tedious jobs. It was also an educational experience that taught essential American values. For example, baseball improved character by emphasizing traits—fair-mindedness, good judgment, and quick thinking—that would be important in life. The sport encouraged respect for authority, self-sacrifice, and teamwork. In sync with progressive educators, baseball offered a way for children to learn from experience. Baseball had a democratizing value as well. It was a great leveler. Fans were drawn from all levels of society and mingled at the ballpark on equal terms. In short, baseball's popularity had much to do with how well it meshed with prevailing American values and beliefs. Although many of the attributes attached to baseball were wildly overstated, the public accepted the myths as true.

Baseball's symbolic function was to demonstrate the continuing relevancy of old values and beliefs in an increasingly modern urban era. Its instrumental function was to teach the dominant WASP belief system and serve as a bulwark against those social developments which seemed to challenge or threaten the core culture. Baseball did this through the rituals of spectatorship and by being transformed into a moral equivalent of the frontier.[2]

Baseball provided heroes and exemplars for young people, but in stressing that baseball built character and established valuable role models, promoters of the game placed it on a shaky pedestal. When such propaganda was expanded to portray baseball owners as selfless, civic-minded, ethical businessmen who sponsored teams more as a public service or to promote hometown pride than to make money, the entire structure became precarious. The editors of *American Magazine* underscored the theme of business ethics in a 1913 editorial that stated, "Baseball has given our public a fine lesson in commercial morals. It is a well paying business...for it must be above suspicion. Nobody dreams of crookedness or shadiness in baseball.... Some day all business will be reorganized and conducted by baseball standards."[3] In truth, many players were not exemplary role models and many team owners less than pillars of honesty. Many owners were actually professional politicians or the business associates of urban political machines. In the early 1900s, all major league clubs had political connections and used those connections to secure lower tax assessments or license fees, or to gain support against others who might want to challenge their business monopolies.

"Black Sox" Scandal

In September of 1920, the game that was said to be above reproach became embroiled in a national scandal. Not long after the favored Chicago White Sox lost the 1919 World Series to the Cincinnati Reds, rumors began to circulate that eight Chicago players, including star outfielder Shoeless Joe Jackson, had conspired to throw the deciding game of the series after allegedly accepting payoffs from professional gamblers. The affair or fix soon became known as the "Black Sox" scandal. The prosecutor's case rested on the confessions of several players, but when the case came to trial, the prosecutor reported that the confessions had been lost. They had, in fact, been stolen from the government files when the state's attorney left office, and later ended up in the office of White Sox owner Charles Comiskey's attorney. The mysterious disappearance of the signed confessions undercut the prosecutor's case, and a trial jury eventually acquitted the players for lack of evidence. Most, however, were of the opinion that wrongdoing had indeed occurred. Comiskey was an autocratic miser who was hated by his underpaid players, almost all of whom had financial problems. Several of the accused players had previously consorted with gamblers. In an oft-told account, a young fan was said to have pleaded with Jackson as he filed out of the grand jury room, "Say it ain't so, Joe. Say it ain't so." In response, Jackson was said to have remarked, "Yes kid, I'm afraid it is." "Well, I never would've thought it," said the boy.[4] Looking to restore baseball's image, the owners hired the game's first commissioner, Judge Kenesaw Mountain Landis, who abruptly banned the eight players from baseball and at least temporarily restored public confidence in the integrity of the game.

Interest in the Outdoors

Closely related to the emphasis on vigor and vitality was the newfound interest in the outdoors and the regenerative benefits that might be derived from a closer association to it. Once again, the evil seemed to be over-civilization. By the end of the nineteenth century (most noticeably after the depression of the 1890s), people were beginning to have doubts about the course of American society. Optimism seemed to be giving way to more sober assessments, doubts, and uncertainties. Nativists blamed the negative popular mood on the flood of new immigrants entering the country, diluting "true American" predominance and weakening American values and institutions. Others blamed big business (the "Trusts") and the amoral value system that seemed to surround it. Still others blamed the process of urbanization and the negative effect it seemed to have on character and morality. Time spent in the outdoors could provide a remedy for the artificiality and effeteness of late nineteenth-century urban life.

Frustrated with social excess, Americans increasingly idealized a simpler past, that, in hindsight, evoked many desirable national characteristics—virility, toughness, manliness—that defined fitness in Darwinian terms. A number of critics, beginning in the 1890s, began to suggest that many of the elements that had shaped the national character were disappearing. Historian Frederick Jackson Turner had underscored this idea in his famous address on the significance of the frontier in 1893 and in a succession of publications in the years afterward. Turner argued that the frontier was the most important influence on the development of the American character, and that living in contact with nature fostered individualism and independence, and instilled confidence in the common man. Ironically, Turner contributed to the general mood of pessimism by suggesting that the frontier (defined as the availability of virgin land that had not been encroached upon by settlement) was gone. Many began to regret nostalgically that this was true.

Boy Scouts

One way of recapturing contact with nature was through the Boy Scouts. Although the official founder of the organization in 1907 was Englishman Sir Robert S. S. Baden-Powell, his efforts had been anticipated in this country by popular nature writer Ernest Thompson Seton. Seton had put forth his ideas for a youth association called Woodcraft Indians in a series of articles for the *Ladies Home Journal* in 1902. When the Boy Scout concept came to the United States during the Progressive Era, it was warmly embraced. In fact, it was Seton who set forth the goals of the Boy Scouts of America in 1910 in the preamble to the Scouts' *Handbook.* According to Seton, a century ago every American boy lived close to nature. But since that time, the country had undergone an "unfortunate change" caused by industrialization and the "growth of immense cities." To Seton, the result was "degeneracy," causing people to become "strained and broken by the grind of the over-busy world." As a remedy for that condition, the *Handbook* proposed that the boys of America would lead the nation back to an emphasis on the "Outdoor Life."[5] The Boys Scouts quickly became the largest youth organization in the country.

One popularizer of this new emphasis was President Theodore Roosevelt. Through his own study of American history and from personal experience, Roosevelt constantly trumpeted the virtues of nature. To counter what he believed to be a drift toward "flabbiness" and "slothful ease," and his own genuine fear that the average American was in danger of becoming over-civilized, he called upon Americans to lead a life of "strenuous endeavor." "As our civilization grows older and more complex," he explained, "we need a greater and not a less development of the fundamental frontier virtues."[6] To that end, Roosevelt, as president, led an energetic campaign to protect parts of the natural environment from economic development. By the time he left office, Roosevelt had created 6 new national parks, 16 new national monuments, 150 new national forests, and 51 new wildlife refuges, and had placed 230 million acres of U.S. land under public protection. Not surprisingly, there was a surge of popular interest in the outdoors. Camping, hiking, and mountain climbing became important facets of what some were soon calling the "outdoor movement." Such pursuits had special appeal to city dwellers who longed to find an escape from stress and toil. Advertisers quickly took note of the trend and grabbed the opportunity to extol the virtues of outdoor recreation. In 1911, for example, the Bangor and Aroostook Railroad, anxious to fill its passenger cars with vacationers on their way to the Maine woods, began to issue its own promotional literature. One typical passage noted that "there's a good deal of the primitive in most of us," and, because of that, "we feel the magic beckoning of old Mother Nature to rise up from the thralldom of business…and to betake ourselves to the woods."[7]

Popular Novels

Popular literature tended to promote the outdoor ideal as well. Two writers who gained notoriety for doing so were Jack London and Edgar Rice Burroughs. In what became one of the most popular novels of the early twentieth century, London's *The Call of the Wild* (1903) told the story of a huge Saint Bernard named Buck, who was stolen from his owner in California and sold in the Klondike region of Alaska to haul sleds. Living in a primitive environment, Buck begins to feel his domesticated habits challenged by the resurgence of primitive wolf instincts. At the novel's end, Buck, who has become increasingly wolf-like, returns to the wild to run with the pack and lead a life that London suggests is more vital, stronger, and nobler than before. Readers had no trouble seeing the moral for their own lives. Similar to London's novel and just as popular was Burroughs's *Tarzan of the Apes* (1914). In telling the story of an English infant raised in the jungle by apes, Burroughs uses Tarzan's experience to show how he benefited from his contact with the primitive environment to become something of a superhero.

Closely related to the emphasis on virility and toughness was Owen Wister's celebrated novel *The Virginian* (1902). Often credited with creating the modern western, Wister, a Harvard classmate of Theodore Roosevelt, used a Wyoming backdrop and a soft-spoken, thoroughly masculine hero figure to offer an instructive contrast of the primitive and the modern. Wister, a completely aristocratic, socially and politically conservative individual, suffered from the same malaise gripping many in society at the time. American culture, to the rabidly nativistic and pessimistic Wister, was being overrun by hordes of immigrants and its values subverted by a combination of greedy materialism and commercialism (Wall Street) and radicalism (labor unions). But it had not always been that way. The old West had been a place where old virtues had taken root, where one's character was constantly put to the test, and where right triumphed over wrong. Gifted, hardworking individuals, like the Virginian, who instinctively knew how to take charge of events and bring about results, rose to the top, while immoral men, lawbreakers, and shylocks were eliminated. In the process they brought law and order to a lawless society and served as noble agents of progress. Cowboy life, as portrayed in novels and short stories, exerted something akin to a mythical attraction for effete easterners suffering from over-civilization. As the prototype of this new genre, *The Virginian* became one of America's most popular novels during the Progressive Era. It sold 100,000 copies during its first three months, 300,000 copies in its first two years, and over 1 million copies by 1920. The novel was made into a play that ran for 10 years on and off Broadway, and Cecil B. DeMille produced the first movie version of the book in 1914.

Popular Music

During the early twentieth century, American popular culture became highly commercialized, with commodities increasingly being mass produced by a growing entertainment industry. One part of this development was in the music industry, as a stream of new musical styles and the popularity of the phonograph changed the nature of popular music. During the last 15 years of the nineteenth century, the established music publishers, who had made a lot of money marketing genteel parlor songs, were challenged by smaller companies that specialized in popular songs that were commonly performed in dance halls, theaters, and beer gardens. These new music publishing firms, many of which were started by Jewish immigrants, were clustered together along a section of West 28th Street between Broadway and Sixth Avenue in New York City known as Tin Pan Alley. As part of the process of providing "hits" for an expanding mass urban market, these firms did extensive market research. Songwriters were usually salaried employees, and the gauging of popular tastes was usually conducted by "song pluggers" who played versions of the songs to audiences in theaters to gauge public reaction. In 1900 the music industry made its profits primarily by selling sheet music to a piano-playing public (there were 100 companies making pianos in 1900) and advertising their product through a nationwide system of vaudeville halls. For the first time, a single song might sell more than 1 million copies. Sheet music sold for between 25 and 65 cents, and the sale of printed music more than tripled between 1890 and 1909. By 1910 the annual sale of sheet music in the United States had reached 30 million copies.

Vaudeville

By the turn of the twentieth century, the most popular theatrical form of entertainment (a descendant of music hall shows and minstrelsy) and the most important vehicle for popularizing Tin Pan Alley songs was vaudeville. Vaudeville shows offered something for everybody—singers, comedians, acrobats, jugglers, dancers—without any connecting theme. Every city of any size had at least one large vaudeville theater (racial segregation dictated that there was a separate chain of theaters for black performers and audiences). Music publishing firms sent out representatives to monitor the vaudeville circuit to make sure performers promoted their songs, and to make sure that local music stores had an adequate stock of the latest sheet music on hand. By 1915 more than $500,000 was being paid to performers to boost sales of popular songs. Typical songs had simple melodies, verses, and a repeated chorus, and many were imbued with a somber spirit—subdued, nostalgic, and, at times, sorrowful. One of the most popular composer-songwriters of the period was Harry von Tilzer (sometimes called the Daddy of Popular Song), whose hits included "A Bird in a Gilded Cage" (1900) and "I Want a Girl (Just Like the Girl That Married Dear Old Dad)" (1911). His songs represented a style that dominated popular taste but was not without its more modern challengers.

Ragtime

One of those challengers was ragtime, and it was beginning to transform popular music. In this new genre, which gained tremendous popularity between 1898 and 1918, African American composers borrowed from the rhythms and harmonies of European marches,

Vaudeville, the Theatre Comique, Detroit, Michigan, between 1900 and 1920. (Courtesy of the Library of Congress)

the syncopated rhythms of African American dances, and the enthusiasm of early African music as played on the banjo or given more unified treatment by traveling brass bands. The cheerful, energetic excitement of ragtime derived from a form of syncopation applied against a steady bass rhythm. The syncopated rhythm challenged the accepted order and regularity of 3/4-time waltzes and the 4/4 time of marches and hymns. "The steady beat of the left hand echoed the rhythm of factory, machine, and train, but the unexpected accents by the right hand, as well as the fast-paced melodies, announced a refusal to be contained by that steadiness."[8]

The king of the ragtime writers was classically trained, African American composer Scott Joplin, who wrote the first popular ragtime tune, "Maple Leaf Rag," in 1898. Capturing the spirit of an emerging popular culture, Joplin's version sold more than 1 million copies and generated huge commercial profits for the sheet-music industry. Ragtime shifted the style of popular piano playing, became a favorite choice at dances, and won a prominent place in most theater and vaudeville productions. Joplin's rags were also widely heard on player pianos (mechanical devices that were activated by piano rolls with punched holes that determined the movement of the piano keys). Ragtime quickly became the newest craze as it invited listeners to cast aside restraint for joy and uninhibited emotion. As Susan Curtis noted, "Whether because it was fascinatingly novel or an emblem of the forbidden 'other,' ragtime offered a chance to break free of the restraints imposed by a Victorian sensibility. Ragtime music countered the genteel imperative for self-control with its irresistible invitation to move to its sensuous rhythm."[9]

Not everyone approved of ragtime. Its exuberant, muscular spirit clashed with the Victorian code of propriety. Many found the music, and the high-kicking dances that it spawned, simply vulgar. The older generation thought it had a pernicious influence on young people. Many whites objected to the new genre because they saw it as primitive and African. Some blacks disapproved because of ragtime's association with cabarets, brothels, and saloons, and because they considered the suggestive lyrics to be racial slurs. Despite the criticism, ragtime's popularity allowed it to be accepted by Tin Pan Alley. As a result, ragtime quickly became commercialized and appropriated by white composers. When composer Irving Berlin contributed music and lyrics for *Alexander's Ragtime Band*, a revue that incorporated the new genre in 1911, ragtime gained acceptance within the mainstream culture. Ironically, although many white Americans seemed to have been drawn to the liberating possibilities (loosening the hold of nineteenth-century Victorian values) of African American music, they remained steadfast in refusing to lessen their own cultural constraints regarding race.

Ragtime encouraged new dance forms as well. Journalist Mark Sullivan, a contemporary of the time, called the "utterly revolutionary" ragtime dances that came with the new music "shocking." In trying to describe the exuberance of the new dance forms, Sullivan used Berlin's "Everybody's Doin' It Now" (1911) as an example of a song that partly described "the not very intricate motions—motions rather than steps—of the parvenu dances, and partly placated scruples against it, the placation consisting of what was coming to be sufficient justification for a good many things."

> Honey, honey, can't you hear funny, funny, music, dear?...
> Can't you see them all, swaying up the hall?
> Everybody's doin' it, doin' it, doin' it.

See that ragtime couple over there,
  Watch them throw their shoulders in the air,
  Snap their fingers, honey, I declare,
  It's a bear, it's a bear, it's a bear! There!
  Everybody's doin' it now![10]

The new dances became popularly known as "animal dances" and included the fox trot, the horse trot, the turkey trot, the crab step, the kangaroo dip, the camel walk, the fish walk, the chicken scratch, the lame duck, the snake, the bunny hug, and the grizzly bear. Despite some mild condemnation from newspapers such as the *New York Sun*—which asked editorially, "Are we going to the dogs by the rag-time route?"—the fad quickly gained acceptance in the great metropolis. As a by-product of the new dance craze, hundreds of new dance halls and cabarets sprang up in cities across America to cash in on the fad. In the bigger cities, hotels and restaurants built dance floors and hired live bands to entertain their customers. Cabarets became the "in" places to try out new dance steps before the onset of Prohibition in 1920. Ragtime dancing and syncopated music made a good match, and soon African American band leaders began to compose ragtime arrangements specifically for the ballroom, and the most popular white orchestras quickly followed suit.

In many towns and in rural communities, however, there was resistance. Newspapers charged that ragtime music and the dances that accompanied it were vulgarizing and corrupting young people, undermining respect for things that had previously been held sacred, and were "responsible for deterioration of manners, taste, and right thinking.... The real danger to the community is the songs that give young folks a false and perverted impression of love and romance, which hold a pure and romantic sentiment up to slangy ridicule." Sullivan mentioned numerous newspaper stories of young women employees being fined or fired for dancing the turkey trot on their lunch hour, but also recounted one story that suggests that the attempts to impose cultural restraints on America's youth were as hopeless then as at other times in American history. As Sullivan told the story:

At Millwood, New York, Grace Williams, eighteen years old, was arraigned on complaint of former Justice of the Peace Ogden S. Bradley, who charged that she was guilty of disorderly conduct in frequently singing "Everybody's Doin' It Now," as she passed his house, and dancing the turkey trot. "Squire" Bradley said that he and his wife thought that both the song and the dance were highly improper and that they had been greatly annoyed. Lawyer Stuart Baker demanded a jury trial. Williams said she sang the song because she liked it, and danced because she could not help it when she heard the catchy tune. Lawyer Baker volunteered to sing the song in court. The prosecuting attorney objected, stating this would make a farce of the trial. Judge Chadeayne overruled him and told Baker to go ahead. The lawyer, who had a good baritone voice, sang the ditty. When he reached the chorus, "Everybody's doin' it, doin' it, doin' it," spectators joined in. The jurors called for an encore. Again taking out his tuning fork to pitch the key, the lawyer sang the second stanza with more feeling and expression, and as he sang he gave a mild imitation of the turkey trot. The jurymen clapped their hands in vigorous appreciation, and after five minutes' deliberation found Williams not guilty.[11]

The Phonograph

Ragtime eventually suffered from competition from two different sources—the phonograph and jazz. The phonograph broadened the base of popular music, and sales of phonographs

The phonograph broadened the base of popular music, and sales of phonographs increased steadily prior to World War I. (Courtesy of the Library of Congress)

increased steadily prior to World War I. It has been estimated that 1 out of every 22 households in the United States had a phonograph in 1904. By 1909 manufacturers were producing over 26 million discs and cylinders every year. By 1920 phonograph companies cut over 100 million records (grooved disks had by then replaced the old cylinder system). The modern record industry was well underway. It might be noted in passing that the phonograph not only allowed various new forms of music the means by which to attract a wider audience, it also had an impact on classical music. The most popular classical vocalist of the Progressive Era was Enrico Caruso, who made his Metropolitan Opera debut in 1903 as the Duke in Verdi's *Rigoletto*. His recording of "Vesti la giubba" from Leoncavallo's *Pagliacci* was the first to sell 1 million copies.

Jazz

Competing with ragtime for popular attention was jazz. Although there has been a great deal of debate about the origins of jazz, "jass" or "hot music" emerged around 1900 in the multicultural environment of New Orleans, Louisiana, where diverse musical traditions converged. The term jazz first appeared around 1915, and the first recorded jazz music was performed by a white group from New Orleans called the Original Dixieland Jazz Band (ODJB). Their recordings of "Livery Stable Blues" and "Dixieland Jass Band One-Step" in 1917 and "Tiger Rag" in 1918 triggered a national craze for jazz music that would peak in the following decade. In its earliest forms, jazz blended many different styles of music—West African rhythms, American spirituals, ragtime, and blues—and always featured a pronounced beat. One historian has called jazz "the folk music of the machine age."[12] Centered on improvisation and complete freedom of expression, jazz created a new sensation. Larry Starr and Christopher Waterman have tried to imagine the impact of "Tiger Rag" on an average white, middle-class listener in 1918 who was accustomed to a menu of ballroom dance music and Tin Pan Alley songs, and conclude that it must have been striking ("exciting or repellant, depending on one's taste") indeed. The unbridled intensity of a song like "Tiger Rag" was an important part of the ODJB's appeal to an audience hungry for excitement and something new, "and perhaps parallel to the effect of early rock 'n' roll records on some listeners in the 1950s."[13]

Amusement Parks

One of the most striking changes in the character of American popular culture during the early twentieth century was the emergence of the new amusement parks. Built to respond to the rapidly growing urban populations and increased leisure time, and assisted by the development of trolley, subway, and train systems that made inexpensive excursions from the city possible, amusement parks spread across the country. Brooklyn's Coney Island with its Luna Park, Steeplechase, and Dreamland; Boston's Paragon Park and Revere Beach; Philadelphia's Willow Grove; Atlanta's Ponce de Leon Park; Cleveland's Euclid Beach; Chicago's Cheltenham Beach, Riverview, and White City; St. Louis's Forest Park Highlands; Denver's Manhattan Beach; and San Francisco's The Chutes all became recreation meccas.

Such parks assembled a variety of popular attractions that reflected the changing cultural mood from one characterized by intellectual and emotional restraint to one that was more vigorous and daring. In addition to the bathing beaches, band pavilions, dance halls, vaudeville theaters, and popular mechanical amusements such as the Ferris wheel or the fun house, the parks often placed visitors in exotic, dream-like environments that glorified adventure. At Luna Park a visitor could view a Japanese garden, a Chinese theater, or the canals of Venice. That same visitor might also experience reenactments of disasters such as burning buildings and earthquakes. At Steeplechase Park a cyclorama called A Trip to the Moon took visitors on a spaceship ride to a lunar landing site, where they were greeted by the Man in the Moon (seated on his throne) and a bevy of dancing moon maidens, who offered travelers bits of green cheese as tokens of their escape from Earth. To compete with Luna Park, Dreamland constructed a 375-foot tower illuminated at night with 100,000 electric lights. Visitors to Dreamland could also experience a three-ring circus, chariot races, and even a Lilliputian village right out of *Gulliver's Travels*. The overall atmosphere was designed to create illusions, allow patrons to forget reality, and, at least temporarily, offer them an escape from social constraints.

Unlike baseball, football, and boxing events, where the public assumed the role of spectators, amusement parks demanded participation. As a consumer, one could feel gay and, at the same time, experience abandon, revelry, and instant gratification. To facilitate that liberation, owners and managers consciously created environments that challenged existing notions of proper conduct and the

Coney Island's Luna Park became a symbol of the rise of a new mass culture. (Courtesy of the Library of Congress)

values associated with genteel culture. As Frederic Thompson, owner of Luna Park, noted, visitors were not looking for seriousness, but rather, "the keynote of the thing they do demand is change. Everything must be different from ordinary experience. What is presented to them must have life, action, motion, sensation, surprise, shock, swiftness or else comedy." Several hundred thousand visitors might come to Coney Island on a Saturday, Sunday, or holiday. During the summer of 1904, 4 million visitors came to Luna Park alone. In his study of Coney Island, historian John F. Kasson concluded that Coney Island's popularity resided in the "way in which it mocked the established social order.... Against the values of thrift, sobriety, industry, and ambition, it encouraged extravagance, gaiety, abandon, revelry. Coney Island signaled the rise of a new mass culture no longer deferential to genteel tastes and values."[14]

Leisure Activities

Although the incomes of laboring families varied widely during the Progressive Era, studies of family budgets in New York

City from 1903 to 1909 indicate that a typical working-class family (four to six members) earned on average $800 per year. Because expenses for rent, food, fuel, and clothing consumed most of the budget, families could afford only the cheapest amusements. Common forms of daily entertainment could be as simple as meeting with friends on street corners or the stoops of tenements to relax and socialize after a day's work. Street musicians and organ grinders often performed for nickels from passersby. For many, entertainment might be simply a walk to a neighborhood park or square, or perhaps casual window shopping in the local business district. An outing to Central Park on Sunday was usually considered a special family excursion.

Leisure activities varied for married working-class women and men in the inner city. Leisure activities for married women tended to be limited and confined. Such constraints were imposed on them by the work rhythms of the home. Household chores—cooking, cleaning, and child care—simply took up all their time. The distribution of family budgets also restricted their participation in recreation. Although working-class husbands were generally allowed a spending allowance for recreation, married women usually received no spending money of their own. The constant pressure to make ends meet on a limited family budget made any expenditure for pleasure a luxury that could not be afforded. As a result, leisure activities for married women tended to be restricted to interaction with neighbors (doorstep gossip) and relatives, and to church functions. It was only after 1905 and the rise of the nickelodeon that large numbers of working-class wives began to enjoy commercialized forms of leisure on a regular basis.

Working men, on the other hand, had a much greater network of leisure institutions to access. Many working men found commercial amusement in the poolroom, billiard hall, or bowling alley. Others participated on baseball teams organized by working men's clubs. The most popular forms of recreation for working men, however, were the saloon and various forms of associational activity. The saloon offered the working man a place for socializing, a refuge from the tedium and toil of the factory, and a clearinghouse for job-related information. A working man could get a free lunch with a nickel beer and enjoy good fellowship. If he was looking for a job, needed a loan, or simply wanted to hear the latest news, a working man headed for the saloon. More than 10,000 saloons were in business in greater New York City in 1900.

Voluntary organizations, such as the fraternal society, mutual benefit association, or lodge combined recreation and camaraderie with important economic services that offered protection against sickness or disability. These kinds of working-class associations were necessary at a time when industrial society offered few social welfare provisions. Voluntary associations were often interconnected with the saloon because such clubs regularly occupied the second-story halls or back rooms of those establishments for their meetings and entertainment.

Increasingly keen on carving out their own separate space for leisure, and consciously seeking to separate leisure from work, were young, unmarried working-class women who were either foreign-born or the daughters of immigrant parents. In 1900 four-fifths of wage-earning women in New York City were single, and almost one-third were between the ages of 16 and 20. For many women in the early twentieth century, new jobs in department stores, factories, restaurants, and offices provided alternatives to domestic work, household production, or sweatshop labor. These new employment opportunities and the declining hours of labor (the 9-hour workday and 54-hour workweek became the legal standard for working women in factories in New York City in 1912 and in mercantile stores in 1914) allowed these young women to reshape the way they spent their free time. As one young woman noted,

The shorter work day brought me my first idea of there being such a thing as pleasure. It was quite wonderful to get home before it was pitch dark at night, and a real joy to ride on the cars and look out the windows and see something. Before this time it was just sleep and eat and hurry off to work.... I was twenty-one before I went to a theater and then I went with a crowd of union girls to a Saturday matinee performance. I was twenty-three before I saw a dance and that was a union dance too.[15]

It has been commented that the new workplace reinforced a working woman's interest in having a good time. On one level, women increasingly sought amusement as a reaction to the drudgery and discipline of the job. Shared social interaction within the workplace only reinforced the new notions of leisure. No longer content with quiet recreation at home, these young, working women sought excitement at dance halls, cheap theaters, and amusement parks. In doing so, they broadened their sphere of autonomy and self-assertion. As Kathy Peiss noted, "It was in leisure that women played with identity, trying on new images and roles, appropriating the cultural forms around them—clothing, music, language—to push at the boundaries of immigrant, working-class life."[16]

Of all the amusements that captivated single working women, dancing was foremost. Outfitted with the best dresses and dancing shoes, they hurried after work to a neighborhood hall or ballroom to enjoy the festive environment, the beat of the orchestra, and the enjoyment of a stream of dance partners. In New York City, thousands of young men and women flocked to such venues each week. By the 1910s, there were over 500 public dance halls in greater New York City. By the second decade of the twentieth century, immense halls and ballrooms began to replace the smaller local establishments. Ranging in capacity from 500 to 3,000 patrons, they served a citywide clientele.

Another arena for diversion and flirtation was the amusement park, with its mechanical rides, sideshow attractions, variety shows, dance pavilions, boardwalks, and beaches. Working women often walked to work or skipped lunch to save enough money for a trip to the amusement park. Young women often sought the excitement of places such as Coney Island with a friend of the same sex (a more protective way of striking up acquaintances with young men). By relying on a form of treating, young women could enjoy a day at Coney Island and have to pay only for their transportation (15 to 25 cents on a commercial excursion boat, or 5 or 10 cents by trolley). "It only costs fare down and back," said one, "and for the rest of it the boys you 'pick up,' 'treat.'" The parks encouraged free, loose, social interaction in which both sexes could enjoy personal freedom. Given the opportunity to meet and enjoy the company of the opposite sex away from parental scrutiny, young single men and women often struck up acquaintances that suggested significant shifts in sexual mores were occurring well before the 1920s. The new amusement parks promoted a free-and-easy sexuality by encouraging closeness and romance. One attraction, known as the Razzle-Dazzle, caused patrons to lose their balance and provided a perfect excuse to clutch each other in the process. The idea was to encourage familiarity, but to do so in a structured way and make it harmless through laughter. Amusement parks "beckoned young women who desired spaces for social experimentation, personal freedom, and unsupervised fun."[17]

THE EMERGENCE OF MASS COMMUNICATION AND MASS CULTURE

Popular Newspapers

The instruments largely responsible for the emergence of modern American mass communication and mass culture—the widely circulated metropolitan newspaper, the mass-market magazine, the mass-produced best seller, national advertising campaigns, and the movies and other forms of mass entertainment—saw their greatest growth during the Progressive Era. The first instrument of modern mass culture was the urban tabloid that became popular during the 1890s. Pioneered by William Randolph Hearst and Joseph Pulitzer, and known to many readers as the Yellow Press, these popular newspapers broke with the proper upper-class and staunchly partisan newspapers of the Gilded Age. Most noticeably, they were far more sensationalistic. To attract customers, newspapers of this new type used splashy, bold-print headlines as lead-ins for stories that often lacked factual accuracy. Appealing to diverse audiences, they also relied heavily on photographs and color comics, provided riveting stories of crime and scandal, gave wide coverage to society and fashion news and sports (Hearst's *New York Journal* created the modern sports page in 1896), offered household tips, and featured a much more lavish use of advertisements (50% of content as compared to just 30% in earlier newspapers). Entertainment was the focus, and a readable narrative, lively style, and numerous illustrations were designed to reach a mass audience of both working-class and middle-class readers. Between 1870 and 1910, the national circulation of daily newspapers increased from less than 3 million to more than 24 million—a pace three times that of the rate of population increase. Pulitzer's *New York World* boasted a circulation of 2 million in 1905.

Popular Magazines

By the turn of the century, the rise of mass-circulation magazines had begun to eclipse old standard publications such as *Scribner's*, *Atlantic Monthly*, and *Harper's*, whose poetry and more serious fiction was designed to appeal to an upper-class readership with more intellectual tastes. The older style of magazine also tended to adhere to what has been called the genteel tradition—the idea that art and literature should underscore morality, refine one's sensibility, and avoid reality. Art and literature, it was thought, should strive to portray the ideal. The new magazines took a different track aimed at a more popular audience. They offered practical advice, gossip, human interest, interviews with celebrities, articles on timely topics, pictures, and photographs. By focusing on popular content and attracting advertisers, which helped keep the magazine's price low, sales soared. Publishers and promoters such as Frank Doubleday started the first national book promotional campaigns, created the modern best seller, and successfully marketed authors (for example, Jack London) who would have been unacceptable to genteel readers.

Popular Novels

Novelists expanded the revolt against the formalism, moralism, and sentimentality that had characterized Victorian culture as they sought to portray life objectively and truthfully. The new quest for realism took a variety of forms. One of the earliest of these was literary naturalism, a style made popular by a group of writers who David Shi has likened to "savage realists."[18] Beginning with Stephen Crane's *Maggie: A Girl of the Streets* (1893), writers began to depict social conditions as they found them. In targeting Irish immigrant life in lower Manhattan, Crane describes the descent of an innocent slum girl into prostitution and suicide. Weary of a constantly warring family and depressed by her low-paying job making shirt collars in a sweatshop, Maggie hopes to find escape and romantic fantasy in a relationship with a 16-year-old bartender and street fighter named Pete. When Pete summarily casts her aside for an older, more experienced woman, Maggie is abandoned. Shunned by her family, she is forced into a brutal struggle for survival. In despair she becomes a prostitute. In the end, beaten down by social and economic forces and finding her life no longer bearable, she drowns herself in the East River. The book was shocking in its candor. Vernon Louis Parrington called *Maggie* "an affront to every instinct of the genteel tradition."[19]

During the early Progressive Era, this new literary style found expression in the popular novels of Frank Norris—*McTeague* (1899), *The Octopus* (1901), and *The Pit* (1902)—and those of Theodore Dreiser—*Sister Carrie* (1900), *The Financier* (1912), *The Titan* (1914), and *The Genius* (1915). In *McTeague*, Norris, who was greatly influenced by the work of Emile Zola, creates a story of character (moral) disintegration prompted by economic circumstances that leads to lust, greed, and then tragedy. In *The Octopus*, Norris develops a story of economic determinism that pits farmers who grow wheat in the San Joaquin Valley of California against the Southern Pacific Railroad monopoly that transports it. As one antagonist, the railroad (the octopus) has monopolized California's agricultural economy through a system of land ownership and rate manipulation aimed at making producers do its bidding. Opposing it are the wheat growers—not simple yeomen, but land barons who control vast estates and who are willing to resort to speculation and bribery to enhance their own wealth and defeat the railroad. In a classic tale of dishonesty and moral and financial ruin, ranchers are killed and pillars of the community disgraced as railroad rates are raised and ranches seized.

In *Sister Carrie,* Dreiser places Carrie Meeber on the path of a typical 18-year-old country girl from a small town in Wisconsin who comes to Chicago with naïve dreams of excitement and riches. When Carrie becomes unable to find work that will pay enough to make even a portion of her dreams a reality, she accepts a life of immorality, first as the mistress of a stylish traveling salesman, and then as the consort of the manager of a fancy saloon. When crime and economic hardship combine to despoil the latter relationship, Carrie abandons her lover and becomes a chorus girl. Eventually finding success as an actress, Carrie is able to obtain riches and celebrity but not happiness. Characteristic of this new genre were the literary themes of poverty, immorality, injustice, and hypocrisy, in pointed contrast to the earlier Victorian themes of comfort, morality, propriety, and honesty. As in *Sister Carrie,* boldness and passion for life had replaced polite sentiments and moral conventions.

A second style of novel that succeeded naturalism and grew in popularity as the era's emphasis on reform intensified was the "progressive" novel (also known as the "problem" novel, the "political" novel, and the "economic" novel). One of the most prominent writers in this school was Robert Herrick—*The Common Lot* (1904) and *The Memoirs of an American Citizen* (1905). In *The Common Lot,* Herrick develops the theme of sin and redemption through the actions of a socially driven architect who compromises his professional integrity only to see one of his buildings collapse, causing the loss of many lives but bringing about his own spiritual salvation. Another who followed similar themes was Brand Whitlock, a reform journalist, lawyer, and politician, who wrote *The Turn of the Balance* (1907), a study of criminal psychology and police brutality. Yet another member of this club was Winston Churchill. Starting out as a writer of romantic historical tales, Churchill shifted his focus as his own political involvement intensified. After serving in the

New Hampshire legislature, he wrote two novels—*Coniston* (1906) and *Mr. Crewe's Career* (1908)—based on his experiences with political bossism and the manipulative influence of the special interests (in particular the Boston and Maine Railroad) on state politics. His own political education made him an outspoken advocate of direct primaries, restrictions on lobbyists, and the need to eliminate the practice of granting free railroad passes to politicians. After an unsuccessful campaign for governor, Churchill wrote *The Inside of the Cup* (1913), a study of the Social Gospel and the need to establish the Kingdom of God in this world.

One final popular and provocative progressive novelist of note was David Graham Phillips. Known to many students of the Progressive Era as the muckraking journalist who wrote "The Treason of the Senate"—a scathing exposé on the unethical relationship that some wealthy U.S. senators maintained with big business, and that appeared in serialized form in *Cosmopolitan* magazine in 1906—Phillips went on to develop his talents as a writer of fiction. Among the more than 20 novels he produced were several problem novels—*Light-Fingered Gentry* (1907) on insurance scandal, *The Conflict* (1911) on local politics, and *George Helm* (1912) on state politics. Eventually, Phillips turned his attention to the "woman question." When he was murdered in 1911, he had just completed a novel titled *Susan Lenox: Her Fall and Rise* (not published until 1917). In writing a "feminist" novel, an increasingly popular genre in the years immediately preceding World War I, Phillips attempted to show that women were products of their environment, particularly their economic environment. In doing so, he tells the story of a woman, desperately poor and lacking opportunities, who begins to accept favors from men and becomes a prostitute. After a series of travails as a fashion model, sweatshop worker, and mistress, she inherits money from a wealthy dramatist who was murdered out of jealousy over her. Armed with the economic resources she never had, she frees herself from her dependence on men and becomes a talented actress and paragon of morality. In the end, Susan has become free "from the wolves of poverty and shame, or want and rags and filth, the wolves that had been pursuing her.... Free to live as *she* pleased instead of for the pleasure of a master or masters."[20]

Artistic Realists

Occupying another niche in American culture during the Progressive Era were the artistic realists—painters who sought to

portray life objectively and truthfully in rebellion against both genteel traditions and the artistic establishment that upheld them. Centered around Robert Henri, an American artist who returned to the
United States in the early 1890s after being exposed to the artistic
ferment in Paris, was a small group of artists—John Sloan, William
Glackens, George Luks, Everett Shinn—who, along with Henri and
later George Bellows, became the nucleus of what was to become
known as the Ash Can School of American art. Sloan, Glackens,
Luks, and Shinn had all worked as newspaper illustrators and had
come into contact with the heterogeneous activity of the city on a
daily basis. They were, by the nature of their profession, trained
as visual reporters absorbed in the human energy that seemed to
emanate from early twentieth-century urban America. In covering the newsworthy stories that made the evening paper, they had
learned the importance of topicality, human interest, and speed. It
was Henri, however, who took these raw talents and their ability
to express the vitality and richness of the American urban environment, and taught them to be painters.

Looking for an alternative to the subject matter (largely land-
scapes and portraits) of their genteel academic predecessors, the
artistic realists found color and excitement in the crowded urban
metropolis. Committed to displaying the unadorned "truth" rather
than decorative "beauty," they soon began to paint the gritty, virile
underside of the city. As Sloan noted, "We came upon realism as a
revolt against sentimentality and artificial subject matter and the
cult of 'art for art's sake.'"[21] These artistic realists loved life, everyday life, and they defended "ugliness" because it was a part of life.
They thought that if they painted life—the slum, the tenement, the
dock, the congested street—truthfully, then beauty would follow.
They had an unabashed sympathy for the lower classes, who they
varyingly depicted, in different styles and attitudes, as crude, colorful, loveable, tender, forlorn, and tragic. "The poor and humble
were to Henri a world of individual types, 'my people...through
whom the dignity of life is manifest.'"[22] Some of the Ash Can painters were social reformers; others were not. Yet as a group, they were
colorful documenters of the diversity of American urban life and,
in their empathy for the slum dweller, their art contained the implication of social reform.

Some of the more noteworthy paintings of the Ash Can group
that vividly portray the daily lives of the masses were done by
Bellows. Like several of the other Ash Can painters, Bellows was
fascinated with crowds of people and gathered spectators—the

dynamic of human activity. He perceived the modern scene as one of energetic social interaction between people at work or play or caught in a moment of daily life. Several of Bellows's paintings are memorable of this genre. "Beach at Coney Island" (1908–1910) expresses the crowded, carnival atmosphere of families who have sought amusement at the beach; "New York" (1911) captures the heterogeneity of urban life in a densely packed canvas filled with delivery carts, horses, trolleys, and working people and shoppers who animate the crowded street scene; and "Cliff Dwellers" (1913) offers a glimpse of life in a densely crowded tenement district that almost overwhelms the viewer with the mass of humanity living there. In "Cliff Dwellers," Bellows makes a direct affront to genteel sensibilities. In lamenting the brutal frankness of the painting, the critic for the *New York Sun* commented,

George Bellows' 'Cliff Dwellers' is appalling.... The dreadful people crowding the street, like naked urchins, the vendors of unhygienic lollypops, the battalion of mothers nursing their infants near the footlights where you have to see them, the streetcar clanging its mad way through the throng, the gentlemen on the fire escapes doing their toilets and the housewives hanging out the wash, can anything in Bedlam or Hogarth's prints equal this?

When the painting was exhibited at the Montross Gallery in October of 1913, however, another reviewer, for the *New York Times,* saw the work in a different light and remarked that the painting's "reality" was its "particular merit." "The scene," noted the reviewer, "is innocent of make-up, just a bit of life outside the theatre, and Mr. Bellows has loved it because it was real and has seen his way to expressing its quality without affectation."[23]

Muckraking Journalists

Yet another form of realism that shared a moment of popular appeal was the riveting journalistic exposé. Investigative reporters pushed aside Victorian propriety to discuss a variety of socially relevant topics that ranged from political corruption to corporate malfeasance to adulterated food products. Investigative journalism was a good fit for the new popular magazines that had begun to appear around the turn of the century. Looking to expand readership through promotional schemes such as reduced newsstand prices and lower subscription rates, editors such as S. S. McClure targeted a readership comprising mainly educated, middle-class

readers in towns and cities. The magazines offered a mix of serialized popular fiction, informative articles on science, technology,
travel, and biography, and, as a centerpiece, at least one prominent
exposé—and readership exploded. Several of the new magazines
had circulations that exceeded 500,000 by 1910.

The coincidental appearance of three articles in the January 1903
issue of *McClure's* magazine (circulated among approximately
400,000 readers) signaled the new type of reform journalism that
would soon become known as muckraking. The articles—one by
Steffens on municipal corruption, titled "The Shame of Minneapo-
lis"; another by Ida Tarbell on the evils of monopoly, "The Oil War
of 1872" (a chapter in her famous history of the Standard Oil Company); and yet another by Ray Stannard Baker on the abuses of labor
during the recent coal strike, "The Right to Work"—seemed to catch
everyone's attention. S. S. McClure, in acknowledging the unique
commonality of the three articles, concluded that they rested on a
previously undiscovered groundswell of public interest. There was
a sudden demand for the magazine on newsstands, and subscriptions increased dramatically. The public response in every part of
the country to the new type of journalism, rooted in hard facts and
in-depth reporting, was simply astonishing. "I doubt," said Baker
of the 1903 issue, "whether any other magazine published in America ever achieved such sudden and overwhelming recognition....
Everybody seemed to be reading them."[24]

For five or six years during the first decade of the twentieth
century (until pressure by advertisers and bankers forced a general change in editorial policy away from exposure), muckraking
became a recognized part of the American cultural, literary, and
political scene. Almost all of the major mass-circulation magazines—
McClure's, Collier's, Munsey's, the *Arena, American Magazine, Hamp-
ton's,* the *Independent,* and even the *Ladies Home Journal*—picked up
on the trend, and essays of exposure began to fill their pages. The
titles of two of the more noted of these magazines—*Everybody's* and
Cosmopolitan—underscored the attempt to capture a diverse, mass
readership. Thomas W. Lawson exposed stock-market practices;
Charles Edward Russell revealed the sordid business practices of
the beef trust; Samuel Hopkins Adams probed patent-medicine
frauds; Burton J. Hendrick disclosed the unethical practices of life
insurance companies; David Graham Phillips took a critical look at
conflict of interest in the U.S. Senate; George Kibbe Turner examined the connection between corrupt politics and prostitution;
and Judge Ben B. Lindsey took a hard look at the criminal justice

system and its impact on juveniles. Nothing seemed to be immune to investigation. By 1912 more than 2,000 articles on "wrongdoing" had appeared in print.

What the muckrakers did was to examine the world around them and report honestly and fully on what they found. When they did, a large number of thoughtful Americans, who had been growing increasingly anxious or indignant about the lawless conditions that existed in so many walks of life, responded. They eagerly read the long, serious, often complicated articles. "Month after month," noted Baker, "they would swallow dissertations of ten or twelve thousand words without even blinking—and ask for more." Baker thought he understood why the articles took hold of the public's attention: "It was because the country, for years, had been swept by the agitation of soap-box orators, prophets crying in the wilderness, and political campaigns based upon charges of corruption and privilege which everyone believed or suspected had some basis of truth, but which were largely unsubstantiated."[25] Political commentator Walter Lippmann drew a similar conclusion in analyzing the literature of exposure in *Drift and Mastery* (1914):

[T]he mere fact that muckraking was what people wanted to hear is in many ways the most important revelation of the whole campaign. There is no other way of explaining the quick approval which the muckrakers won. They weren't voices crying in the wilderness or lonely prophets who were stoned. They demanded a hearing; it was granted. They asked for belief; they were believed.... There must have been real causes for dissatisfaction, or the land notorious for its worship of success would not have turned so savagely upon those who had achieved it."[26]

Finley Peter Dunne, who created the Mr. Dooley series, and who was about as perceptive a political commentator as there was at the time, understood the moment. As saloon keeper Mr. Dooley pointed out to his patron, Mr. Hennessy, across his Archey Road bar,

Time was when.... [t]h' magazines...was very ca'ming to th' mind.... Th' idée ye got fr'm these here publications was that life was wan glad, sweet song.... But now whin I pick me fav'rite magazine off th' flure, what do I find? Ivrything has gone wrong. Th' wurruld is little better thin a convict's camp.... All th' pomes be th' lady authoressesses that used to begin: "Oh, moon, how fair!" now begin: "Oh, Ogden Armour, how awful!".... Graft ivrywhere. "Graft in th' Insurance Comp'nies," "Graft in Congress," "Graft in th' Supreem Court,"...Why, if Canada iver wants to increase her popylation all she has to do is to sind a man in a balloon over th' United States to yell: "Stop thief!" At th' sound iv th' wurruds sivinty million men, women, an' little scoundhrelly childer wud skedaddle f'r th' frontier,... Th' noise ye hear is not th' first gun iv a rivolution. It's on'y th' people iv the United States batin' a carpet.[27]

Celebrated in the popular magazines, the muckrakers became the journalistic voice (one writer called them publicity men) for reform. And for six or seven exciting years, they carried a reform message to millions (it has been estimated that during the heyday of muckraking, the magazines that led the crusade for exposure had a combined readership that ranged anywhere from 3 million to 20 million in a nation with an entire population of less than 80 million in 1900) who might not have otherwise gotten the message.

Muckraking Cartoonists

Enhancing the social importance of the muckraking journalists who used the literature of exposure to arouse public indignation were the muckraking cartoonists. The stories of franchise grabs, food adulteration, tax dodging, and especially monopoly control of the marketplace that were the staple of reform journalists could be portrayed with equally telling effect by the political cartoonist. The most influential and creative of the new breed of early twentieth-century cartoonists was Frederick Burr Opper. Drawing primarily for Hearst's newspaper syndicate, Opper achieved acclaim quickly. According to Benjamin Orange Flower, editor of *Arena* magazine, no one was "more potent in arousing the American people to the essential criminality, oppression and peril to the public of the trusts, the privileged interests and the political allies by which they have been able to plunder the people, than the cartoons of Frederick Opper."[28] Flower rooted Opper's comic genius in low comedy, which added an original quality of buffoonery to Opper's craft that was both hilarious and hard-hitting. Using a simple pen-and-ink technique, Opper created absurd effigies of power and venality. He drew the trusts as a giant bully—grinning, obese, and predatory—who always oppressed the meek, little, puppet-like figure Opper labeled "The Common People." His symbol of the trust made perfect sense. He represented the greed of the millionaire tax dodger, the avaricious corporate tycoon, the Wall Street swindler, and the bribed politician who had betrayed his public trust. Opper's symbol of The Common People was just as apt: a foolish, frightened, insignificant dwarf. But he was weak and powerless only because he relinquished his sovereign power to others. It was time The Common People reclaimed what was rightfully theirs.

Opper's closest rival for artistic creativity, trenchant political comment, and popular appeal was Homer Calvin Davenport. After Davenport's successful stints at newspapers in San Francisco and Chicago, Hearst lured him to New York to draw for the *Evening Journal* and later for the *New York American*. Davenport's drawings were humorous, but not outrageously funny in the manner of Opper's. They are most often analyzed in terms of their savage force and power. His weapon was the broadsword, not the rapier. The best example of his style can be found in his harsh depictions of "The Trusts." He drew his figure to resemble a crude, primitive, Neanderthal type—a barbarian. He called his creation "The Brute." Bearded, clothed in only a grass skirt, and often carrying the blacksnake whip of the slave driver, The Brute personified evil, lawlessness, and oppression. Such a figure could not help but generate an intense feeling of antagonism. Such a feeling might arouse a reader's moral indignation and perhaps compel him or her to think or act. It has been said that Hearst was certain that he could pictorially shame an entire nation into moral purpose.

Motion Pictures

While investigative journalism enlightened and aroused a national audience, the motion picture amused and captivated people; it was perhaps the most influential innovation in mass culture after the turn of the century. Although inventor Thomas Edison had perfected the kinetoscope (a peep-show cabinet at which one person could pay a penny and, by hand, revolve a drum to give motion to 50 feet of tiny pictures that passed before his or her eyes) in 1893 and projected moving pictures on a large screen in 1896, it was not until 1903 that Edwin S. Porter demonstrated the commercial possibilities of the new medium. Each of the two films he produced and directed that year—*The Great Train Robbery* and *The Life of an American Fireman*—told a simple story. In the first, a gang of robbers hold up a train, flee, and are apprehended. In the second, a mother and child are rescued from a burning building. Audiences were delighted that film could be used as a vehicle for narrative and not just as a method to view a scene. Porter invited the viewer to make a personal identification with the action of the story through his or her own inner life of fantasy and dreams.

Nickelodeons

The next step was the commercialization of the product. The earliest movies started out as novelties, often used as "chasers" to signal the end of a show in a vaudeville theater. In 1905 John P. Harris and Harry Davis of Pittsburgh expanded on the idea when they transformed their vaudeville house into a full-time movie theater. The owners gave their new theater a luxurious appearance, added piano accompaniment to the program to give it a grander air, charged an affordable $0.05 admission, and christened their new venture with the dignified name Nickelodeon. Their first feature, Porter's *The Great Train Robbery*, was a huge success, filling the theater's 96 seats with customers from 8:00 A.M. until midnight. Nickels poured in so rapidly that the owners averaged over $1,000 a week.

Initially disdained by the well-to-do, these nickelodeons found profitable homes in working-class neighborhood storefront theaters. Within three years, there were from 8,000 to 10,000 nickelodeons in operation nationwide. Admission prices were kept low, seating was open, viewings followed convenient schedules, and the lack of spoken dialogue allowed non-English-speaking immigrants to enjoy them as well. Programs were short enough (lasting 20 to 60 minutes) for the casual viewer to stop by on the way home from work and catch a program that often included a single-reel melodrama, a comedy, and a novelty. In the evenings and on Saturday afternoons, whole families would go together and sometimes take in all the local programs in a single outing. By 1910 approximately 26 million people (more than one-fourth of the population) attended movies each week. By 1920 the number of weekly moviegoers had increased to 50 million, and the number of movie theaters had grown to 15,000.

At first, the guardians of public morality took a dim view of the new medium. Some saw the popularity of movies as a form of mass delirium they called "nickel madness." Others regarded movies as just another example of the corrupt institutions and evil practices that had always plagued the poor, immigrant-based, working-class districts of the new industrial city, and placed theaters in the same class as saloons, brothels, and gambling dens. To more than a few middle-class reformers, the shock was more that they, as self-appointed directors of American culture, had lost control over the behavior and values of the lower class. Workers and immigrants seemed to have found their own source of entertainment and cultural diffusion. Movies told their story and depicted their values without condescension.

Silent Movies

By the end of the first decade of the twentieth century, films had begun to evolve as an art form. As the film industry shifted its base of operation from New York and New Jersey to Hollywood, California, producers began to create "feature" films that were designed to appeal to the middle class. As producers lured the middle class with more sophisticated films, they also modernized the moviegoing experience. Ornate movie palaces that rivaled opera houses in grandeur soon replaced the old nickelodeons. The Strand Theater, which opened its doors on Times Square in New York City in 1914 and could seat 3,000, displayed carpeted lounges, crystal chandeliers, original oil paintings, comfortably padded seats, an orchestra, and a battalion of uniformed ushers. The program included a comedy, a newsreel, a travelogue, and a feature film. Many of those identified as custodians of culture hoped that movies might impart middle-class values to the lower class. Producers, however, were more interested in entertaining the masses than in spreading high culture. The movies did offer a mass audience a sophistication of sorts, in that they conveyed a manner of speech, fashion, social etiquette, and social attitudes to the masses for the first time. Movies helped set the style of modern life.

One of the earliest technical and artistic innovators of the silent movie era was David Wark Griffith. Though other directors had used such technical devices as the close-up, slow motion, camera eye fade-ins and fade-outs, shadow and profile lighting, and film editing, Griffith showed how these techniques could be combined to create a different type of storytelling. Some have called this approach photographic realism. Griffith used editing to convey events occurring simultaneously or to depict different events over time. He instructed his actors to avoid the exaggerated gestures and pantomimed emotions that had been a staple of the nineteenth-century stage and to act in a more lifelike manner. Actors were told to assume a role rather than address the camera directly. Griffith also used the most modern techniques to create suspense and emotion and to focus the audience's attention more directly on the individual actors. In doing so, Griffith inadvertently contributed to the development of the star system. As the star system developed, salaries skyrocketed. One of the earliest of the screen idols, Mary Pickford, saw her salary jump from less than $400 a week in 1914 to $10,000 a week in 1916. Charlie Chaplin, who started out earning $150 a week making Keystone comedies in 1913, turned his tremendous popularity into a $1 million-per-year movie contract in 1918. Kevin Starr has sought to capture the dynamic that linked viewer and screen idol in the early days of film:

Through its star system Hollywood took ordinary Americans—which by and large the stars themselves were, in terms of talent and frail humanity—and endowed them with a quality of transcendence that flattered star and audience alike. Remaining ordinary, the stars glorified the ordinariness of those whose adulation made their careers possible. They touched ordinariness with a glamour of appearances and possibilities for which each individual in the audience of millions secretly yearned, sitting in a movie theater of an evening or on a weekend afternoon in a respite from routine, dreaming of the someone or something that might await them in the day, the week, the month, the year ahead.[29]

Closely tied to the development of the star system was the creation of a new type of publicity medium, the fan magazine. The first such publication, *Motion Picture Magazine,* was distributed by the Vitagraph Pictures sales department to promote Vitagraph-produced motion pictures. The magazine was distributed to exhibitors who, in turn, handed them out to their audiences. The demand quickly became so great that the company began to sell the most recent issues on newsstands. Other film companies quickly saw the commercial potential in fan magazines and soon stepped in with their own publications. Over time the magazines began to devote more and more attention to the personalities of the stars themselves. As the major movie stars increasingly became the focus of public attention, the star policy gradually evolved into a system of production.

Advertising

In tandem with the growth of the Hollywood star system, America's advertising industry also refined its approach, made widespread use of brand names, illustrations, and trademark identity, and created snappy slogans and colorful packaging to generate mass consumer demand. Advertisers also made greater use of psychology to attract buyers by suggesting that their products could enhance one's social and psychic well-being or transform the buyer's life. One very popular theme was to suggest that women would have more time to enjoy leisure outside the home if they would buy a certain product. An advertisement for Van Camp's Pork and Beans in *Collier's Weekly* in September 1915 promised to save the housewife "100 hours yearly." Campbell Soup Company wanted her to "get some fun out of life" and not allow the "three-meal-a-day problem" to tie her down to a life of "constant drudgery." *Cosmopolitan* ran an ad for a vacuum cleaner manufacturer in June 1915 that encouraged the housewife to just "Push the Button—and Enjoy the Springtime!" The *Ladies Home Journal* echoed the theme of the richer, fuller existence that awaited the smart consumer in April 1918 in an ad that had one woman tell her friend, "I don't have to hurry nowadays. I have a Florence Automatic Oil Stove in my kitchen."[30] By stressing instant gratification, advertisers helped to undercut the earlier Victorian emphasis on thrift and self-denial. Advertisers helped to shift the emphasis from saving to spending as they constantly prodded Americans to give in to the desire for consumption. All these new modern forms of mass communication ultimately served to break down localism and isolation, and helped to overcome divisions based on class and ethnicity, to create a basis for more standardized forms of information, entertainment, and consumption. In doing so, they created a more democratic American culture.

The Automobile

If Americans during the Progressive Era were the first generation to go to the movies, they were also the first to embrace the automobile. When the first nickelodeon opened for business in 1905, there were about 78,000 cars in this country (only 300 had been in existence 10 years before). But whereas movies had emerged as a medium for the masses, the automobile, at first, gained popularity as a toy for the mechanically inclined and an expensive amusement for the well-to-do. The explanation had to do with cost. Although the price of an expensive car might run as high as $7,000, a Reo Runabout could be purchased for less than $500 (a folding seat capable of holding two extra passengers was an additional $25) and touring cars for about $780 in 1911. It was the cost of upkeep and operation, however, that kept many potential owners out of the driver's seat. An article on the subject that appeared in 1907 estimated that the repair costs for a six-month driving season included $100 for new tires, $96 for minor parts, $70 for work on the engine, and $45 for gasoline. Extras could include a cape top and a glass front window, a speedometer, and a horn, in addition to an expensive outlay for motoring clothes. Unless a garage was available, an owner had to pay to store the car during the winter. Woodrow Wilson, then president of Princeton University, warned that the conspicuous consumption that went with car ownership actually promoted socialistic sentiment. To the worker and the farmer, the new motorist was "a picture of the arrogance of wealth."[31] That sentiment was soon to change.

One individual who played a key role in making the automobile affordable to the masses, and who became a prominent spokesperson for the new consumer culture that began to emerge in the early twentieth century, was Henry Ford. Determined to produce a lightweight, durable, affordable car for the American people, Ford spent the first five years of his company's existence experimenting with different models aimed at that goal. Finally, in 1908 Ford announced the appearance of a "universal car," the Model T. The new model was boxy in appearance, open-top in design, and offered in only one color—black. The car weighed only 1,200 pounds and was propelled by a 4-cylinder, 20-horsepower engine that the driver started with a crank. The car's suspension system gave it great flexibility, and a high clearance allowed it to navigate badly rutted roads. It could do 45 miles per hour on a smooth, straight surface. Simple to operate and easy to repair (it was said that anyone handy with a screwdriver, pair of pliers, wrench, and some wire could fix most problems and get the car running if it broke down), the earliest model sold for $850. After the initial offering, refined mass production techniques and increased demand worked both to drive down the price of the Model T ($780 in 1910; $600 in 1912; $490 in 1914; and $360 in 1916) and increase sales (5,986 cars in 1908; 19,293 in 1910; 78,611 in 1912; 260,720 in 1914; and 577,036 in 1916). The new cars, commonly known as "tin lizzies" or "flivvers," began to pour out of Ford's Detroit factory to be snatched up by millions of eager middle- and working-class consumers. By 1920 Fords would comprise almost one-half of all cars driven in rural and urban America.

The car culture created by the Model T changed the way ordinary Americans lived their daily lives. Economically, automobile manufacturing quickly became a dominant component in the American economy and triggered the growth of related industries such as petroleum, steel, rubber, glass, and paint. By 1919 there were 230 companies assembling passenger cars and 372 assembling trucks in the United States. More than 1,000 additional firms manufactured car bodies, parts, and accessories. Automakers and their suppliers employed some 600,000 workers. Supporting the automotive industry were more than 27,000 car dealers employing more than 230,000 workers. By that year there were more than 5.5 million motor vehicles registered in the United States. A year later the number of registered vehicles would surpass 8 million, far more than the rest of the world combined. Socially, the automobile necessitated tremendous expansion in road construction, stimulated real-estate development, and nurtured the growth of a new service industry that included gas stations, roadside diners, and motels. It took America to work and then from work to play. According to one assessment, the Model T "democratized mobility, opened up the suburbs, brought the farmer to town, emptied the churches on Sunday...and moved courtship off the front porch and into the back seat."[32] Soon, the ability to purchase a car on the installment plan would forever change the way consumer credit became an important part of everyday life.

William Leach has argued that from the 1890s on, "American corporate business...began the transformation of American society into a society preoccupied with consumption, with comfort and bodily well-being, with luxury, spending, and acquisition, with more goods this year than last, more next year than this. American consumer capitalism produced a culture almost violently hostile to the past and to tradition, a future-oriented culture of desire that confused the good life with goods."[33] Historian Steven Watts continued that theme in his biography of Ford, arguing that despite its practical impact, Ford's Model T represented a new, more far-reaching vision of the "good life" in America. Coming to prominence amid the collapse of a Victorian value system that emphasized hard work ("producerism"), self-control, thrift, and delayed gratification, Ford popularized a new creed of self-fulfillment through consumption. "In a new atmosphere of consumer abundance, Ford became a principal architect of a cultural order stressing standardized experiences, collective self-consciousness, and widely dispersed leisure among a popular audience." Acquiring an automobile was a way to enhance a person's sense of self. "With his new car for the people," stated Watts, "Ford certainly changed how his fellow citizens lived. But, even more significantly, he changed how they thought about what was important."[34] Although never remiss in praising his car's utilitarian features, Ford constantly stressed the pleasure and satisfaction that one would find by owning a Ford. Millions of

Americans seemed to agree. Between 1910 and 1923, when competitors finally began to cut into Ford's lead, car sales skyrocketed.

Motoring

The growing popularity of the automobile also broadened the already burgeoning interest in recreation. It was now easier to participate in sports such as golf and tennis; engage in outdoor activities such as camping, hiking, hunting, and fishing; and travel to the beach, enjoy a holiday picnic or weekend excursion, or set out on a vacation by car. Many of the advertisements of the Ford Motor Company echoed this general theme. The Model T, consumers were told, offered the prospect of exciting experiences through greater mobility. "No Ford owner ever doubted the ability of his car to go wherever he decides to travel," noted one advertisement. "He tours in it, travels in it, hunts in it, climbs mountains and crosses deserts." Another 1913 promotion touted the possibilities of tourism— "Every day is 'Independence Day' to him who owns a Ford."[35] To encourage touring, *American Motorist*, the magazine of the American Automobile Association, published the "Motorist's Creed" in 1917, which stated in part,

I believe that nothing…can do more to broaden the outlook of the people and educate them to a proper knowledge of their country and its greatness than the Automobile.

   I believe that my physical welfare and my mental growth call for frequent journeying into new territory, with the resultant meeting of new people and the absorption of new ideas.

   I believe the Automobile promotes joy and dispels gloom, increases health, banishes disease, and stimulates mental and moral growth.[36]

Between 1910 and 1920, several hundred thousand middle-class families responded to the siren call and began to tour the countryside—camping along the roadside, sleeping in tents, and cooking meals over campfires. In the vernacular of the time, these early auto-campers—the precursors of an era of mass motoring characterized by an elaborate service and commercial infrastructure of gas stations, garages, campgrounds, cabin courts, and highway eateries that would soon pop up everywhere—called their excursions "gypsying." Eventually, the popularity of this new type of motoring spawned the production of pamphlets, manuals, and travel diaries all designed to promote motor camping. Tourists kept journals to share with friends. Journalists recounted transcontinental journeys for newspapers and magazines. In hyping the driving experience, promoters shared the same themes—the intrigue of adventure, the pleasures of being liberated from hectic routines, and the freedom to chart one's own course. "You are limited," said one observer, "only by the quality of the roads and in no other way." Yet these early auto-campers were recreationists more than social rebels. They were looking to "mitigate its [the city's] harsh effects through periodic, ritualistic contact with a somewhat tamed wilderness," returning revivified after several weeks of touring to home and job.[37]

In an interesting extension of the liberation theme, the advertising department of the Ford Motor Company made a special effort to target the "new women." In a pamphlet entitled *The Woman and the Ford* (1912), the company claimed that the Model T's ease of operation made it a car for women. Taking advantage of the car's durability and reliability, vigorous women who "crave exercise and excitement [and] who long for relief from the monotony of social and household duties" could avail themselves of the opportunity to roam the countryside and experience new things. In fact, the notion of possible escape from Victorian constraints was the pamphlet's main theme.

It's woman's day.... She shares the responsibilities—and demands the opportunities and pleasures of the new order. No longer a "shut in," she reaches for an ever wider sphere of action—that she may be more the woman.

And in this happy change the automobile is playing no small part. It has broadened her horizon—increased her pleasures—given new vigor to her body—made neighbors of far away friends—and multiplied tremendously her range of activity. It is a real weapon in the changing order.[38]

Early twentieth-century motorists had to be prepared. Potential drivers had to take a comprehensive course of instruction to learn both how to drive and how to make necessary repairs. To be properly equipped, a driver needed a full set of tools, tire-changing equipment, an extra set of spark plugs, tire chains for muddy roads, and an extra supply of gasoline, not to mention a duster, a raincoat, an umbrella, and a pair of goggles to ward off the elements. Women passengers needed long linen dusters, lap robes, and hats secured with long veils knotted under the chin. As long as automobiles had to be cranked by hand to start, it was assumed that women would generally not be drivers or owners. With the invention of the electric starter in 1910, however, that changed. Automobile manufacturers, looking to expand sales, encouraged women to learn how to drive.

The proper attire for women automobile passengers included long linen dusters, lap robes, and hats secured with long veils knotted under the chin. (Courtesy of the Library of Congress)

As women began to move their feet to operate the pedals of the car, long skirts became an inconvenience. According to journalist Mark Sullivan, the problem directly affected fashion, with the hems of women's skirts rising (from roughly the knob of the anklebone to the top of the shoe) to accommodate their new roles.

The "sport" of motoring was also hazardous. Fast driving quickly became a public problem. What was one person's thrill was another's nuisance. Automobiles frightened horses, upset carriages, and severely injured pedestrians. To combat careless or reckless driving, a number of states began to impose speeding limits. In New York the maximum speed in congested areas was 10 miles per hour, 15 miles per hour in outlying areas, and 20 miles per hour on the open (country) road. Many of the suggestions for driving safety also served to combat the prejudice that the early automobile aroused among non-motorists. In the end, the appeal of the automobile was just too strong. The motorcar brought freedom from earlier restrictions. It tremendously shortened time and distance. It broadened the market in which an individual could sell his labor. It also broke up the old community of organized society and substituted a much larger one. "The process…gave rise to ferment and flux in every area of life."[39]

The Airplane

If Americans felt liberated by the advent of the automobile and understood firsthand the impact that the new leap in technology had on their everyday lives, they were just beginning to have their collective imagination stirred by the promise of manned flight. Although the era of the barnstorming aviator and the heroic exploits of intrepid fliers such as Charles Lindberg would be part of the popular culture of the 1920s, Americans in the Progressive Era began to sense the special significance of flight and what it might mean for their future. But it took some time. When the Wright brothers, two former bicycle mechanics from Dayton, Ohio, made the first successful human-controlled, motor-powered, heavier-than-air flight at Kitty Hawk, North Carolina, on December 17, 1903, the event was not widely noted or publicized. Only a handful of people (men from a nearby coastal lifesaving station had been summoned as witnesses) saw the first flight (it lasted 20 seconds and covered a distance of 120 feet), and only one person bothered to take a photograph of the plane as it left the ground. No newspaper reporters were present.

When stories of the event did appear in print, many readers thought that it was either a hoax or merely another flight by a lighter-than-air craft commonly known as an airship or dirigible. Most people would have to see an airplane to understand that controlled flight had taken place. After making improvements to their prototype, the Wrights finally made another public demonstration of their flying machine for the U.S. Army at Fort Meyer in Virginia in September 1908. During a two-week demonstration period, tens of thousands of spectators watched as the Wrights completed short test flights. This time the flights were widely reported in the newspapers, and press accounts included detailed descriptions of the plane and its performance as well as photographs of the plane in flight. Millions read about the new invention and studied the

The machine used by Glenn H. Curtiss to fly from Albany to New York City in 1910. (Courtesy of the Library of Congress)

photographs intently, but the news still seemed to challenge credulity. The suggestion that humans had developed a way to fly was both impossible to explain and difficult to believe. In the end, people just had to see for themselves.

In 1909 Wilbur Wright made a series of flights around New York City. Crowds estimated at over 1 million watched him fly along Manhattan, out over New York Harbor, and around the Statue of Liberty. In January 1910, in Los Angeles, California, 30,000 attended the first air show. Later that year a crowd estimated at over 1 million watched as a plane flew over Chicago. "Never," said a minister who witnessed the spectacle, "have I seen such a look of wonder in the faces of a multitude. From the gray-haired man to the child, everyone seemed to feel that it was a new day in their lives."[40] Later in 1910 Glenn H. Curtiss, a mechanic and former motorcycle racer, flew his own plane from Albany, New York, to Governor's Island in New York Harbor. The crowds that watched his achievement were larger than those that had turned out to watch Wright's earlier flights. The *New York Times* devoted six full pages to covering the story. That same year the *New York World* assigned a full-time reporter to follow developments in aviation, and other major dailies quickly followed suit. Magazines also began to feature articles and stories about flight. Soon both Curtiss and the Wrights were training a number of pilots to stage exhibitions in their aircraft at county fairs, racetracks, and air races—anywhere a promoter could guarantee a crowd and pay an exhibition fee. For the public, each new record or "first" (such as the first flights by a scheduled airline in 1914 or the start of government airmail service in 1918) inspired even greater wonder. More than any other achievement, the miracle of flight reinforced the feeling that Americans had truly entered the modern era.

NOTES

1. Steven Mintz and Randy Roberts, eds., *Hollywood's America: United States History through Its Films* (St. James, NY: Brandywine Press, 1993), 2.

2. Steven A. Reiss, *Touching Base: Professional Baseball and American Culture in the Progressive Era* (Westport, CT: Greenwood Press, 1980), 7–8.

3. Ibid., 21.

4. Eliot Asinof, *1919: America's Loss of Innocence* (New York: Donald I. Fine, 1990), 291.

5. Roderick Nash, *Wilderness and the American Mind* (New Haven, CT: Yale University Press, 1982), 148.

6. Ibid., 150.

7. Ibid., 150, 153, 155.

8. Susan Curtis, *Dancing to the Black Man's Tune: A Life of Scott Joplin* (Columbia: University of Missouri Press, 1994), 66.

9. Ibid.

10. Mark Sullivan, *Our Times: America at the Birth of the Twentieth Century*, ed. Dan Rather (New York: Scribner, 1996), 409.

11. Ibid., 410–411.

12. Sean Dennis Cashman, *America Ascendant: From Theodore Roosevelt to FDR in the Century of American Power, 1901–1945* (New York: New York University Press, 1998), 72.

13. Larry Starr and Christopher Waterman, *American Popular Music: From Minstrelsy to MP3* (New York: Oxford University Press, 2010), 57.

14. John F. Kasson, *Amusing the Million: Coney Island at the Turn of the Century* (New York: Hill and Wang, 1978), 66, 50.

15. Kathy Peiss, *Cheap Amusements: Working Women and Leisure in Turn-of-the-Century New York* (Philadelphia: Temple University Press, 1986), 43.

16. Ibid., 62.

17. Ibid., 126, 186.

18. David E. Shi, *Facing Facts: Realism in American Thought and Culture, 1850–1920* (New York: Oxford University Press, 1995), chapters 10–11.

19. Vernon Louis Parrington, *The Beginnings of Critical Realism in America, 1860–1920* (New York: Harcourt, Brace and World, 1958), 328.

20. Page Smith, *America Enters the World: A People's History of the Progressive Era and World War I* (New York: Penguin Books, 1985), 913.

21. Shi, *Facing Facts,* 254.

22. Milton W. Brown, "The Ash Can School," *American Quarterly* 1 (Summer 1949): 132.

23. Marianne Doezema, "The Real New York," in *The Paintings of George Bellows* by Michael Quick, Jane Myers, Marianne Doezema, and Franklin Kelly (New York: Harry N. Abrams, 1992), 119.

24. Ellen F. Fitzpatrick, *Muckraking: Three Landmark Articles* (Boston: Bedford Books, 1994), 109.

25. Ray Stannard Baker, *American Chronicle: The Autobiography of Ray Stannard Baker* (New York: Charles Scribner's Sons, 1945), 183.

26. Fitzpatrick, *Muckraking,* 111.

27. Finley Peter Dunne, *Mr. Dooley on Ivrything and Ivrybody*, ed. Robert Hutchinson (New York: Dover Publications, 1963), 241–244.

28. B. O. Flower, "Frederick Opper: A Cartoonist of Democracy," *Arena* 33 (June 1905): 587, 589.

29. Kevin Starr, *Inventing the Dream: California through the Progressive Era* (New York: Oxford University Press, 1985), 320.

30. Cashman, *America Ascendant,* 59, 60.

31. Foster Rhea Dulles, *A History of Recreation: America Learns to Play* (New York: Appleton-Century-Crofts, 1965), 314.

32. John A. Jakle and Keith A. Sculle, *Motoring: The Highway Experience in America* (Athens: University of Georgia Press, 2008), 15.

33. William Leach, *Land of Desire: Merchants, Power, and the Rise of a New American Culture* (New York: Vintage Books, 1993), xiii.

34. Steven Watts, *The People's Tycoon: Henry Ford and the American Century* (New York: Vintage Books, 2005), xii, 112.

35. Ibid., 126–127.

36. Jakle and Sculle, *Motoring,* 27.

37. Warren James Belasco, *Americans on the Road: From Autocamp to Motel, 1910–1945* (Cambridge, MA: MIT Press, 1979), 8, 16.

38. Watts, *People's Tycoon,* 127.

39. Sullivan, *Our Times,* 390.

40. Joseph J. Corn, *The Winged Gospel: America's Romance with Aviation, 1900–1950* (New York: Oxford University Press, 1983), 4.

4

Citizen Activism and Civic Engagement

Although the Progressive Era is commonly viewed by historians as a complex, multifaceted period in the emergence of modern America, most have continued to emphasize reform as the dominant characteristic of the time. The more difficult questions, however, are those that deal with the nature of that reform impulse, its timing, and its overall impact. What were the origins of what has come to be called progressivism? Why did this major shift in social and political consciousness occur when it did? What factors combined to give this reform era its general thrust? And what impact did the various reform efforts have on the development of modern America?

THE ORIGINS OF PROGRESSIVISM

The roots of progressivism can be found in the Gilded Age of the latter part of the nineteenth century. Numerous groups during that time believed that certain changes would improve society. Demands for civil service reform, the eight-hour day, woman suffrage, vice and temperance reform, nonpartisan balloting, factory inspection, trust-busting, preservation and conservation of natural resources, tax reform, ending child labor, creating more efficient local government, and railroad regulation were topical then and would remain vital issues during the Progressive Era. During the Gilded Age, young social scientists such as Lester Frank Ward and economists such as Richard T. Ely were starting to challenge current conservative, laissez-faire-oriented economic thinking. They suggested that scientific procedures could be applied to the study of the political economy and argued that a more activist federal government could be a means to improve society. Although the issues were numerous and the intellectual environment fertile, reform during the Gilded Age never coalesced into a nation-defining movement. Individuals and groups acted in seeming isolation, and there was no common program around which to rally disparate groups. The general prosperity of the Gilded Age seemed to assure many people that industrial capitalism might yet solve its own problems and marginalized critics as pessimists or alarmists.

The Impact of the Depression of the 1890s

According to historian David Thelen, what served to change this pattern and align the various reform groups behind a common banner was the severe depression of 1893–1897.[1] Key to this event was the way in which it dramatized the failures of industrialization. By 1894 20 percent of the workforce was without a job, walking the streets of the major cities and wandering from town to town looking for work. During 1893 and 1894, numerous bands of unemployed workers (referred to in the press as "industrial armies") marched on Washington, D.C., to demand federal relief. Paralyzing labor disputes, such as the Pullman Strike in Chicago in 1894, suggested that the specter of social revolt was not a fantasy. But workers were not the only ones affected by the economic collapse. Over 500 banks failed, and roughly 16,000 businesses were pulled into bankruptcy along with them. Seventy-four railroads went into receivership. Added to the genuine human suffering were numerous examples of business embezzlement and corruption (graft). Just as sensational were the reports that not all suffered equally. Flaunting the stereotype of the Gay Nineties, the rich staged extravagant parties and banquets, sailed their sumptuous yachts, and attended glitzy theatrical events. As Thorstein Veblen noted in his depression-inspired book *The Theory of the Leisure Class,* the rich engaged in ostentatious displays of wealth through a lavish lifestyle characterized by "conspicuous consumption."

Unable to escape the hardship, and with no economic upturn in sight, Americans of all social classes wanted to know what had caused the collapse and what could be done about it. When the nation's political leaders failed (primarily through ineffective attempts to manipulate the currency supply and the tariff) to alleviate the crisis, the national mood soured. Angry, frightened, and disillusioned with their political leaders, Americans became increasingly receptive to new ideas. Looking to broaden their understanding of the political economy, they attended hundreds of discussion groups or clubs in their search for remedies, and participated in an expanding adult education movement that was often connected with boards of education, farmers' institutes, churches, or universities. In 1890 26,632 people attended free lectures offered by the New York Board of Education. By 1898 that number had increased to 509,135. The Yellow Press (newspapers) of the 1890s and later popular muckraking magazines sensed the thirst for answers and fed the popular hunger for information.

The everyday experiences of Americans during the depression made the ideas that were being suggested by the new social scientists increasingly intriguing. Some economists connected to the American Economic Association (formed in 1885 to attack the emphasis on economic individualism and promote state intervention in the economy) used as their touchstone the ideas of Henry George. George, an economic thinker who had published his famous book *Progress and Poverty* in 1879, had advanced the notion that land ownership and economic opportunity were linked, and that the way to create opportunity was to make land available. The way to do this was through a new "single tax" on all monopolized, unimproved land, land that was being held for speculative purposes.

The importance of *Progress and Poverty* to later social scientists was manifold. It offered a new ethical approach to economics. It argued that individuals had an obligation to aid the less fortunate and undercut the prevailing notions of self-help and individualism. It offered an environmental explanation for social ills and posited that conditions under which people lived (in this case, unjust tax laws), rather than heredity or individual character, determined social outcomes. It argued that collective action (such as the formation of unions) or state intervention (the passage of new laws) could improve living and working conditions. It also suggested that taxation could be used as a means to redistribute wealth. During the 1890s social scientists began to advocate mechanisms such as income, inheritance, franchise, and corporate taxes as means by which the wealthy would be required to contribute to the general welfare, or the municipal ownership of public utilities whereby costs could be lowered to consumers and efficiency of operation enhanced. It was only a short step for these new social scientists to conclude that if government should prove to be a captive of vested interests and an impediment to change, new participatory devices—municipal home rule, the initiative, referendum, recall, direct primary, woman suffrage, and the direct election of U.S. senators—could be adopted to further democratize the political process and facilitate change. Political conceptions, like economic and (eventually) legal ones, would have to evolve with changing social conditions.

The depression of the 1890s ended much of the fragmentation that had previously plagued the reform effort. It generated a broad set of new issues in which all individuals, especially those living in cities, could feel a common cause. The rapid growth in the size of cities and the sharp increase in the number of people who lived in them necessitated a tremendous expansion in the goods and services required by urban consumers. To accommodate the need for expanded services, municipalities granted franchises to street railway, gas, water, and electric companies. In return for having the city grant a monopoly to these various corporations, urban consumers expected to receive safe, efficient service at a reasonable price. This same civic understanding carried over to the retail sale of basic necessities such as food, coal, and ice. During the depression of the 1890s, people living in urban environments began to feel betrayed. Reformers exposed numerous examples of corporate arrogance by which privately owned gas, electric, and transportation (streetcar) companies maintained or increased rates during the depression without making any improvements in service and failed to display any genuine concern for the health or safety of their customers. The reformers also showed that "as local governments raised taxes to meet the higher costs resulting from massive unemployment, wealthy individuals and corporations often dodged taxes through favoritism purchased from governmental officials."[2] As a result, individuals began to identify with their roles as consumers, taxpayers, and citizens as much if not more than their occupational roles as workers. It was this broader focus that would give progressivism its activist thrust at the grassroots level. Individuals and groups began to mobilize behind issues that cut across class lines. When progressive reformers commonly spoke of "the people" or the "public interest" against the "selfish" or "special interests," they were speaking of this new political coalition, which expressed itself in numerous and varied ways throughout the Progressive Era.

CITIZEN ACTIVISM

The St. Louis Streetcar Strike

One example of the way in which this new dynamic manifested itself was the St. Louis Streetcar Strike of 1900. Five years before the strike, and during the depression of the 1890s, Lee Meriwether, Missouri State Labor Commissioner, gained public attention for advocating that the property of municipal franchises be fairly assessed for tax purposes. The *St. Louis Post-Dispatch* quickly joined the issue by alleging that street railway companies in the city had obtained tax breaks after applying pressure on local tax boards. Public displeasure with the streetcar companies increased with reports of accidents caused by fenderless cars, increased fares, and damage resulting from uncontrolled street construction. The comments of Meriwether and the concerns of the public eventually forced the mayor to persuade the board of assessors to increase the tax assessments on street railway property in 1899.

The street railway issue in St. Louis, however, was not over. In May of 1899, the *Post-Dispatch* accused the state legislature of betraying the public interest by enacting legislation that would allow one street railway corporation to purchase the properties of other street railways and consolidate the streetcar service into one corporate entity. Lamenting the action, one state official warned that the passage of the bill would leave the people of St. Louis with "no protection in the manner of service that the monopoly will furnish. The monopoly will do as it pleases."[3] Having been given the authorization to do so by the state legislature, the United Railways Company quickly acquired, with one exception, the railway lines, properties, and franchises of all the independent railroad companies in St. Louis. As they moved to reorganize the railway system in the city, company officials promised the public more efficient service and improved facilities. Alarmed by what the newly consolidated system might mean to their own livelihood were the employees who wanted the new company (now operating under the name St. Louis Transit Company) to recognize their union and bargain collectively with it. In March 1900 the workers submitted a list of demands that included union recognition, a 10-hour day, the elimination of split shifts, a standardized wage scale, and the right to arbitrate future grievances. When the company refused to meet their demands, 3,325 employees of the company went out on strike.

Initially, the strike had a decided labor-versus-capital focus with the main point of contention being union recognition. But the apparent class consciousness was actually part of a broader citizen consciousness that would be sharpened as the strike spread to involve the entire community. To one St. Louisan, the company, as a quasi-public concern, owed "a duty not only to those who are entitled to dividends on its stock, but to the people of the city and State as well. It occupies the public streets...and is the grantee of certain public franchises to be used for the benefit of the public." One day after the start of the strike, sympathizers in many parts of the city began to organize a boycott of the transit company. Many people could be seen wearing small pieces of cardboard attached to their lapels that read, "I will walk until the street car companies settle." Other labor organizations in the city created a chain-letter system in which a member would ask a friend to walk downtown with him from a residential section of the city. Each friend would

Woman boarding a New York City streetcar by jumping onto the running board, 1913. (Courtesy of the Library of Congress)

be asked to exert the same influence on another. Support from the community grew. Soon all manner of conveyance—furniture vans, tallyhos, carryalls, ice and milk wagons, sprinkling carts, and bicycles—could be seen transporting people. One observer noted that it was "very amusing at first, those that didn't walk rode in anything from a handsome carriage down to an old coal wagon. There were…all kinds of wagons, all *crowded*.…The entire width of the street was packed with vehicles." The *Post-Dispatch* reported that "Silk Hats and Shirt Waists are Side by Side in Delivery Wagons and Furniture Vans."[4]

It did not take long for the strike to affect everyone. Strikers and their wives suffered from lost wages, small businessmen felt the pinch of declining sales, and consumers endured the inconvenience of supplemental transportation. When the company brought in scabs to operate the cars, animosities intensified. Women were especially evident along the streetcar routes, verbally abusing the carmen, conductors, and policemen who rode the nearly empty cars. As the strike continued, violence increased. Sympathizers cut down so many streetcar wires that the company was forced to hire detectives in an effort to reduce such incidents. On some lines, crowds piled stones and rubbish on the tracks to impede the progress of the cars. Small dynamite charges were placed on the tracks as well. A crowd estimated to number more than 1,000 built a huge bonfire on the car track at one major intersection. Mounted policemen with drawn sabers routinely charged the crowds to break them up, only to see the crowds reform after their departure. Obstructing the flow of streetcar traffic soon triggered legal action, and a court injunction was issued to restrain strikers from interfering with the operation of mail cars. The injunction also allowed for an increased number of deputy marshals. After 11 people were shot in South St. Louis during an altercation between armed company employees and riotous crowds, the city's police chief formed a posse comitatus to preserve order. To many, the armed strikebreakers, saber-wielding police, and newly formed posse served as graphic examples that property rights seemed to take precedence. As one spokesperson for a citizen's group commented, it seemed as if it had become government "of monopoly, by monopoly, and for monopoly."[5]

Eventually the strike took a political turn. Realizing that the existing franchise grant would be nearly impossible to overturn, the *Post-Dispatch* again raised the issue of franchise taxation. Soon both major political parties publicly declared their support in favor of the equitable taxation of corporate franchises. Another group, known as the Franchise Repeal Association, held mass meetings to discuss the possibility of municipal ownership of the street railway system as an alternative to private operation. On another front, Missouri Attorney General Edward C. Crow initiated legal action to annul the consolidation of the street railway system in St. Louis.

For many St. Louisans, however, the strike ended badly. In early July, after the strike had lasted almost two months, strike leaders admitted defeat and accepted the reality that their union would not be recognized by the company. In doing so, they also admitted that they were powerless to prevent the company from continuing to employ non-union strikebreakers or to stop the company from permanently blacklisting many strikers. Attorney General Crow's legal suit lingered on the court calendar until it was ultimately dismissed early in 1901. The state's Board of Equalization refused to increase the taxes of quasi-public corporations in the state even though 40,000 voters signed a petition in support of the idea. Adding insult to injury was the recognition that promises of improved service had proved to be false. Mayor Rolla Wells acknowledged after the strike that several delegations had come to his office "bitterly complaining that frequently, large numbers of persons were left standing at the street intersections in the shivering cold as cars rapidly passed them by without stopping," and had informed him that stones were often hurled at the cars by angry citizens. To observe the service for himself, the mayor visited some of the street corners and intersections "and watched the waiting, indignant groups, and saw for myself that there were good grounds for the popular uproar."[6]

The St. Louis Streetcar Strike exhibited a complex interaction of people in a rapidly changing urban environment. Despite its outward appearance as a labor issue, the strike actually developed a cross-class sense of community consciousness. Complaints of inefficient and discourteous service, unsafe operations, tax inequities, and monopoly control of a necessary public service converted the strike into a broader community action. People altered their lifestyles and everyday patterns to support the boycott of the streetcar company by walking or taking alternative forms of transportation. The transit company, as the antisocial product of legislative-derived monopoly, caused the emotions of many St. Louis residents to merge. In the process, the public welfare became foremost, and people articulated positions from new perspectives. The intense feelings generated against the street railway monopoly contributed to the showing of Meriwether, who gained 28 percent of the vote in St. Louis while running for mayor on a municipal ownership ticket in 1901. In an apparent effort to save face, the Democratic state legislature did pass a diluted franchise tax law in 1901. As one state senator remarked, "I am mighty glad the assembly passed a franchise bill. I would hardly have dare[d] to go home if it had not."[7]

St. Louisans had confronted the monopolization of a necessary public service during the transit strike. As consumers, they registered concern about the way streetcar service operated, and they showed increased interest in the idea of municipal ownership. As taxpayers, they supported the call for increased taxes on quasi-public corporations. As citizens, they turned their attention to franchise privileges and the police protection readily granted to the corporation. As workers, they were reminded just how dependent their lives were without a recognized union to bargain for them. But in their daily lives, people also had to contend with the nagging problem of making means and ends meet.

CONSUMERS CONFRONT MONOPOLY

When President William McKinley ran for reelection in 1900, he did so behind a slogan that promised the American worker a "full dinner pail." The worst aspects of the previous depression had passed, but people were still concerned about the relationship between wages and prices. Real hourly earnings for workers in all industries rose slightly between 1898 and 1902, but the cost of living index moved upward at the same time. By 1902 it had increased 9 percent above the 1898 level. Similar results appeared in the retail price index for food as prices jumped 8.3 percent between 1898 and 1902. Such increases created problems. In St. Joseph, Missouri, the director of the Board of Charity worried that monthly grants of money (usually not more than $5 per family) would not be sufficient to keep up with rising food prices. Basic items such as meat and potatoes had increased markedly. The cheapest kind of beef had increased in price from 5 cents per pound to 12.5 cents per pound in just one year. Potatoes had more than doubled in price over the past 12 months, from 40 to 50 cents per bushel up to $1.05. According to the director, an allotment that had once been adequate for the purchase of 20 pounds of soup meat and 2 bushels of potatoes would now have to be stretched to buy 12 pounds of meat and 1 bushel of potatoes.

As price increases continued during the early twentieth century, consumers began to make the connection that their declining purchasing power was directly linked to corporate consolidation or, in the term most commonly used at the time, the trusts. Over 100 trusts had formed in the year 1899 alone, more than doubling the number in existence before that time. By 1903 the number had grown to over 300. Occasionally, newspapers helped readers understand this process. The *St. Louis Post-Dispatch* found, in August of 1899, that prices were higher on nearly every necessity. This trend occurred during a time of plentiful crops and when the amount of manufactured products exceeded previous years. These figures seemed to call into question the presumed laws of supply and demand. To the editors of the *Post-Dispatch,* conditions should have caused a decrease in prices, not an increase. Their conclusion was that the trusts had forced prices up to "make dividends for largely over-capitalized combinations."[8] In the case of meat, the most popular charge was that the major meat packers—Armour, Swift, and Morris—had formed a pool to dominate the industry by controlling and regulating the shipments of dressed meats to the markets.

The Beef Trust

As the price of meat advanced 3 to 4 cents per pound early in 1902, charges of market manipulation gained credibility. The *Lamar* (Missouri) *Leader* commented that with the price of beef "soaring among the clouds" and the manufacturers of tinware forming a trust, the average working man would find the promised "full dinner pail" to be "chimerical." The editors of the *St. Joseph Daily News* noted that four consecutive years of price increases had forced the poor to quit using all but the cheapest grades of beef. Market butchers blamed price increases on a conspiracy of the meat packers. They asserted that the increase in the price of dressed meat seemed to be well out of proportion to the increase in the price of cattle. Those who actually raised beef agreed. One Missouri stockman concluded that "the packers raise is way out of proportion to the increase in the price of cattle. The big fat steers which can be bought for 6 cents a pound now have not been below 5 cents for the past five years. It is certainly hard on the common people."[9]

Meat packers and consumers offered differing explanations for rising beef costs and the effects of those increases on working-class families. In responding to public criticism, the packers cited a rise in the price of cattle feed caused by a drought that had produced a lighter-than-normal corn crop. They also accused farmers of holding out for higher prices, and argued that artificial scarcity and growing consumer demand had made the cost of beef dear to consumers. On occasion they blamed the victims, suggesting that workers had appetites that did not suit their budgets. According to one agent for the Armour Company in Houston, Texas, the average worker with a wage of $2 or $3 a day "wants porterhouse, demands porterhouse and, in the past, has been able to get porterhouse because the market was easy and within reach of his purse."[10]

Workers held a different view. Alois Bilker, a St. Louis street sweeper who earned $1.50 a day offered his own opinion on the price of meat.

We have meat but once a day now at our house. It is too high to expect a poor man to serve it at every meal. As long as I have had a family I do not know when it was so high. Nowadays we buy round steak, cut as thin as paper almost, for twenty cents or perhaps fifteen cents, and we are lucky in getting it at that. Generally we have to buy shoulder and neck pieces, because we get more of that part of the cow for the money. We have to fall back on beans and cheap things to take the place of meat. There is much grumbling down in my neighborhood around Geyer Avenue. We all believe that a few rich men get together and make the prices. That story about higher beef and scarcity of corn and so on may do for some, but we do not believe that it is necessary to send up the price of meat the way they do.

To Mr. Bilker, the assumed inability to purchase select cuts of meat concealed an inability to purchase a sufficient quantity of meat or any meat at all. In a nearly tragic story, a 17-year-old boy attempted suicide with morphine. When asked to give a reason for his near-fatal attempt, the boy replied that he had to support his mother and sister on his wages of $7 a week earned setting type. He had lost his job the previous week, but had managed to find work as a pantry boy at a hotel. But "my earnings," he explained, "would not meet our expenses. Meat was so high and all the world seemed against me."[11]

Others, viewing the situation from perhaps a different angle, offered their own suggestions to the problem of high meat prices. Noticing the increase in the price of beef products, Harvey W. Wiley, head of the Bureau of Chemistry of the U.S. Department of Agriculture (USDA), encouraged consumers to alter their diets and adopt cereal substitutes in place of beef products. The editor of the *Baltimore American* joked along similar lines as he put his suggestion to rhyme.

Mary had a little lamb,
    With mintsauce on the side;
    When Mary saw the meat trust's bill,
    It shocked her so she cried.
Mary had a little veal—
    A cutlet, nicely broiled.
    Her papa, to pay for that veal,
    All morning sorely toiled.
Mary had a little steak—
    A porterhouse quite small,
    And when the bill came in, she sighed;
    No dress for me next fall.
Mary had a little roast—
    As juicy as could be—
    And Mary's papa simply went
    Right into bankruptcy.
Mary isn't eating meat;
    She has a better plan;
    She vows it's ladylike to be
    A vegetarian.[12]

Consumer Protest

In numerous cities consumers began expressing attitudes of resistance to what they perceived to be trust imposition. Although the increase in the price of meat had not been proved to be a conspiracy, "an impression of this kind could result in nothing else than general agitation and resentment." In the smaller meat shops in St. Louis, butchers found their customers "complaining lustily." As the consumption of meat dropped off, fish became the new staple for many. Butchers and consumers soon began to unite to resist the "extortion" of the "Beef Trust." As one retail butcher put it, "Our interests are the same as those of the public." In Indianapolis, Indiana, grocers discontinued the sale of beef and beef products and notified suppliers that they would not resume the trade until prices were substantially reduced. Several butcher shops also closed or refused to buy from the major Chicago packinghouses.[13]

Workers, yielding to their roles as consumers, used their existing forms of organization to boycott the trust. In Bloomington, Illinois, 2,000 employees of the Chicago and Alton Railroad agreed that none of their members would eat meat for 30 days. They were joined by 400 workers in Bellefontaine, Ohio, and 5,000 members of the Central Labor Union of Amsterdam, New York. In Dayton, Ohio, protesters began an endless chain-letter campaign against the Beef Trust. Thousands of letters called attention to the high price of meat and encouraged consumers to refrain from eating beef for one week.

Popular outcry against the Beef Trust in Missouri provoked legal action from the state's attorney general, who charged that the state's antitrust law prohibited packers from conspiring to fix wholesale and retail prices of all beef, pork, and dressed meats. The Beef Trust hearings began in Jefferson City before the Missouri Supreme Court in May of 1902. During questioning, retail butchers from Kansas City and St. Louis testified that the major Chicago packers (Armour, Swift, Cudahy, and Morris) fixed the prices for meat, and that they levied fines on anyone they dealt with for selling at a lower price. During the second day of inquiry, testimony revealed that salesmen employed by the major packing companies undersold their smaller competitors with the intention of driving them out of business. In addition to allegations that the trust fixed prices and sought to destroy competition, further testimony revealed that the trust also forced consumers to purchase an inferior product.

When the public learned that the big packers had actually sold diseased meat to St. Louis customers, the term "concession" beef entered the consumer vocabulary. Under this practice wholesalers sold "ripe," "aged," "stale," or "beginning to spoil" meat to butchers at a reduced price, after the major packing firms had granted a similar price reduction to the wholesaler. During the hearings, one St. Louis meat dealer testified that he had seen meat that had been rubbed to remove "whiskers," painted to restore a healthy color, and preserved with ammonia. Confident that he had obtained sufficient evidence, the attorney general asked for a writ of ouster against the major meat-packing firms in the state. In the writ he charged that a combine of packing companies fixed the prices of 90 percent of all the meat sold in the state. Final judgment in the case, which was rendered in March of 1903, ended in a victory for the state. To be allowed to continue to do business in Missouri, five major meat-packing companies—Armour, Hammond, Cudahy, Swift, and Schwarzschild and Sulzberger—were each fined $5,000 plus court costs.

The information revealed in the Missouri hearings, the anticipation of other legal suits by the federal government and other states, increased newspaper coverage of the growing scandal, and persistent high prices intensified popular reaction. In Lynn, Massachusetts, approximately 1,700 employees of General Electric Company formed an anti-beefeating league. Members pledged to refrain from eating meat for 30 days, and organizers expected an additional 5,000 company employees to join before the end of the boycott. Members of the Central Labor Union in Portland, Maine, and 2,500 Santa Fe Railroad employees in Topeka, Kansas, agreed to boycott meat for one month as well. Continued high meat prices in St. Joseph, Missouri, and Omaha, Nebraska, caused consumers to switch to a fish diet. In New York City, angry Jewish consumers conducted a food riot. Five hundred Jewish women formed the Ladies Anti-Beef Trust Association and threatened to start their own cooperative meat store if kosher meat did not come down in price. To one editor, these actions seemed to be part of a process. People stopped eating eggs when dealers pushed the price too high. Stung by high prices, they cut down on butter, coffee, and sugar in the same manner. They then "revolted and they stopped eating meat...when their common sense told them that the prices asked were asked only because the beef barons thought they had the supply so thoroughly cornered that they could charge anything they pleased."[14] When beef prices finally stabilized in mid-May, 1902, local butchers concluded that it was the direct result of popular agitation and legal prosecutions.

IMPURE DRUGS AND FOOD

Among the numerous consumer-related issues raised during the Beef Trust investigation, one that gained a good deal of public attention was the sale of an impure product to consumers. The topic was not a new one. One of the dilemmas of the late nineteenth century was how to regulate drugs and food. In an environment where scientific knowledge and official supervision were woefully inadequate, quackery and deception in the sale of drugs flourished. Because patent medicine manufacturers were not required by law to put labels on their bottles that showed the ingredients, consumers purchased medicines at their own risk. These nostrums were ineffective, often harmful (many contained habit-forming ingredients), and dishonestly advertised. Working to prevent any meaningful regulation of the industry were drug manufacturers (organized as the Proprietary Association of America); numerous popular newspapers, magazines, and medical and religious journals that accepted deceptive patent medicine advertisements; and a sizeable portion of the public who still embraced the practice of using patent medicine home remedies as alternatives to potentially risky and almost certainly expensive medical care.

Just as difficult as regulating drugs was the effort to maintain the purity of food. As food processing shifted from the home to the factory, ethical standards in the "industry" declined, and companies debased their products to stay competitive. To reduce costs some companies added chicory to coffee, ground rice to flour, and mixed husks and dirt to ground pepper; and sold a mixture of glucose and hayseed that had been flavored and colored as raspberry jam. Although such adulterations were not necessarily health threatening, they were dishonest. A more serious problem for consumers was related to food preservatives that could be harmful. To reduce spoilage, food was commonly refrigerated. But because that process had not been perfected by the 1890s, food manufacturers turned to chemical preservatives such as salicylic acid, borax, and formaldehyde. State laws governing food preparation were weak, and inspection and enforcement were essentially nonexistent. A state could not even regulate an out-of-state manufacturer. As a result, consumers lacked adequate protection.

CITIZEN ACTIVISM

The Woman's Christian Temperance Union

One of the first organizations to focus on pure food and drugs was the Woman's Christian Temperance Union (WCTU), which approached the issue primarily from the vantage point of home protection. By the mid-1880s the WCTU had expanded its campaign against alcohol abuse to include stimulants and narcotics such as opium, laudanum, morphine, "loco-weed," and the hidden, addictive ingredients (such as cocaine) in many patent medicines. As early as its annual convention in 1884, the organization publicly denounced the use of patent medicines containing alcohol. The national body also created a special Department of Non-Alcoholic Medicine to assist state activists who were promoting the teaching of physiology and hygiene in the public schools, with the purpose of emphasizing the dangers of using stimulants and narcotics. In 1902, as an indication of the growing interest in the topic, the superintendent of the WCTU's Department of Non-Alcoholic Medicine sent out 15,600 pages of literature that included the informational pamphlets "Patent Medicines" and "Safe Remedies." Prior to the death of WCTU president Frances Willard in 1898, the entire organization, including the Department of Legislation, the *Union Signal* (the official publication of the organization), and the central committee all supported pure food and drug activism.

In 1902 the WCTU's Department of Health requested all local and state unions to place the entire energies of their organizations behind the drive for pure food and drug legislation. State bodies seemed more than ready to comply. Most of the unions committed congressional candidates to vote for a pure food and drug bill and sent petitions and resolutions to Washington, D.C., urging incumbent politicians to take action. The Massachusetts WCTU sponsored lectures and debates that featured public officials, physicians, and lawyers to broaden interest in food and drugs, and distributed a barrage of pure food and drug leaflets. In 1902 Massachusetts state chemists, at the request of the state WCTU, assayed a large group of food supplements to inform the public of their alcohol and nutritive content. In 1902 WCTU unions in 50 counties in New York joined efforts to fight against proprietary medications, demanding truth in labeling and adequate law enforcement. In Ohio 61 county and 144 local women's temperance unions maintained active campaigns to alert the public to dangerous drugs.

The General Federation of Women's Clubs

Joining the efforts of the WCTU in the crusade for pure food and drugs was the General Federation of Women's Clubs (GFWC) founded in 1890 to organize women's clubs nationwide. By 1900 the federation's membership had increased to more than 150,000 members organized in nearly 600 clubs in 30 states. Five years later the membership had more than doubled. Although their emphasis shifted from home protection to altruism and service, and they concentrated more on adulterated foods than drugs, an examination of GFWC reports between 1902 and 1904 indicate considerable pure food and drug activism in a majority of the clubs. One club woman from Cranford, New Jersey, Alice Lakey, developed a special interest in the pure food issue. Frustrated in her own efforts to procure unadulterated food, she joined the domestic science department of her local village improvement association and soon became its president. In 1903 she wrote the U.S. secretary of agriculture requesting information on pure food and drugs, and asking for suggestions for a speaker who might come and address one of her meetings. The secretary recommended Harvey W. Wiley, chief USDA chemist. Their meeting began a useful collaboration to win support for pure food and drug legislation.

By 1904 Lakey's Cranford Village Improvement Association and the New Jersey Federation of Women's Clubs had started to petition members of Congress to enact a pure food bill. That same year Lakey convinced the membership of the GFWC at its biennial convention in St. Louis to form a special Pure Food Committee. The committee wrote thousands of letters, distributed circulars to every state, sponsored lectures, and presented exhibits (Wiley supplied examples of adulterated food for the exhibits and even printed a popular pamphlet, *Some Forms of Food Adulteration and Simple Methods for Their Detection*) to promote public interest in the topic. The contacts that Lakey made in her efforts brought the federation into contact with state and federal officials. Once organized, state and local affiliates distributed information to be used in newspaper articles, and sent delegations to lobby their state and national legislators to support pure food and drug regulation. Women in other national organizations that affiliated with the GFWC, such as the National Congress of Mothers' Clubs, the National Council of Jewish Women, and the Women's Educational and Industrial Union, joined the effort. Lakey's work in New York led her to recruit the National Consumers' League to the cause. By 1905 consumer advocates affiliated with the GFWC had laid a solid foundation aimed at obtaining national regulation.

The National Consumers' League

Adding yet one more level to the citizen activism coalescing behind pure food and drug legislation was the National Consumers' League (NCL). Organized in 1899 to unite consumers for the protection of women and children from exploitation in the garment trades, the league, through the efforts of Lakey, embraced the cause of pure food and drugs in 1905. The NCL agreed to conduct its own investigation of conditions under which food products were prepared and the working conditions of the employees who prepared them, and to disseminate information about food adulteration, and appointed Lakey to head its own Pure Food Committee. The committee eventually included an impressive list of club women, temperance advocates, chemists, public health officials, physicians, and journalists. Because the NCL reached out to a wide range of consumer advocates, was openly activist (the consumer boycott was the weapon it used to force employers to improve working conditions for women and children), had a close association with trade unions, and because its membership was open to both men and women, it appeared to be a natural vehicle to promote the cause. As one historian has noted, "The formation of this [Pure Food] committee was the key to securing federal regulation. In effect, it created an activist network of the nation's leading pure food...and drug advocates that defined consumer objectives more clearly and spoke with more authority for American consumers than either the N.W.C.T.U. or the G.F.W.C."[15] Members of the Pure Food Committee sent out personal letters (Lakey reportedly mailed more than 500 letters herself) urging greater effort from reform groups and officials. They wrote articles for the press and gave public lectures. As a result, letters and petitions began to pour into the offices of senators and representatives in Washington.

Harvey W. Wiley

One individual who became very concerned about the unethical and harmful practices of food and drug manufacturers and an advocate for federal regulation was Harvey W. Wiley, chief USDA chemist. Soon after accepting his new post in the mid-1880s, Wiley began to focus his attention on food adulteration, hoping to protect both consumers and producers by establishing general standards of purity. Under Wiley's direction, the USDA issued a series of reports in the late 1880s as part of a general study of the chemical composition and adulteration of numerous food products. The data collected from those studies informed a pure food bill proposed by Senator Algernon Paddock of Nebraska in 1892. The measure sought to forbid the addition of any poisonous or harmful ingredient to food or drugs that might be injurious to the consumer; make it a misdemeanor to knowingly traffic in adulterated products; and require products to bear truthful labels. But commercial interests that feared they might be adversely affected by the bill managed to kill it. When the bill was reintroduced in Congress in December 1897, Wiley again worked closely with congressional leaders in hopes that it might pass. Once again, Congress refused to take any action on the measure.

The "Poison Squad"

In 1902 Wiley did something that finally got the public's attention and helped break the grip that special interests had on pure food legislation. He decided to conduct tests on the effects of certain food preservatives on humans by using as guinea pigs 12 human subjects from his department. Beginning in December of 1902 and running until June of 1903, the 12 volunteers were fed a regulated diet that included certain chemical compounds to determine their effects.

During the first experiment, boric acid and borax were added to the diets of some of the subjects. Other tests with different sets of volunteers were made by adding salicylic acid and salicylates, sulfurous acid and sulfites, and benzoic acid and benzoates to food. A final experiment with formaldehyde closed out the tests in December 1904. The published results showed that all those ingredients were harmful to the metabolism, digestion, and health of the volunteers. The experiments convinced Wiley that it was unhealthy to include certain preservatives in foods, unethical to claim effectiveness for drugs that were really ineffective compounds of alcohol and water, and immoral to include drugs in compounds that might cause physical harm or lead to addiction. The press gave extensive coverage to Wiley's experiments, and when one reporter dubbed the original 12 volunteers the "poison squad," the term captured public attention.

Muckrakers Join the Battle

Although Wiley had excited public interest, his experiments had not been sensational enough to outrage them. That would be accomplished by the muckrakers, who joined the pure food and drug crusade at just the right moment. Leading the journalistic effort was Edward Bok, editor of the widely circulated *Ladies Home Journal*. In a series of articles during 1904–1905, written with the help of some investigative reporting by journalist Mark Sullivan and materials supplied by the Medical Temperance Department of the WCTU, Bok revealed to his women readers that the patent medicine industry cheated sick and trusting consumers by selling letters that they had written asking for medical advice to other nostrum dealers, and that those same trusting women had often dosed themselves and their children with harmful or addictive cure-alls. Supporting the work of Bok was Norman Hapgood, editor of *Collier's*. On June 3, 1905, the magazine printed a riveting, full-page cartoon titled "Death's Laboratory," which showed a human skull with patent medicine bottles serving as teeth; this captured everyone's attention. Hapgood then set journalist Samuel Hopkins Adams to work on an exposé of the patent medicine industry. First appearing in serialized form on October 7, 1905, as "The Great American Fraud," the series created a sensation. The most powerful effect of the Adams articles was the challenge they made to the curative claims of scores of patent medicines. In writing the articles, Adams saved his harshest attack for the secret formulas of "the opium-containing soothing syrups, which stunt or kill helpless infants; the consumptive cures…[that] destroy hope where hope is struggling against bitter odds for existence; the headache powders which enslave so insidiously that the victim is ignorant of his own fate; [and] the catarrh powders which breed cocaine slaves."[16]

The public was now angry. On December 5, 1905, a pure food and drug bill was introduced in the Senate by Welden Heybern. When reactionary forces in the Senate moved to block its passage, "[p]ublic indignation against this treachery seethed."[17] Aided at this point by the American Medical Association, which lobbied heavily for the bill; by President Theodore Roosevelt, who publicly endorsed the measure; and by the continued efforts of the muckrakers (the February issue of *Ladies Home Journal* made an appeal for action and encouraged its readers to send a copy of the bill, which it printed, to their representatives in Washington), the Senate passed the bill on February 15, 1906, and sent it to the House, where passage was still uncertain.

Publication of *The Jungle*

At that moment the country was shocked by the publication of Upton Sinclair's novel *The Jungle*. Omitted in the general debate over food preservatives and patent medicines was any specific mention of the conditions under which meat was prepared at the packing plants. Prior journalistic accounts and even the Missouri Beef Trust investigation of 1902 had generated little national attention. Sinclair, a socialist, had written his novel to arouse the public to the oppressive working conditions in the Chicago packinghouses and to the exploitation experienced by those who worked there. As he moved into his topic, Sinclair offered readers some information regarding food and drugs—milk was "watered" and treated with formaldehyde; tea, coffee, sugar, and flour were "doctored"; canned peas were colored with copper salts; and fruit jams were treated with aniline dyes.[18] But what really caught his audience's attention were the gruesome descriptions of contaminated meat. Readers were informed that hams were treated with formaldehyde; that rotten meat and other refuse swept from the factory floor often went into sausages; that diseased cattle were often butchered and then treated and sold as healthy meat; and that men had actually fallen into rendering vats to be sold as lard. Readers, fearful for their own health, were outraged. The novel sold 25,000 copies in its first six weeks.

The popular reaction to *The Jungle* revitalized the debate over the pure food and drug bill that was still being considered. The public demanded protection. Prompted to take some action, President Roosevelt sent a team of investigators into packingtown to examine the operations of Chicago's leading meat packers and to check the authenticity of Sinclair's allegations. As the team did so, Senator Albert J. Beveridge introduced a meat inspection bill in Congress. When the investigators issued their report and confirmed the main charges made by Sinclair, a storm of indignation swept the country. Although the packing companies lobbied heavily (and with some success) to weaken the proposed legislation, they could not defeat it. Swept up in the furor, both the Pure Food and Drug Act and the Federal Meat Inspection Act, arguably the two most important pieces of legislation passed by Congress during the Roosevelt presidency, became law on June 30, 1906.

Historians continue to debate the question of who deserves the credit for the passage of pure food and drug regulation. Some like to credit the muckrakers such as Bok, Hapgood, and Adams, who, although they did not become thoroughly engaged in the issue until between 1903 and 1905, aroused the general public to indignation. Others acknowledge the service of Wiley, whose blend of scientific expertise, showmanship, and political maneuvering ultimately carried the day. Still others credit professionals such as the American Medical Association, which lent its considerable legitimacy to the cause at a crucial juncture, and the politicians such as Heybern and Beveridge, who demonstrated their mastery of the art of political compromise to gain majority support. Others applaud Roosevelt for using the weight of his office and the force of his personality to broker the various interests.

A recent study by Lorine Goodwin, however, makes a case that it was women, through organized groups such as the WCTU, GFWC, and NCL, who created a coalition of consumers that became strong enough to challenge the special interests, and then, "[w]orking as a block of consensus within the national conscience," were able to mobilize those consumers into a body that was influential enough to propel the cause of pure food and drugs into the state and then national arena. These female activists played a major role in defining objectives and in keeping the issue alive over a considerable span of time, and then "forged the connecting link between consumer, professional, and legislative forces, and were able to consolidate support" for national regulatory legislation. As Wiley graciously noted, pure food and drug legislation was a "victory of the women of this country, whose influence was felt as irresistible." He also noted that there was "something wonderful in the power which organized effort can develop."[19]

CIVIC AND SOCIAL REFORMERS

One especially contested area for reformers during the Progressive Era was in the operation of the city—in deciding how a municipality should be governed and how it might better serve the needs of the people who lived there. Historians have tended to couch this debate in terms of "political" progressives versus "social justice" progressives. Both types of progressives took an activist approach to the problem as they perceived it, and both embraced the new emphasis on expertise and in using the methodology of social science to identify and confront social problems.

Political Progressives

A growing number of progressive businessmen and professionals believed that the way to improve governance was to remove politics from the control of political bosses and party politicians, and to create new mechanisms of government. Central to their thinking was the belief that professional experts, uniquely trained in political science, economics, the law, or business, should be put into office. As historian Maureen A. Flanagan has suggested, these political progressives saw government as "instrumental," and believed that their expertise could improve efficiency and generate "democratic opportunity" for everyone.[20]

Several administrative innovations characterize this approach to achieving a better governed city. Home rule was one reform that had the potential to open avenues for applied economic science. Given increased control over their affairs, cities could manage their own finances and improve municipal efficiency, and meddling state legislatures could be restrained from interfering in municipal affairs. Organizations such as the National Municipal League drafted model home-rule charters that featured a strong (expert) mayor and a small city council elected at large rather than by party-controlled districts. Such an electoral reform, they reasoned, would also reduce the influence of immigrants and the lower classes that many political progressives saw as sustaining corrupt government. Some political progressives favored municipal government run by a commission or a city manager, in which experts would be hired to manage municipal government. With the appointive power to designate other of the city's administrative officers, they could further extend the scope of expertise. Other popular reforms were the secret ballot, the nonpartisan ballot, and the direct primary (to replace nomination by party caucuses). In Wisconsin, Governor Robert La Follette popularized the Wisconsin Idea, whereby he used professors from the University of Wisconsin to prepare reports and do statistical studies that formed the basis for reform legislation he presented to the state legislature. La Follette also created nonpolitical commissions of experts to supervise the operation of factories and railroads and to revise the state's tax structure.

Social Justice Progressives

Many social justice progressives, however, tended to reject the thrust of the political progressives. Settlement house workers such as Jane Addams, cofounder of Hull House in Chicago and a leader in the national settlement house movement (there would be more than 500 settlement houses in the country by 1920), were concerned about social conditions and the degradation of life and work in America's cities. Their primary purpose was to assist immigrant families, especially women, in adjusting to urban life. To that end, they created playgrounds; started day nurseries and kindergartens; gave working women places to meet and started boarding cooperatives for working girls; and offered classes in nutrition and health care as well as in basic homemaking skills such as cooking and sewing. They provided instruction in the English language and vocational training in areas such as woodworking, pottery, and telegraphy.

These progressives also challenged the dominant cultural thinking that regarded poverty as a direct result of personal failure, and they adopted the belief that environmental factors were more important in shaping human development. To alleviate the distress of poverty, ways of improving the environment would have to be designed. It was on that point that Addams and other social justice progressives disagreed with political progressives. Upper-class business and professional types, she argued, "are almost wholly occupied in the correction of political machinery and with a concern for the better method of administration, rather than with the ultimate purpose of securing the welfare of the people. They fix their attention so exclusively on methods that they fail to consider the final aims of city government."[21] For Addams and others, the city needed to be governed more as a home than as a business. City government should look after the welfare of the people who lived there. It should be concerned with issues such as sanitation, public health, clean and safe streets, education, recreation, care of the poor and sick, and maintaining a moral environment.

Reformers such as Addams did not reject scientific expertise; they just wanted to use it to meet people's needs and improve their health in a more direct manner. During a typhoid outbreak in Chicago in 1902, Dr. Alice Hamilton, who was an expert in bacteriology, and Addams discovered the typhoid bacillus in the city's water supply. They charged that city engineers had not cleaned up the drinking water. The two women also uncovered a network of institutionalized corruption connected to Chicago's water pollution ordinances. Municipal engineers, politicians, and health inspectors had colluded in not enforcing ordinances in lower-income neighborhoods. The women discovered a secret account, called the "stay book," that listed hundreds of complaints against the health department that had not been followed up on by city officials as a favor to anyone with political connections. To Hamilton and Addams, professional expertise would always be compromised unless it was also motivated by a desire to provide social justice.

During the 1890s and early twentieth century, Addams became increasingly involved in numerous public campaigns to improve human conditions in the urban-industrial environment. Provoked by the stench of uncollected garbage in her ward, and convinced by scientific evidence that cleaner streets would reduce the overall death rate, she campaigned for more effective garbage collection and even served for a time as supervisor of garbage collection for her ward. She also helped organize a community improvement association to lobby city government to pave the streets and build public baths, parks, and playgrounds. Ever the activist, Addams also helped form consumer cooperatives in an effort to secure lower prices for coal and better-quality milk, and she joined the successful effort to establish the first juvenile court in the United States in 1899.

As Addams expanded her reform efforts, she found herself sharing concerns with a group of the country's earliest sociologists. One of her initial efforts in this regard was the house-to-house social investigation of the area surrounding Hull House to determine the nationality and income of the people who lived there. Published as *Hull House Maps and Papers* (1895), the collaborative effort of the residents of Hull House was an outgrowth of an earlier investigation of the sweatshop trade in Chicago conducted by Florence

Kelley, another Hull House worker. *Hull House Maps and Papers* was the first systematic analysis of a poor section of a major American city. It contributed to the emerging field of urban sociology, and encouraged Addams and others to make Hull House a laboratory where college instructors and graduate students could combine research with hands-on social work. Sociological data gathered through investigation could be used to spur legislative action, such as adopting building codes for tenements, abolishing child labor, and improving factory safety.

Responding to a void left by many professional planners and male scientists who largely studied the environment outside the home, Ellen Swallow Richards, a trained scientist and instructor of sanitary chemistry at the Massachusetts Institute of Technology, focused her attention on the household and how it might benefit from expertise. Richards worked to create better sanitary conditions for food and clean water, and played a leading role in developing sewage treatment and promoting food inspection laws in Massachusetts. But she also wanted to raise the popular consciousness of the need for sanitation inside the household as a means of improving public health. She was a leader in what was called the home ecology (later home economics) movement and an advocate of "scientific housekeeping." Her work with the Boston Women's Education and Industrial Union led to the creation of public kitchens that, by 1912, served lunch to nearly 10,000 public school children each day in the city's South End.

Rural women used Richards's ideas to demand improved health standards in their communities as well. Farm women in Illinois criticized the USDA's policy of promoting the modernization of farm work while ignoring the need to modernize the home through indoor plumbing and electrification. They also demanded improvements in education and better access to health care for their children. As early as 1898, farm women who were members of Farmers' Institutes in Illinois organized a separate department of household science. Topics of discussion and investigation included domestic hygiene, child nutrition, and household sanitation. These were the same types of concerns that urban women were rallying behind in their crusades against smoke pollution and garbage removal. As Flanagan has noted, the "environment for these progressive women was inside the home as well as outside; one could not flourish without the good of the other being taken care of. Public attention and public funding had to be directed toward both and not just given on the basis of economic development."[22]

VOTES FOR WOMEN

Women's activism in an organized context was nowhere more evident during the Progressive Era than in the battle to obtain the vote. For many women, the issue was one of citizenship and equal rights denied. For others, the vote was seen more as a means to advance a social program or achieve a political goal such as temperance. Many working women and immigrant women saw the vote as necessary for self-protection and a means to address issues such as industrial safety, legal equality, and equal pay for equal work. Labor leader Leonora O'Reilly argued that women needed the vote "to do justice to our work as home-keepers. Children need pure milk and good food, good schools and playgrounds, sanitary homes and safe streets."[23] But progress was slow. In 1900 only four states, all west of the Mississippi River, had granted full voting rights to women, and there was a growing feeling within the National American Woman Suffrage Association (NAWSA) that the movement had lost its momentum. A new generation of suffrage leaders, however, was about to modernize operations and adopt techniques that were more in tune with modern, urban, industrial America. In doing so, they attempted to shed their outdated, nineteenth-century image. "Votes for women" became a more popular slogan than "woman suffrage." New contacts were made with wealthy women who could contribute money for campaigns and with working-class women in an attempt to broaden the movement's middle-class base.

The Woman Suffrage Movement

Early indications that life was returning to the campaign came with two new organizations—the Boston Suffrage Association for Good Government and the College Equal Suffrage League. Both of these groups experimented with new, bolder methods of activism. Advocates spoke on street corners, canvassed door-to-door in urban and suburban neighborhoods, conducted open-air meetings (previously regarded as unladylike), held torchlight parades, and toured the state using public transportation, giving speeches at every stop. The recruitment of working-class women intensified. Wage-Earners Suffrage Leagues were formed in San Francisco, Los Angeles, New York City, and elsewhere. In 1907 the Women's Trade Union League established a Suffrage Department. Settlement house workers organized immigrant women to demand the vote. Pro-suffrage literature was often printed in a variety of languages and designed to explain how woman suffrage could raise wages and improve working conditions for women workers.

In 1907 Harriot Stanton Blatch, the daughter of Elizabeth Cady Stanton, started the Equality League of Self-Supporting Women. The organization was a coalition of upper-class women, career women, and working women from factories, garment shops, and laundries in New York. The Equality League, whose membership grew to 19,000 by late 1908, was the first to send a delegation of working-class women to testify before a state legislature on behalf of woman suffrage. Carla Silver, one of the witnesses, told the legislators, "To be left out by the State just sets up a prejudice against us. . . . Bosses think and women come to think themselves that they don't count for so much as men." The league also initiated the first of the grand suffrage parades that would characterize the suffrage movement during the second decade of the twentieth century. In many of these parades, large divisions of working women would march under the banners of their trade union. A modest action by today's standards, these spectacles, with thousands of women from various classes (often clad totally in white and holding American flags) marching in dignified fashion down a major urban thoroughfare, brought tremendous attention to the movement. By 1910 attitudes seemed to be changing as well. As one Nebraska college student noted in a letter to her mother, women students were no longer "afraid of antagonizing the men or losing invitations to parties by being suffragists."[24]

It was not long before these new techniques started to pay dividends. In Washington and California, suffragists conducted well-organized and creative campaigns that employed billboards, newspaper editorials, plays, church sermons, and, in California, fleets of automobiles, to gain the franchise via referenda in 1910 and 1911, respectively. These victories were actually part of a grassroots resurgence in the western states, where suffragists mounted successful referendum campaigns for the vote in Kansas, Oregon, and Arizona in 1912. The Progressive Party, running on a broad reform platform, endorsed woman suffrage in 1912, and the state of Illinois passed a law allowing women to vote in presidential elections in 1913 after a more all-inclusive referendum failed.

The suffrage campaign in New York in 1915 was especially noteworthy for the scope of its activism. Carrie Chapman Catt remembered the organizing efforts there in some detail.

[T]he Empire State Campaign Committee…was organized and took charge of the campaign. Plans for simultaneous action for the workers in all parts of the State were formulated and executed with such precision that every woman engaged in suffrage…knew that she was companioned by hundreds of other women who on that day were doing the same thing. There were "canvassing squads," processions with banners and music, meetings of every kind, peripatetic headquarters, gaily decorated and supplied with speakers and workers who went the rounds of each county visiting every town and post office. On Mother's Day, hundreds of churches had ceremonies and appeals for the new order, and on the Fourth of July, the Woman's Declaration of Independence was read from the steps of fifty court houses…[T]here was a strongly organized press department…devising and spreading broadcast suffrage publicity in the 26 languages in which newspapers were published in New York State.

The New York City campaign was even more intensive.

There were barbers' days, days for firemen, street cleaners, bankers, brokers, business men, clergymen, street car men, factory workers, students, restaurant and railroad workers, ticket sellers,…lawyers, ditch diggers and longshoremen. No voter escaped. Each one of these days had its own literature and attractions and called forth columns of comment in the newspapers. Evening demonstrations took place daily and brought interested and thoughtful crowds. There was a bonfire on the highest hill in each Borough, with balloons flying, music, speeches, and tableaux illustrating women's progress…Torchlight processions were formed upon twenty-eight evenings with Chinese lanterns, balloons, banners and decorations in yellow and ending in a street rally at some important point in the City. There were street dances on the East Side, in honor of political leaders; there were Irish, Syrian, Italian, Polish rallies; there were outdoor concerts…There were open air religious services on Sunday evenings, with the moral and religious aspect of suffrage discussed.… Bottles containing suffrage messages were consigned to the waves from boats and wharves with appropriate speeches. Sandwich girls advertised meetings and sold papers. Sixty playhouses had theatre nights, many with speeches between the acts. There were innumerable movie nights with speeches and suffrage slides.… Just before election day a great procession possessed Fifth Avenue, the entire suffrage forces of the State uniting in it.… Twenty-five bands made music for 30,000 marching men and women.[25]

Although state referenda were defeated in New York, New Jersey, Massachusetts, and Pennsylvania in 1915, NAWSA regrouped, raised more money, and pushed ahead.

Under the leadership of Catt as president and Maud Wood as head of congressional lobbying in Washington, D.C., NAWSA adopted the Winning Plan—a strategy whereby suffragists would continue to work for the franchise in individual states (in the hope that newly enfranchised women would add political clout to the campaign), and would increase pressure on Congress to pass a constitutional amendment. To facilitate the latter tactic, NAWSA maintained detailed files on each congressman and senator and carefully selected individual women to meet with them. In the 1916 election campaign, both the Democratic and Republican parties endorsed woman suffrage but left the decision up to the individual states. At the time America entered World War I in 1917, woman suffrage was receiving front-page coverage in newspapers all over the United States and commonly featured in popular magazine articles. The nation seemed to be growing more supportive. NAWSA, with 2 million members, had become the largest women's voluntary organization in the country, and 4 million women in 11 states could vote. When women secured the vote through a popular referendum in New York in 1917, it gave the suffrage movement a tremendous morale boost and added the significant electoral clout of that state to their campaign.

While NAWSA worked to mobilize its vast membership behind the Winning Plan, other suffragists were concluding that a more radical form of protest was needed to achieve a federal suffrage amendment. Key individuals behind this new approach were Alice Paul and Lucy Burns. Both had taken part in the more militant suffrage movement in England, where British suffragettes had developed a strategy of holding the party in power responsible for refusing to grant women the vote, and had used tactics that centered on demonstration and confrontation. In 1912 Paul and Burns approached the leaders of NAWSA and asked to have the freedom to pursue a more aggressive strategy that would seek to maximize publicity through newsworthy protests. Appointed to the Congressional Committee within NAWSA, they soon had the opportunity to try out their approach. The first step in this plan was to hold a massive suffrage parade down Pennsylvania Avenue in Washington, D.C., on March 3, 1913, the day before the inauguration of President Woodrow Wilson. The idea was to apply immediate pressure on the new president to force him to confront the issue and perhaps capture the attention of Congress by means of a dramatic public display. On the day of the event, 8,000 women participated. Leading the procession of 26 floats, 10 bands, and 6 sections of marching units was a young woman riding a white horse and wearing a flowing white dress with a banner that read, "Forward Out of Darkness, Forward Into Light."

The huge crowd of predominantly male onlookers, however, did not appreciate the spectacle and began to jeer and taunt the marchers. As emotions escalated, men disrupted the parade and roughed up many of the female marchers. When the police could not control the unruly mob, the U.S. Department of War called in the cavalry to restore order. The ensuing chaos seemed irrelevant to Paul. She had made suffrage front-page, headline news across the country and generated a great deal of enthusiasm among suffragists and their sympathizers.

Paul pressed forward with her program of direct action through a variety of forms. Immediately after the parade, the Congressional Committee began an intensive lobbying campaign. The committee coordinated an assembly of delegates (one from every congressional district in the country) who carried resolutions and petitions from their districts, on behalf of a federal suffrage amendment, directly to their senators and representatives in Congress. It marked the beginning of an unceasing lobbying effort. Paul's group also started *The Suffragist*, a weekly magazine intended to address a national audience. By the end of 1913, the Congressional Committee had led organizing campaigns in a half-dozen states, started a Men's League for Woman Suffrage, distributed over 120,000 pieces of literature, and raised over $25,000 in donations. But the boldness, independence, and success of Paul's new organization threatened the leadership of NAWSA. Disputes over tactics and control over newly acquired financial resources soon led to a split. Unwilling to be hamstrung by the larger, more conservative body, Paul withdrew her group from NAWSA and began to function as the Congressional Union.

Following the program of the British suffragettes, Paul decided to challenge the Democratic Party (the party in power) in the off-year elections in 1914. To convince Democrats that their current passivity on the suffrage question was inexpedient, Paul targeted for defeat party candidates running for election in the nine western states where women had already gained the vote. The plan was, once again, a bold one. What Paul was doing was asking women who already had the vote to help their un-enfranchised sisters by abandoning their loyalty to party in favor of gender solidarity. The Congressional Union then sent two organizers into each of those states. One organizer would open and operate a state headquarters, talk to the press, distribute literature, and direct speakers. The other would stump the state, speaking in support of a federal amendment and urging women voters to vote against Democrats. Despite being vilified in the party press, Paul made suffrage the issue every-one talked about. Of the 43 Democratic candidates targeted by the Congressional Union, only 20 won election to office. Although the explanations offered for the party's defeats were varied and hotly debated, the Congressional Union had added a new element to the political debate over suffrage.

Although NAWSA sharply criticized her election tactics as coun-terproductive, Paul, seemingly unfazed, moved ahead with new ideas to keep her membership active and "The Question" con-stantly before the public. The Congressional Union pressed ahead with its organizing efforts, creating branches in 19 states by the end of 1915, 36 by the end of 1916, and all 48 states a year later. Paul then decided to call a national convention of women voters to be held in San Francisco in September 1915 and scheduled to coin-cide with the Panama-Pacific International Exposition. After three days of meetings and speeches, the delegates completed an 18,000-foot-long petition bearing 500,000 signatures. The petition was ulti-mately presented to Congress, but only after a carefully planned and highly publicized 3,000-mile trip across country in an auto-mobile dubbed the Suffrage Flyer. Paul next organized a National Women's Party (NWP) to act as a balance of power in the upcoming national election. She immediately sent a delegation of 23 organiz-ers on a tour of the western states aboard a train called the Suffrage Special to generate support for the new party. As a result, more than 1,500 delegates from those states convened in Chicago on June 5–7, 1916, to formally launch their new party. Members of the NWP appeared before the resolutions committees of both the Democratic and Republican parties, and although they stopped short of endors-ing a federal amendment, they added suffrage planks to their party platforms for the first time. The NWP approached the 1916 election as it had two years before, but in a contest complicated by the war in Europe and the possibility of American involvement, President Woodrow Wilson won reelection as most voters (and many suffrag-ists) favored the candidate who promised continued peace.

The electoral defeats of 1916 convinced Paul that she needed to increase the level of protest. Beginning in January 1917, members of the Congressional Union known as the Silent Sentinels began to picket in front of the White House. Before the United States entered World War I in April 1917, the public seemed to be sympathetic to the effort. But when Paul announced that her anti-administration stance would continue uninterrupted during the war, the public's attitude quickly shifted to derision. NAWSA had thrown its support behind Wilson's war policy, and privately hoped that by showing that women were "patriotic" Americans by working to support the war effort, women would be rewarded with the vote at the end of the conflict. Paul viewed suffrage and the war as separate issues and refused to relax her fight for suffrage. After Congress's declaration of war in 1917, NWP (the Congressional Union had been absorbed by the NWP in March) picketers began to carry banners bearing quotations from the president's own speeches to highlight what they saw as the hypocrisy of fighting a war to achieve democracy abroad while ignoring disenfranchised citizens at home. Paul intended the banners to embarrass the president, but an emotionally charged public caught up in wartime propaganda had no tolerance for such criticism. They ripped poles from protesters' hands and destroyed them. Some women suffered physical injury in the process. The police began to arrest the protesters on the pretext of obstructing traffic, but released them without penalty. When the picketing continued, picketers were then sentenced to three nights in jail. When they persisted, the sentences were increased to 60 days in the dark, dank Occoquan Workhouse. These repressive tactics soon backfired, and public outrage forced Wilson to pardon all prisoners confined at the workhouse.

Woman suffrage pickets at the White House, 1917. (Courtesy of the Library of Congress)

As the picketing continued, confrontation between angry crowds and picketers increased. Crowds began to act more like mobs, and women picketers were assaulted. More and more uniformed servicemen began to take part in the harassment as self-appointed defenders of the administration (their participation was eventually ended by military order). When Paul was arrested in October, authorities saw an opportunity to single her out as an example. Sentenced to seven months in the Occoquan Workhouse, Paul began a hunger strike. After a week of confinement, she was forcefed nourishment. When she still refused to cooperate, she was transferred to the prison psychopathic ward in the district jail in a failed attempt to cast doubts about her sanity. Even before Paul's famous hunger strike, the NWP decided on yet another tactic to draw attention to the cause. It created a Prison Squad composed of previously jailed picketers (dressed in clothing identical to their prison uniforms) who toured the country to inform the public about their treatment. Their public testimony alarmed many within the Democratic Party who feared political repercussion. Abruptly, on November 28, authorities released all suffrage prisoners. Picketing would continue, but the punishments were never as severe as before. The picketing campaign was an ordeal for the NWP. Thousands of women had picketed, roughly 500 had been arrested, and 168 had served harsh prison sentences. But Paul would always argue that their efforts created a sense of urgency that shortened the timetable for passage of a federal amendment.

Eventually the conciliatory approach of NAWSA, with its 2 million members, and the more militant approach of the Congressional Union/NWP and its 35,000 members began to have an effect on national politicians. As one historian has noted, "Although the NWP and the NAWSA were hostile to each other,... their two approaches were complementary, the former raising the political stakes by its radical efforts, the latter negotiating with congressmen to move the amendment forward."[26] When the House of Representatives agreed to bring the question of a suffrage amendment up for a vote in January of 1918, President Wilson lobbied for its successful passage. However, when the Senate continued to delay a vote on the suffrage amendment, Paul again went on the offensive. Beginning in September 1918, the NWP began burning copies of Wilson's "war for democracy" speeches in urns dubbed the Watchfires of Freedom in Lafayette Park across from the White House. Two weeks later Wilson gave the Senate only 30 minutes' notice, and then proceeded to the Capitol to address that body and urge it to immediately approve the suffrage amendment. Although the president's speech, in which he linked the success of the war to suffrage, only inched the Senate closer to passing the federal suffrage amendment, it was an important political turning point. Final Senate approval of the measure, delayed primarily by recalcitrant southern, states'-rights Democrats, finally occurred on June 4, 1919. Ratification by two-thirds of the states, a process that was equally hard fought but greatly assisted by the organizational strengths of the two suffrage associations, took an additional 14 months. The Nineteenth Amendment to the U.S. Constitution, a product of a tremendous grassroots organizing effort, became effective on August 26, 1920.

POLITICAL EMPOWERMENT

The effort put forth by American women to obtain the vote during the Progressive Era was part of a larger struggle to expand the bounds of popular democracy. As society wrestled with the harsh realities that accompanied rapid urban and industrial growth, many felt increasingly ignored as participants in the political system. It seemed as though policymakers identified issues and established priorities in a political environment increasingly susceptible to the influence of economic power. As a result, many issues of concern to workers, farmers, consumers, and taxpayers were ignored. Concluding that their elected representatives no longer represented their interests, many Americans looked to alter the existing situation. Some sought to create new political parties; others to capture control of existing parties. Still others favored altering voting procedures, and favored reforms such as the direct primary, nonpartisan elections, enfranchising women, allowing for the direct election of U.S. senators, or enacting corrupt-practice laws to limit the influence of money in political campaigns. A growing number of individuals, however, began to come to the conclusion that the legislative process itself needed to be expanded. Maybe it would be better if voters were allowed to bypass irresponsible or unresponsive political bodies and create or veto laws on their own. As this idea gained momentum during the Progressive Era, it became known as direct legislation or, more commonly, the initiative and referendum. Under the initiative, a certain percentage of voters could, by petition, propose a law that would have to be approved at the polls. Under the referendum, a certain percentage of voters could request, again by petition, that a law passed by a legislative body be submitted to them for final approval.

The Direct Legislation Movement

Americans learned about the initiative and referendum from the Swiss, who had developed a system that allowed voters to decide questions regarding taxation, public finance, grants to corporations, and public works—operations commonly left to legislators and other officials. To many outside observers, the process had the appearance of direct democracy, and it seemed to work. The first American to argue that such a purely democratic system would work in this country and provide a cure for the nation's political ills was a social reform editor and trade unionist named J. W. Sullivan. Sullivan's book, *Direct Legislation by the Citizenship through the Initiative and Referendum,* published in 1892, was the first volume to argue the relevancy of direct legislation for the United States. The book sold between 10,000 and 15,000 copies a year for the first three years of publication. Sullivan believed that this popular legislative procedure would greatly enhance the process of representative government in this country. It would revive voter interest in politics and encourage the public debate of vital issues. Citizens would feel like participants in the political system. In the process, voters could force state and local government to become more responsive to questions of importance to voters and hold legislators more accountable.

The idea soon caught the attention of Eltweed Pomeroy, owner of a small New Jersey company that manufactured ink. Pomeroy began to publish the *Direct Legislation Record* in January 1895. He designed the *Record* to be a quarterly newsletter that would help popularize direct legislation, serve as a bulletin for sharing news and correspondence on the subject nationwide, and offer advice to other advocates on how they might organize direct legislation leagues and introduce direct legislation amendments in their state legislatures. By 1895 direct legislation leagues had been organized in more than a half-dozen states. The growing popularity of the issue convinced Pomeroy to call a national conference on direct legislation to be held in St. Louis on July 21, 1896, the day before the Populist Party convention in that city. At the meeting, delegates elected Pomeroy president of a new National Direct Legislation League and chose delegates to represent the league in every state and territory. They also convinced the Populists to add a resolution to their party platform recommending the initiative and referendum. The defeat of the Populists in that year's election did not deter Pomeroy. He advised state organizations to lobby their legislatures; work to influence municipal and civic leagues, farmers' alliances and granges, and trade unions to pass resolutions in favor of the initiative and referendum, and then have those resolutions sent to each member of the legislature and to the press; and circulate petitions as an indication of broader public support. Organization and mobilization, Pomeroy believed, would yield success.

The first state in which voters approved an amendment to their state constitution allowing for voters to initiate and refer laws by popular petition and vote was South Dakota in 1898. Leading the grassroots movement in that state was Henry Loucks, editor of the *Dakota Ruralist*, who took the first steps toward organizing initiative and referendum leagues in every county and supplying other newspapers in the state with printed matter pertaining to the reforms. Some voters were enthralled by the new idea. As one farmer described his reaction, "[W]hen I first heard of this movement I thought it a good thing. When I learned a little more about it I said 'that is just what we want.' When I heard the matter explained last night I could not go to sleep till 2 o'clock." Reflecting on those early organizing efforts during the 1890s from the vantage point of 1915, Loucks recalled clearly what triggered the political revolt in the state and how direct legislation became a central part of the reform program. "Our experience," he said, "was that the railroad and allied corporations controlled the political machines of both political parties, and thru them our conventions and legislatures. We were discouraged by the failure of our representatives to do the will of the people even when promised in platform pledges. The legislative sins of ommission [sic] and commission were many."[27]

Although voters in South Dakota used the initiative and referendum infrequently over the next 20 years (voters considered 9 initiated ballot propositions and 15 referred measures during that time), it encouraged direct legislation activists in other states to work toward the same goal with renewed optimism. The adoption of the process in South Dakota also seemed to encourage the legislature to seek popular approval on numerous important issues by asking voters to decide on 38 proposed constitutional amendments between 1908 and 1918. In doing so, voters rejected woman suffrage in 1910, 1914, and 1916, but approved the proposal in 1918. They also approved laws for taxation of corporate stocks and bonds, road improvements, the irrigation of public lands, the establishment of a system of rural credits, and prohibition.

Following South Dakota in the procession of states adopting what became known as the I & R during the Progressive Era was Oregon in 1902. Like voters in South Dakota, many in Oregon had come to the conclusion that corporations, through their political influence, controlled the selection of legislative officers and committee assignments, and directed legislation in their interest. They also felt that the legislature, which met for only 40 days every two years, was notoriously unproductive. Taking the lead in organizing voters behind the idea of direct democracy as a way to lessen the influence of corporations and break legislative gridlock was William S. U'Ren, who organized a Joint Committee on Direct Legislation (comprised primarily of farmer and labor groups) in 1893. Using nearly $600 in funds collected through donations, the joint committee published 50,000 pamphlets in English and another 18,000 in German proclaiming the merits of the I & R. The printers' union printed the materials, women's groups sewed the covers, and farmers and workers distributed the information. The joint committee also furnished printed material to newspapers and circulated 1,500 copies of J. W. Sullivan's book. Lecturers spoke to the Grange, the Farmers' Alliance, and various teachers' meetings to explain and promote direct legislation.

Responding to the increasing popularity of the idea and to the inclusion of numerous influential supporters on its executive committee (the joint committee evolved in to the Non-Partisan Direct Legislation League in 1897), the legislature passed a direct legislation amendment in 1899. But under Oregon's constitution, a proposed amendment had to pass both houses of the legislature in two consecutive sessions. To guard against any legislative backsliding, U'Ren and the league worked to keep the issue before the public. Supporters wrote articles, delivered speeches, distributed pamphlets, conducted house-to-house canvasses, interrogated political candidates, and continued to gather endorsements. When the legislature convened again in 1899, U'Ren worked the halls as a lobbyist. The result was again a victory. All that remained in this long, tedious process was for voters to formally approve the amendment. They did so at the election in 1902 by a vote of 62,024 to 5,668.

Over the next decade, Oregon voters, spurred on by U'Ren's new advocacy group, the People's Power League, actively used the I & R. Voters considered 2 initiatives in 1904, 10 initiatives and 1 referred statute in 1906, 11 initiatives and 4 referred statutes in

1908, 25 initiatives and 1 referred statute in 1910, 28 initiatives and 3 referred statutes in 1912, and 19 initiatives in 1914. At general elections between 1904 and 1914, the Oregon electorate was asked to consider 104 ballot measures brought to their attention by either the initiative or referendum process and approved 39 (38%) of them. Among the voter-initiated issues of a more significant nature that were considered during this period were local option liquor, a direct primary law, home rule for municipalities, woman suffrage, the recall of public officials, a corrupt-practices act, a presidential preference primary, prohibition, an employer liability law, and a law establishing an eight-hour day on public works projects. In their vigorous use of direct democracy, the citizens of Oregon made a revolutionary political statement. And in doing so, they placed their state in the vanguard of progressivism.

Another state that actively embraced the I & R was Arizona. During Arizona's territorial period, railroad and mining companies controlled the legislature, and it was common practice for their paid lobbyists to bribe legislators to obtain favorable legislation. Judson King, a national organizer for the Direct Legislation League, stated that Arizonans had been living "at the mercy of Federal judges, governors and office holders, appointed from Washington at the dictation of railroads and mining interests" for a generation. "The People," said King, "were helpless and knew it."[28] At issue were the tax privileges enjoyed by corporations in the state and the threat that costly and intrusive labor legislation might be enacted. Mines worth $100 million were officially assessed at only $2 million. Much of the land that had been granted to the Santa Fe Railroad was either untaxed or undervalued. As a result, many small businessmen and property holders felt they were being asked to bear most of the territorial tax burden. Also upset was organized labor, which felt blocked in its attempts to gain protective labor legislative for its members. During the 1899 session of the territorial legislature, measures to impose a bullion tax on minerals, regulate hours for miners, prohibit the issuing of scrip (which had to be spent at company-owned stores), and create the office of mine inspector were all defeated by corporate lobbyists.

George W. P. Hunt, perhaps Arizona's most important politician during the Progressive Era, introduced the first direct legislation bill in the 1899 session of the legislature. Supporting the measure was the Western Federation of Miners, which wrote to Hunt, "We want to see if it is possible for one bill for the benefit of labor to become a law at the hands of the Arizona legislature."[29] The bill passed the legislature, but Governor Nathan O. Murphy, a political appointee of the McKinley administration and said to be closely associated with mining and railroad interests, pocket vetoed it. Direct legislation did not get a second hearing in the legislature until 1909, when Hunt introduced essentially the same measure he had proposed 10 years before. This time the bill passed the upper house only to have the lower house postpone any consideration of it. But proponents got a second chance to push their cause in 1910, when President William Howard Taft signed the Enabling Act giving Arizona and New Mexico permission to draw up constitutions and apply for statehood.

Realizing that delegate selection to the constitutional convention would be key, organized labor, led by the Bisbee Miner's Union, decided to mobilize and formed an alliance with the Democratic Party on a platform that included the initiative and referendum. Supporting them were woman suffragists and prohibitionists, who found the idea of the initiative appealing should the convention decide not to include their demands in the new constitution. As the campaign for delegates heated up, the I & R became the central topic of discussion and attained what one historian described as "shibboleth status on par with statehood and, in an earlier era, free silver."[30] In an effort to enlighten voters on the merits of direct legislation, proponents circulated a pamphlet, "Code of the People's Rule," written by Senator Jonathan Bourne of Oregon, a national authority on the topic. Additional publicity came from a number of territorial newspapers that explained how the I & R worked in other states. The National Direct Legislation League sent its best organizer to Arizona to lend his support. The result was a major victory for the Labor-Democratic alliance, which claimed to have the support of 41 of the 52 delegates chosen.

With the election of Hunt as president of the convention, the inclusion of the I & R was a foregone conclusion. The final version adopted by the convention allowed voters to initiate amendments to the state constitution and enact state laws, as well as refer statutes passed by the legislature. Also included in the new document was a provision allowing for the recall of all public officials, including judges. This last provision was important to organized labor because they believed that judges were often unfairly biased in favor of employers in labor disputes. Overall, the new Arizona Constitution was an extremely progressive document, and some thought it might be too radical for the conservative Republican administration in Washington. Those fears soon proved to be true.

Although Arizonans overwhelmingly approved their new constitution at a special election on February 9, 1911, with 77 percent of the vote, it failed to meet the approval of President Taft (apparently because of the provision allowing for the recall of judges). As a result, Taft vetoed the congressional resolution allowing for the admission of Arizona as a state! Seeing no alternative, voters agreed to delete the offending provision, and Arizona officially became a state on February 14, 1912. Ironically, only nine months later, Arizonans approved an amendment to their constitution reinstating the recall of judges by a popular vote of almost five to one. Although Arizona voters initiated only 1 constitutional amendment in 1912 (woman suffrage, which passed), they initiated 15 ballot propositions in 1914 (including statewide prohibition, which passed), 10 in 1916, and 7 in 1918.

Between 1898 and 1918, voters in 22 states ratified amendments allowing for the statewide initiative and/or referendum. In each state, the same motivating factors were evident. Voters in South Dakota and North Dakota confronted monopoly-controlled transportation, grain elevator, and marketing agencies, and either a single-party-dominated state government or a powerful political machine. In both of those states, calls for the regulation of transportation rates as well as the storage, grading, and weighing of grain; the equitable taxation of real property; and legislation to regulate interest rates were all ignored. Oregonians thought their political system was controlled by influential corporations and stymied by legislative gridlock. Voters in Washington complained of corporate-influenced politics, discriminatory railroad rates, tax inequities, and wasteful expenditures. Californians felt subservient to the legislative influence of the Southern Pacific Railroad, Montanans to the mining magnates and cattle barons, and Arizonans to the railroad and mining interests. Colorado used the terms "Lobby" to describe corporate influence over state politics and "Big Mitt" to denote the political control that telephone, water, gas, electric, and streetcar monopolies exercised over city government. In Missouri voters referred to those same interests as the "Big Cinch" in St. Louis and the "Lobby" in Jefferson City, and could talk knowingly about bribery and corruption in politics at both the state and local levels. Oklahoma voters complained of corporate tax dodging and patronage-driven politics that seemed to ignore the interests of farmers and workers. Voters in Michigan and Ohio complained that single-party control of the state legislature prevented meaningful reform. Voters in Maine resented tax concessions granted to timber companies, and working-class voters in Massachusetts were increasingly critical of a legislature that seemed unwilling to address the concerns of organized labor. In each state, frustrated voters were driven to conclude that they had become politically powerless.

But maybe that could be changed. The initiative and referendum might be a way to force legislators to share power with voters by allowing them to create law and veto legislation directly, whereas the recall would allow voters to immediately discipline irresponsible officials. With these new reforms, perhaps the most significant political changes of the Progressive Era, voters could recapture the power to directly influence the making of policy. But this would require an activist electorate. To that end, proponents held public meetings, interrogated political candidates about their position on I & R, organized speaker's bureaus, and conducted any number of mass-mailing campaigns. They encouraged prominent labor organizations, farm associations, and municipal and civic leagues to pass resolutions in support of direct legislation; and they drew up model bills, lobbied legislators, and encouraged voters to create or join direct legislation leagues. Historian Carlos Schwantes has called direct legislation a "protean reform" that united workers, farmers, and the middle class.[31] Perhaps that is not surprising because direct legislation offered the best means to correct political, economic, and social abuses as defined by each particular group. Many of the ballot propositions put forward by petition during the Progressive Era were ill-conceived, superfluous, or even spiteful, but the "failures" should not negate the achievements. Included in the list of voter-initiated accomplishments were woman suffrage, direct primary laws, the recall, corrupt-practices laws, workmen's compensation, child labor and eight-hour laws, public utility regulation, and modifications to existing tax structures, to name but a few. The consideration of over 400 ballot propositions under the I & R process between 1898 and 1918 offers a striking indication that voters did gain a voice.

What is striking about the Progressive Era is not just its uncommon fascination with reform, but the tremendous level of citizen activism and civic engagement that played such a fundamental part in bringing about change. The depression-generated anger toward "an establishment of corporations and politicians that deliberately thwarted the will of the people and refused to respond to change" led individuals to create a new yardstick defined as the public interest. It became, during the late 1890s and first two decades of the twentieth century, the new way of evaluating individuals and corporations. This new assessment of the political economy led to an increased interest in radical economic programs such as municipal ownership and progressive taxation; in radical political programs such as woman suffrage, the direct election of U.S. senators, corrupt-practices acts, the direct primary, home rule for cities, and the initiative, referendum, and recall; and in a greater acceptance of the idea of federal regulation to curb abuses. Many of these reforms were the direct result of a surge of activism at the grassroots level that found formal expression as coalitions of workers, farmers, consumers, taxpayers, and citizens. Those living during the Progressive Era comprised a generation that had different ideas about democracy than those of the generations that immediately preceded or succeeded them, and they possessed a more expansive (many today would say naïve) sense of economic, social, and political possibilities. Some would come to call this new popular spirit the "insurgent" spirit. As one historian has stated, "This insurgency against political establishments was the progressive's contribution to the radical tradition."[32]

NOTES

1. For a further discussion of this argument see David P. Thelen, "Progressivism as a Radical Movement," in *Main Problems in American History*, vol. 2, ed. Howard H. Quint, Milton Cantor, and Dean Albertson (Homewood, IL: Dorsey Press, 1972), 149–158. See also David P. Thelen, "Social Tensions and the Origins of Progressivism," *Journal of American History* 56 (September 1969): 323–341.

2. John Whiteclay Chambers II, *The Tyranny of Change: America in the Progressive Era, 1890–1920* (New York: St. Martin's Press, 1992), 148.

3. Steven L. Piott, *The Anti-Monopoly Persuasion: Popular Resistance to the Rise of Big Business in the Midwest* (Westport, CT: Greenwood Press, 1985), 57.

4. Ibid., 61–62.

5. Ibid., 66.

6. Ibid., 69.

7. Ibid., 70.

8. Ibid., 73.

9. Ibid., 76–77, 79–80.

10. Ibid., 77.

11. Ibid., 77–78, 79.

12. Ibid., 78.

13. Ibid., 81, 82.

14. Ibid., 86.

15. Lorine Swainston Goodwin, *The Pure Food, Drink, and Drug Crusaders, 1879–1914* (Jefferson, NC: McFarland and Co., 1999), 156.

16. Mark Sullivan, *Our Times: America at the Birth of the Twentieth Century,* ed. Dan Rather (New York: Scribner, 1996), 233.

17. Louis Filler, *Crusaders for American Liberalism* (Yellow Springs, OH: Antioch Press, 1964), 155.

18. Upton Sinclair, *The Jungle* (New York: New American Library, 1960), 79.

19. Goodwin, *Pure Food, Drink, and Drug Crusaders*, 265, 260.

20. Maureen A. Flanagan, *America Reformed: Progressives and Progressivisms, 1890s–1920s* (New York: Oxford University Press, 2007), 82.

21. Ibid., 87.

22. Ibid., 175–176.

23. Ibid., 133.

24. Nell Irvin Painter, *Standing at Armageddon: The United States, 1877–1919* (New York: W. W. Norton, 1987), 247, 248.

25. Carrie Chapman Catt and Nettie Rogers Shuler, *Woman Suffrage and Politics: The Inner Story of the Suffrage Movement* (Seattle: University of Washington Press, 1970), 287–290.

26. Ellen Carol DuBois and Lynn Dumenil, *Through Women's Eyes: An American History* (Boston: Bedford/St. Martin's, 2009), 476.

27. Steven L. Piott, *Giving Voters a Voice: The Origins of the Initiative and Referendum in America* (Columbia: University of Missouri Press, 2003), 24, 25.

28. Ibid., 141.

29. Ibid., 142.

30. Ibid., 144.

31. Carlos A. Schwantes, *Radical Heritage: Labor, Socialism, and Reform in Washington and British Columbia, 1885–1917* (Seattle: University of Washington Press, 1979), 93.

32. David P. Thelen, *The New Citizenship: Origins of Progressivism in Wisconsin, 1885–1900* (Columbia: University of Missouri Press, 1972), 312.

5

The Progressive Era and Race

Most histories of the Progressive Era describe the period as one of reform in which society wrestled with the negative results of industrialization. Most reform-minded progressives sought to check the increase in corporate power, confront problems related to rapid urban growth, ease the widening class conflict in society and defuse labor violence, reduce political corruption, expand government regulation of business and transportation, lessen the control of Wall Street bankers, create a more equitable tax system, protect consumers, conserve natural resources, broaden democracy, and regulate morality. There seemed to be a new interest in social justice, in having the law evolve in relation to social need, and in helping the less fortunate. But for all their commendable efforts, most progressives never confronted racism, and a number supported various programs aimed at social control. Caught up in a surge of white supremacy at home and abroad, most Americans embraced ideologies of biological or cultural racism that denigrated non-Anglo-Saxon ethnic groups and people of color.

THE "BIOLOGICAL REPUBLIC"

One area that attracted the attention of a number of Americans after 1900 was the new pseudo-science of eugenics. Though behaviorists stressed the importance of environment in determining human behavior, eugenicists looked to improve the human race through heredity or better breeding. Leading the new interest in this area was Charles B. Davenport, who in 1910 established the Eugenics Records Office at Cold Spring Harbor on Long Island, New York, which served as the center for eugenics research until 1940. Those drawn to eugenics often argued that the superior white, Anglo-Saxon race was committing a form of racial suicide by not producing enough offspring. Theodore Roosevelt, who embraced the "race suicide" argument, became convinced that the way to improve the genetic stock of the nation was to encourage the reproduction of people with desirable traits; he favored offering tax breaks to white families who would have more children. Others, however, focused their attention on discouraging the reproduction of people with undesirable traits and supported the idea of sterilizing allegedly inferior or dangerous people for the good of society. From 1907 to 1917, 17 states passed legislation that allowed for the sterilization of unfit individuals. The numerous international expositions held during the late nineteenth and early twentieth century lent support to this way of thinking and served as a way to spread scientific racism to the masses. Exhibits at these fairs were designed to contrast primitive villages with modern western science and technology, and in doing so, projected a form of white supremacy. College textbooks and popular magazines presented eugenics to an even wider audience, prompting one historian to note that more articles on the topic of eugenics appeared in print between 1910 and 1914 than on slums and poverty.

Two of the most noted popularizers of scientific racism were Madison Grant and Lothrop Stoddard, who both favored applying scientific knowledge to questions about immigration and race. Grant, a Nordic or Anglo-Saxon racialist who published the widely read *The Passing of the Great Race* in 1916, was primarily concerned about the "new immigrants" and thought the flood of recent immigrants from southern and eastern Europe was pushing the nation toward a racial abyss. Convinced that such a dire result was imminent, Grant argued that America's preservation required it to exclude all inferior racial and ethnic groups. Stoddard, in contrast, focused his attention on black-white relations and his book *The Rising Tide of Color against White World Supremacy* (1920) was said to have inspired the leaders of the Ku Klux Klan.

The arguments advanced by the eugenicists were used to justify restriction, exclusion, and discrimination. Intellectuals promoted

the idea that the human race could be neatly divided into heredi-
tary types. Teutonic peoples topped the "civilized" list, and Medi-
terranean, Oriental, and African peoples languished at the bottom.
In response to the growing concern about the rising number of
immigrants, immigration officials in 1907 added the character-
ization of "physical degeneracy" to the list of reasons that might
be used to exclude new immigrants. The intention was to create
a stringent medical test that would be administered by medical
examiners at Ellis Island and used to exclude anyone deemed to be
mentally or physically defective. The provision suggested just how
strongly the theory of innate degeneracy had taken root in society.
That same year Congress created the United States Immigration
Commission (known as the Dillingham Commission) to study the
immigration problem and recommend solutions. When the commission finally issued its report in 1911, it agreed that immigration
from southern and eastern Europe did pose a threat to American
society and culture, and called for the adoption of a restrictive
literacy test to selectively limit the overall number. The Boston-
based Immigration Restriction League quickly became the most
effective of several lobbies for such a law. Both presidents William
Howard Taft and Woodrow Wilson vetoed efforts to impose such
a test on newcomers, but in the months before the United States
entered World War I, Congress overrode Wilson's veto and passed
the Immigration Act of 1917. The new law prohibited entry into
the country for any prospective immigrant who was 16 years or
older and could not demonstrate the ability to read in any language. The measure served as a precursor to the quota-based legislation passed during the 1920s designed to severely restrict the
number of southern and eastern Europeans and to exclude Asians
entirely.

With the outbreak of war, there was a surge in antiforeign sentiment against "hyphenated Americans." At the urging of the American Psychological Association, the U.S. Army began to administer
intelligence tests to new recruits to identify potential officers, match
recruits with appropriate jobs, and exclude the mentally deficient.
The tests were heavily slanted in favor of native-born recruits
from middle-class backgrounds who had attended high school.
With such a built-in cultural bias, it is not surprising that new
immigrants and southern blacks recorded the lowest scores. To
defenders of the tests who regarded them as measures of innate
intelligence, low scores could only serve as proof of inborn mental inferiority. To many Americans who read or heard about the

outcomes, the authority of experts and the U.S. government had been added to the arguments of intellectuals such as Grant and Stoddard to underscore the debasing influence of various ethnic and racial groups.

THE ERA OF "JIM CROW"

During the Progressive Era, the primary racial divide in the country was white and black. Most Americans either acquiesced in the entrenchment of Jim Crowism or simply ignored the problem. As a result, segregation, disenfranchisement, economic and educational discrimination, peonage, race-baiting, lynching, and race rioting intensified for African Americans. One scholar has concluded that the Progressive Era, for all its liberal rhetoric and legislative accomplishments, marked the "nadir" of African American life after emancipation. As historian David W. Southern has noted, however, the "history of African Americans always has two sides. One side relates what whites have thought about and done to blacks...The other side traces the aspirations and strivings of blacks to make a life for themselves in a hostile white world."[1]

Disenfranchisement

The 1890s are historically significant for ushering in the era of Jim Crow (the term derived from the name of a poor, ragged minstrel character) when blacks were legally disenfranchised and segregated in the South. Although the black vote was reduced through intimidation and fear after ratification of the Fifteenth Amendment in 1870, white southerners sought to institutionalize the process during the 1890s. Beginning with Mississippi in 1890 and spreading to all 11 former Confederate states by 1911, white southerners amended their state constitutions to eliminate black voters without totally disenfranchising poor, illiterate white voters as well. They accomplished this by a series of legal contrivances that included property qualifications, residency requirements, literacy tests, "good character" and "understanding" tests administered by white voter registrars, and the adoption of the all-white primary.

Another very effective method used to prevent hundreds of thousands of black men (and perhaps tens of thousands of white men as well) from casting their ballots was the poll tax. Poll taxes were personal taxes of from $1 to $2 per year, the payment of which was required for voting. Anyone wishing to vote was required to pay his poll tax long before the day of the election and to retain his receipt for several months to prove that he had paid his tax. In addition, the potential voter had to show that he had paid taxes for every year since turning 21. Perhaps the most ingenious method of disenfranchisement was the "grandfather clause," which stated that only citizens whose grandfathers were registered to vote on January 1, 1867, could cast their ballots. Although such blatantly discriminatory devices as the grandfather clause would be successfully challenged in court, a combination of the other tactics effectively eliminated the black vote in the South. Louisiana was a typical example. Although 130,334 black voters were registered in 1896, after that state altered its constitution in 1898, the number of registered black voters dropped to 5,320 in 1900. By 1904 the number of registered black voters was fewer than 1,000.

Segregation and "Separate but Equal"

Jim Crow had a social dimension as well as a political one. Beginning in the 1890s, governing bodies at the state and local levels in the South began to enact laws that legalized segregation in public facilities, a legislative process that accelerated in the early twentieth century. Starting with railroad cars and schools, such laws soon included hotels, theaters, restaurants, train depots, hospitals, parks, playgrounds, cemeteries, washrooms, and drinking fountains. In June 1892, Homer A. Plessy, a person of mixed ancestry, was arrested after he purchased a first-class railway ticket and attempted to ride in a coach designated for white people. Plessy's arrest was part of a planned legal challenge to a Louisiana segregation law passed in 1890 that called for equal but separate accommodations for white and "colored" races traveling on passenger railways in the state. The legal challenge, organized by the American Citizen's Equal Rights Association, a group composed of blacks and Creoles (French-speaking people of mixed ancestry), argued that the existing law deprived people of color of equal protection under the law as guaranteed under the Fourteenth Amendment to the Constitution. Finally, on May 18, 1896, after a lengthy judicial process, the U.S. Supreme Court in the case of *Plessy v. Ferguson* upheld (by a vote of eight to one) the Louisiana segregation law. In doing so, the majority on the court accepted the argument that racial segregation was within the police powers of the state to maintain public order.

Segregation laws were legal as long as the facilities were "separate but equal." In dissenting to the majority opinion, Justice John Marshall Harlan argued that the Constitution was "color-blind" and that the court's decision relegated blacks to a status of legal inferiority. As one historian noted, "After the Plessy decision, southern states and cities passed hundreds of laws that created an American apartheid—an elaborate system of racial separation."[2]

Black Resistance to Segregation

Even though the Supreme Court had rendered its verdict, black people resisted segregation especially on streetcars. For many, the electric street car was the dominant mode of transportation in urban areas. As cities across the South began to segregate those cars after 1891, blacks resisted with boycotts and sit-ins. There were at least 25 streetcar boycotts in southern cities between 1891 and 1910. Blacks refused to ride segregated cars in Atlanta, Augusta, Jacksonville, Montgomery, Mobile, Little Rock, and Columbia. They walked to work or took horse-drawn conveyances. Although such boycotts had only limited success (in Atlanta and Augusta), the boycotts inflicted financial damage on the streetcar companies. In Portsmouth and Norfolk, Virginia, and in Chattanooga and Nashville, Tennessee, blacks tried to form alternate transportation companies. Black citizens in Nashville organized a black-owned bus company in 1905 and contributed $25,000 to its operating budget, but they could not maintain enough capital to keep the venture going for longer than a few months.

Violence toward Blacks

Accompanying the institutionalization of Jim Crow in the South was a marked increase in white violence toward blacks. During the decade of the 1890s, there were an average of 187 lynchings a year in the United States. There were 245 lynchings during the first two years of the twentieth century, and an average of nearly 89 lynchings a year during the century's first decade. The practice took on an even sharper southern-black focus as well. Although over 80 percent of the lynchings occurred in the South in the 1890s, 92 percent occurred there during the following decade. The proportion of blacks lynched increased as well, from 72 percent of all people lynched during the 1890s to almost 90 percent during the ensuing decade. Throughout the Progressive Era, the practice remained a national disgrace. The white mobs who participated in these community spectacles defended their actions as a legitimate form of law enforcement and the only way to punish black men accused of raping white women. In reality, whites used lynchings to control and subjugate blacks through terror and intimidation.

One individual who became especially incensed by the practice was journalist Ida Wells, who had been shocked and horrified when three people she knew who ran a successful and competitive grocery store in Memphis, Tennessee, were brutally murdered in 1892. The incident, which was not connected to the crime of rape, opened her eyes to "what lynching really was. An excuse to get rid of Negroes who were acquiring wealth and property and thus keep the race terrorized and 'keep the nigger down.'"[3] In Wells's mind, white fears of black uprisings during slavery had given way to white fears of black rule during Reconstruction, which, in turn, had been replaced by white fears of black advancement after 1877. "Legalized segregation and political disenfranchisement served as reminders that the black man was still regarded as inferior. Lynching was a form of intimidation, while rape served as the metaphor in the southern white mind for any challenge to white supremacy." Wells went on to lead a national crusade against lynching and to publish two influential pamphlets on the topic—*Southern Horrors* (1892) and *A Red Record* (1895). She persuasively argued that the "public justification for lynching as the defense of southern white womanhood was really a façade to conceal a racist agenda contrived by southern white men to maintain power." Wells understood that the only way to stop lynching was to have the government enact a federal anti-lynching law and to establish a federal bureau to investigate and publicize the details of every lynching. Both the later Niagara Movement and the National Association for the Advancement of Colored People (NAACP) would continue the anti-lynching campaign into the twentieth century. Under pressure from the NAACP, the U.S. House of Representatives finally passed an anti-lynching bill in 1922, only to have southern opponents kill the measure in the Senate.[4]

Wells also raised a protest against the slander of black women. Whites commonly charged that black women were "congenitally immoral and as mothers were incapable of instilling sexual morality in their sons and daughters. From this perspective, whites argued that black women could not be 'ruined' by white men."[5] In fact, the implication was that black women were always eager to satisfy white lust. Also working to restore the reputation of black women was the National Association of Colored Women (NACW), founded in 1896, an organization composed largely of middle-class women. Because the two dominant agencies of influence in the black community—the Republican Party and the black church—were controlled by men, black women needed an organizational forum to discuss issues important to them. By 1900 the NACW had grown to 300 clubs and approximately 18,000 members. By 1914 the NACW had 1,000 clubs and 50,000 members. Although the initial focus of the NACW was on moral uplift, the organization would broaden its social agenda during the Progressive Era.

Racial Bias

Also designed to further the mandate of white supremacy in the South was a racially biased justice system. Those who operated that system—police, judges, lawyers, and juries—were almost always white. Lower-class whites tended to dominate southern police departments and meted out heavy-handed justice to blacks. At the same time, white judges handed down sentences to blacks that were far more severe than those given to whites and often shockingly disproportionate to the crime committed. A judge might sentence a black man to three years in jail for stealing a bicycle, but sentence a white man to three months in jail for the theft of a car. White juries almost always found white violence against blacks justifiable. Conversely, a black assault on a white person brought severe retribution on the black offender (provided he had not already been taken from his jail cell and lynched).

The southern justice system had other racially biased inventions. One of these was the convict lease system, whereby a prisoner could be leased to a private employer. Penal reformers regarded this as another form of human slavery and targeted it for elimination; every southern state with the exception of Alabama had been compelled to end the practice by 1920. Southerners, however, quickly replaced convict leasing with the chain gang. Under the chain gang system, a prisoner worked for the state rather than for a private employer. Like convict leasing, law enforcement agencies channeled those, primarily black, who had committed petty crimes onto the chain gang. In the state of Georgia in 1904, 124 men and 25 women worked on the Bibb County chain gang. Of those 149 prisoners, 56 had been convicted of drunkenness, 40 of disorderly conduct, 18 for fighting, 12 for loitering, 4 for reckless driving, 2 for throwing rocks, and 12 for violating minor city ordinances. Most of the prisoners were put to work on road construction projects for terms of six months or more.

Law enforcement agencies in the South often sentenced blacks who had committed petty crimes to the chain gang. (Courtesy of the Library of Congress)

Economic Hardship

By 1900 an entrenched caste system had imposed a burden of severe social and economic suffering on southern blacks. At the start of the twentieth century, 90 percent of African Americans lived in the South. Of an American population of 76 million in 1900, 11.5 percent or 8,883,000 were black. Although blacks comprised about one-third of the population of the southern states, they made up 60 percent of the population in South Carolina and Mississippi and more than 40 percent of the population in Alabama, Florida, Georgia, and Louisiana. In 1900 50.4 percent of blacks worked in agriculture. Although many blacks hoped to own land in the South, three-fourths were too poor to own any land at all. Most black farmers lived in poverty and understood that they had little chance of escaping the economic system as they knew it. In the southern countryside, black families often lived in log huts with dirt floors and no glass or screens in the windows. The total living space might be as small as 200 square feet. The diet for most black farm families consisted of fatback (pork), corn bread, and molasses. With a diet consistently lacking in protein and vitamins, children were vulnerable to chronic anemia and diseases related to vitamin deficiency.

Sharecroppers

Most black families were sharecroppers, allowed the use of someone else's land for a share of the crop. The landlord usually provided a place to live, a horse or mule to work the land, tools, and seed, as well as food and clothing. In return, the sharecropper gave to the landlord from one-half to three-quarters of the crop. Under this system, verbal agreements were more common than written contracts, and black sharecroppers had to accept the monetary value assigned to their crops and to the goods provided by the white landowner. It was a system rampant with cheating and exploitation. As one Mississippi sharecropper explained, "I have been living in this Delta thirty years, and I know that I have been robbed every year; but there is no use jumping out of the frying pan into the fire. If we ask any questions we are cussed, and if we raise up we are shot, and that ends it."[6]

Tenant Farmers

Other black farmers were renters, which was preferable to sharecropping. A tenant paid a set amount to rent a given number of acres. Payment might be in cash (perhaps $5 per acre) or in commodity (perhaps two bales of cotton per each 20 acres farmed). Tenants probably owned their own tools and farm stock. As one renter put it, "You see, a sharecropper don't ever have nothing. Before you know it, the man done took it all. But the renter always have something, and then he go to work when he want to go to work. He ain't got to go to work on the man's time. If he didn't make it, he didn't get it."[7]

The Crop-Lien System

Under the southern crop-lien system, many sharecroppers and tenants were also indebted to the local furnishing merchant for food, clothing, tools, and farm supplies. Under this pernicious system, a tenant would mortgage his crop to the merchant as security against which he could borrow to obtain necessary supplies. The merchant rarely advanced cash, but instead, offered credit at his country store. Taking advantage of this inescapable system (the farmer had to have credit or starve), the furnishing merchant gouged the helpless farmer by charging exorbitant rates of interest. Where the going rate of interest might have been 6 percent, it was not uncommon for the furnishing merchant to command rates of from 20 to 35 percent. Compounding the poor farmer's woes were the prices he was forced to pay for goods at the store. The insidious crop-lien system, which victimized poor white as well as black farmers, allowed the merchant to set a two-tiered pricing structure—cash and credit. Although the amount of markup for credit customers varied widely, it was at least 25 percent above retail cost and usually much higher. If the sharecropper or tenant could not repay the merchant, the merchant was legally entitled to a portion of the crop after the farmer had received his payment. Most often finding himself in debt, the farmer was informed that he could not move off the land until his debt was paid. This perpetual state of bondage was commonly known as debt peonage, in reality a new form of enslavement.

Nonagricultural Labor

Nonagricultural labor for blacks was equally harsh. Working as blue-collar laborers, fewer than 3 percent of blacks nationally held skilled jobs in 1910. And no matter how skilled a black worker might be, he always received wages that were lower than those of his white counterpart. With racial discrimination firmly entrenched, white employers offered the lower-paying and more arduous jobs to blacks. In 1910 blacks held 24,647 of the 28,674 jobs in the turpentine industry, regarded as the worst type of work available. Turpentine workers labored long hours in hot, humid weather at isolated worksites near insect-infested swamps. Poorly paid, they were forced to spend their hard-earned wages at company stores that charged exorbitant prices. Blacks made up 39.1 percent of the steelworkers in Birmingham, Alabama, in 1907, but they held the unskilled positions that paid the least and had the greatest risk of injury. Blacks comprised about one-half of the workers in the tobacco plants, but they were assigned the unskilled jobs that required hauling and stemming leaves by hand. In the textile industry, blacks were usually excluded from work in southern cotton mills because that work was reserved for poor white workers to prevent them from dropping below blacks on the ladder of economic status.

Black women faced even more limited job opportunities than did black men. Approximately 80 to 90 percent of black working women toiled as cooks, maids, and laundresses. They commonly worked a six-day workweek of 10- to 14-hour days for $2 to $3 a week. Although only a small part of the population in northern cities, black women comprised almost 30 percent of those who worked as servants by 1920. The dominant culture stigmatized married women who worked outside their homes during the Progressive Era, yet more than one-third of married black women in New York City were forced to do so in 1910; the comparable figure for married white women was only 4.2 percent. As an indication that racial discrimination in hiring had no sectional boundaries, more than 60 percent of black men and more than 80 percent of black women worked at menial jobs in northern cities.

Housing

Housing for blacks who lived in cities was not much better than on the farm. By 1900 more than one-fourth of the African American population nationally lived in urban environments. In the South approximately one-third of the urban population was black. Almost every town or city in the South had a large population of blacks, who were usually confined to the poorest residential areas. Black sections of towns often lacked water and sewage systems, paved streets, streetlights, and other basic municipal services. In Louisville, Kentucky, in 1909, 53 percent of the black population lived in substandard housing, whereas only 15 percent of foreign-born whites fell into that same category. In observing these deplorable living conditions, a northern minister visiting the South described the "wretchedness" as "pathetic" and the poverty "colossal." As one historian has noted, "The conditions in which urban blacks lived was a testament to the power of racism and the lack of power by African Americans."[8]

Between 1890 and 1900, approximately 200,000 blacks left the South to try to improve their lives in the North and West. In 1900 Washington, D.C., had a black population of 86,000, and New York, Philadelphia, and Baltimore each had more than 50,000 black residents. By 1920 all of those cities and Chicago had black populations that exceeded 100,000. As larger numbers of blacks began to migrate to northern urban centers, residential segregation intensified and ghettos formed. An example of this process was Harlem, which was home to two-thirds of all blacks living in New York City in 1920. Low wages and high rents in urban areas placed a severe strain on many black inhabitants. Slumlords charged higher rents to blacks than whites because housing was in great demand. The same supply-and-demand dynamic allowed landlords to devote little attention to the maintenance of the property they rented. Many black families who lived in the city were forced to take in boarders to make ends meet.

Health and Family Stability

Poor health and a tenuous family life were two by-products of poverty, substandard diets, a lack of social services, and minimal medical care. The average life expectancy for black males at the turn of the twentieth century was 32.5 years, 16 years less than for white males. In South Carolina, 16 percent of black babies died before the age of one, a figure almost twice that for white babies. In 1915 in Cleveland, Ohio, more than twice as many blacks as whites died from pneumonia, and the black tuberculosis rate was more than four times that of whites. Tens of thousands of both white and black southerners suffered from pellagra and rickets, the result of improper nutrition, and a similar number became victims of hookworm. The black rate of syphilis was eight times that of whites. Nationally, the death rate for blacks was double that of whites. Black families were also less stable than white families during the Progressive Era. Because of the high death rate for black males, about 20 percent of black women between the ages of 33 and 45 were widows. Single females headed almost 20 percent of black households in Chicago, almost 24 percent in New York City, and nearly 34 percent in urban Georgia. Partly because more than 80 percent of all urban black women worked outside the home and had no access to adequate child care facilities, juvenile delinquency rates were higher for blacks than for whites. The number of black children born out of wedlock was 12.6 percent as opposed to 1.7 percent for native whites.

Education

Another problem plaguing African Americans, especially those who lived in the South, was a substandard education. At the beginning of the twentieth century, southern states spent roughly twice as much per capita on white students as they did on black students. In states such as Mississippi and South Carolina, the ratio was 10 to 12 times as much. Even in more moderate southern states such as North Carolina, the black share of educational money declined between 1900 and 1915. Black students often had only secondhand textbooks that applauded slavery and Jim Crow. Black students also had shorter school terms than did white students. Black urban schools were crowded, and class sizes were larger than those for whites. In many sections of the South, a dilapidated shanty might serve as a school. Black poet and essayist James Weldon Johnson remembered teaching 50 children in a crudely built church in rural Florida without a blackboard or desks. Public education for black children usually stopped at the sixth or seventh grade. Public high schools for blacks in the South were nonexistent. Regardless of the level of schooling, white school officials emphasized industrial training for black students over a more liberal arts oriented curriculum.

Compounding problems for black education was the lack of qualified teachers and the low salaries paid to teachers. Only 20 percent of African American teachers had obtained more than a grammar school education. In 1915 the average monthly salary for elementary school teachers in Georgia was $60.25 for white men and $45.70 for white women. For black male and female elementary school teachers, the comparable figures were $30.14 and $21.69.

African American school in Anthoston, Kentucky, where the tobacco harvest has severely reduced the attendance, 1916. (Courtesy of the Library of Congress)

Some northern philanthropists provided money to black education. Julius Rosenwald, president of Sears, Roebuck and Company, donated liberally to build black schools, subsidizing the construction of 100 black schools in Alabama alone in 1914. The Anna T. Jeans Fund, the Phelps-Stokes Foundation, and numerous northern religious denominations also contributed money to black education. The Rockefeller-backed General Education Board (GEB) spent $58 million between 1902 and 1909 on southern education. Ironically, 90 percent of GEB money went to white education. The reform-minded administrators of the GEB operated from the assumption that an educated southern white population would be less racist and more willing to accept the accommodationist ideas of black leaders such as Booker T. Washington. In the final analysis, the good news–bad news scenario for black education between 1900 and 1920 was that the overall illiteracy rate for southern blacks declined from two-thirds to less than one-half, and literacy rates were far higher for younger blacks. At the same time, however, educational inequality during the Progressive Era increased, and blacks fell even farther behind whites.

BLACK LEADERS

Thomas T. Fortune

Trying to address the many problems confronting African Americans in their daily lives were a series of exceptional black leaders. One of these was Thomas T. Fortune, editor of the *New York Age*, who established the National Afro-American League in 1890. In his opening address to nearly 100 delegates representing 23 states at the inaugural meeting of the organization in Chicago, Fortune looked to encourage black resistance to white oppression: "It is time to face the enemy," he said, "and fight him inch by inch for every right he denies us.... Let this League be a race League."[9] Fortune hoped to spread state and local chapters of his militant league throughout the South, where they would be encouraged "in their efforts to break down color bars, and in obtaining for the Afro-American an equal chance with others in the avocations of life [and]...in securing the full privileges of citizenship."[10] He also advanced a number of strategies to improve black life that included self-help and the promotion of education. The Afro-American League supported civil rights and black voting, denounced segregation laws and the exclusion of blacks from public places, and condemned the convict lease system and lynching. Fortune favored peaceful methods to achieve his ends, but he warned whites that if they continued to use violence, blacks would respond. "[I]f others use the weapons of violence to combat our peaceful arguments," he said, "it is not for us to run away from violence. A man's a man, and what is worth having is worth fighting for."[11] But for all its noble objectives, trying to establish a militant black organization in the South just as Jim Crow began to intensify was doomed to failure. The Afro-American League continued until the mid-1890s but was unable to make any progress.

Booker T. Washington

In 1895 another black leader, Booker T. Washington, delivered a famous speech at the Cotton States Exposition in Atlanta, Georgia, in which he laid out a different program for black advancement. Washington was a former slave who had risen by hard work to become head of the Tuskegee Institute in Alabama. Tuskegee stressed black self-reliance and self-discipline and emphasized the teaching of vocational skills that would enable blacks to become economically independent. From that perspective, Washington used his speech, known as the Atlanta Compromise, to prescribe his program for interracial cooperation in the South. He encouraged blacks to be willing to start at the bottom, learn industrial skills, commit themselves to hard work, and focus on economic advancement. Seeking conciliation rather than confrontation, Washington also asked blacks to tacitly accept segregation and disenfranchisement and to defer demands for social and political equality. "In all things that are purely social," he said, "we can be as separate as the fingers, yet one as the hand in all things essential to mutual progress." It was best, he thought, not to make defiant demands. "The wisest among my race understand," he stated, "that the agitation of questions of social equality is the extremest folly, and that progress in the enjoyment of all the privileges that will come to us must be the result of severe and constant struggle rather than of artificial forcing."[12] If southern whites would recognize the economic potential of trusting blacks and would enable black opportunity (provide jobs), they would be repaid for their efforts with greater economic prosperity and racial harmony. Over time, African American advancement in education (vocationally emphasized) and their contributions to southern economic growth would win white support for broadened civil rights. Washington's program, seen in the context of worsening race relations, had appeal. The speech was warmly received by both white and black audiences and by those who read it when

Booker T. Washington, head of the Tuskegee Institute and proponent of interracial cooperation. (Courtesy of the Library of Congress)

it was widely reprinted in the press. Washington seemed to offer practical solutions to the problems of everyday life.

W. E. B. Du Bois

In 1903 William Edward Burghardt Du Bois, the most prominent black intellectual of his era, published *The Souls of Black Folk*, in which he challenged the accommodationist ideology of Washington. In his mind Washington conceded too much, practically accepting "the alleged inferiority of the Negro races," and withdrew "many of the high demands of Negroes as men and American citizens." Blacks, argued Du Bois, needed their constitutional rights, including the right to vote and to have access to higher education for talented members of the race. In his criticism, Du Bois raised a most important question: "Is it possible, and probable, that nine millions of men can make effective progress in economic lines if they are deprived of political rights, made a servile caste, and allowed only the most meagre [sic] chance for developing their exceptional

W. E. B. Du Bois, director of publications
and research for the NAACP and editor
of *The Crisis.* (Library of Congress)

men? If history and reason give any distinct answer to these questions, it is an emphatic *No.*"[13] Du Bois believed that Washington's
economic-centered program would result in the creation of a cheap,
submissive supply of labor for an industrializing South and result
in further exploitation rather than economic progress for blacks. He
further believed that racial advancement for blacks was the responsibility of the black elite, who he called the Talented Tenth. "Work
alone," he argued, "will not do it unless inspired by the right ideals and guided by intelligence. Education must not simply teach
work—it must teach Life. The Talented Tenth of the Negro race
must be made leaders of thought and missionaries of culture among
people."[14] They would gain the respect of white society, serve as
role models for other blacks, and raise the race.

To give organizational stature to his ideas, Du Bois issued a call
for black leaders to organize a campaign for black equality. Fifty-
nine men signed the call, and 29 of them ultimately convened in
Niagara, Canada, (a major terminus on the Underground Railroad) on July 11, 1905, to rekindle a militant abolitionist movement
and demand full citizenship for black Americans. What grew out
of that meeting (held on the Canadian side of the border because

no American hotel would grant them accommodations) was the Niagara Movement. In a tone that reminded one of Fortune's militant stance 15 years before, the declaration of principles adopted by the delegates included calls for restoring to blacks the right to vote, ending segregation, and enacting complete equality in economic opportunity and education. At the second annual meeting of the organization held at Harper's Ferry (the site of John Brown's martyrdom), Du Bois expanded his demands to include social equality. In his address to the country, given on the final day of the conference, Du Bois reinforced his commitment to an ideal. "We claim for ourselves," he stated, "every single right that belongs to a freeborn American, political, civil and social; and until we get those rights we will never cease to protest and to assail the ears of America."[15] Although the Niagara Movement continued to meet for two more years and eventually grew to 400 members, internal disagreements, insufficient funding, the lack of an official publication for publicity, and attacks from those who supported Washington prevented it from becoming an effective civil rights organization.

INCREASED RACIAL TENSIONS

Race Riots

As the Niagara Movement struggled to sustain itself as the nucleus of a new twentieth-century civil rights movement, two race riots occurred that had a significant impact on that development. The first of these was the Atlanta Race Riot of 1906, which occurred 11 years after Washington's famous address there. The riot took place in the midst of a race-baiting gubernatorial campaign between Hoke Smith and Clark Howell that centered on the issue of disenfranchising black voters. Smith's own newspaper, the *Atlanta Journal,* claimed that Howell favored granting blacks political equality. To the editors of the *Journal,* political equality led directly to social equality, which, in turn, led directly to assaults on the "fair young girlhood of the South." Political empowerment, argued the editors, would encourage "the Negro" "in his foul dreams of a mixture of races." As historian Nell Painter noted, "By this analysis, black voting automatically entailed racial amalgamation of the most brutal sort, which was the only kind of black male/white female miscegenation that white supremacists could imagine."[16]

Adding to tensions in the city was the opening of Reverend Thomas Dixon's play *The Clansman*. Based on Dixon's 1905 novel of the same name, the play was as widely popular as the novel had been. *The Clansman*, set in South Carolina during Reconstruction, argued that the black population was inherently incapable of self-government, featured the attempted rape of a white woman by a black man, and praised the Ku Klux Klan as the only agency that could assure the continuation of civilization and guarantee white supremacy. The book and the play, rooted in the question of black empowerment, further inflamed white minds about black sexuality and its evil consequences.

Sensationalistic journalism did the rest. Just before the riot, several newspapers ran special editions alerting readers to the "torrid wave of black lust and fiendishness" (there had allegedly been four recent rapes of white women in the city by black men).[17] On the night of September 22, 1906, a white man mounted a soapbox, held up one of the incendiary newspapers, and asked a gathering group if southern white men were going to tolerate such crimes. By midnight a crowd estimated at between 10,000 and 15,000 began to roam the streets of the city's black neighborhoods looking for victims. The governor immediately ordered 3,000 militiamen to Atlanta, but they largely ignored the white mob. Instead, they went to the Brownsville section of the city (an area of black colleges as well as the homes of many respectable black families) to disarm blacks. The militia rounded up professors and students and marched them through the streets of the city to prison. The riot continued for five days and, at its end, 25 blacks had died (at least four had been beaten to death) and approximately 150 had been wounded or injured. There was one white fatality.

The Atlanta Race Riot was important on several levels. News of the riot greatly alarmed blacks, especially educated blacks, because the city's black population was something of a model of what the race could accomplish as entrepreneurs and educators. The National Negro Business League had recently met in the city to highlight black progress in business, and the city's black college graduates were touted as pillars of refinement and respectability. One of those especially shocked by the event was Du Bois, who was a professor at Atlanta University when the violence occurred. In a sense, the riot radicalized him. As Painter described his reaction, "[He] interpreted the riot as a political and economic phenomenon that disillusioned him thoroughly about the prospects of racial harmony in the United States."[18] It also hardened his stance in opposition to Booker T. Washington. Du Bois viewed blacks in the riot as victims of white supremacy and became even more convinced that southern whites could not be trusted to protect the interests of southern blacks.

Two years later angry white citizens in Springfield, Illinois, attacked black residents after an alleged charge of sexual assault. The riot erupted when a white woman accused a well-known black man of attempting to rape her, a charge she later recanted. Although the police were able to prevent the accused man from being lynched, by actually sneaking him out of town, an enraged mob decided to attack the entire black community. After two nights of violence, in which the mob looted, burned, assaulted, and killed eight blacks, city authorities were forced to ask for the state militia to restore order. Although the identities of many of the leaders of the mob were known and 190 whites were indicted for participating in the riot, only two whites were convicted of any crime. The August 1908 riot, however, assumed historical importance. Occurring in Abraham Lincoln's hometown and burial place, it revealed that racially motivated white mob violence was no longer unique to the South. For many in the Niagara Movement, the Springfield Race Riot once again offered proof that accommodationism did not work.

The Creation of the NAACP

One of those appalled by the violence in Springfield was William English Walling, a well-known settlement house worker, labor leader, and socialist. After visiting Springfield in the aftermath of the riot and talking to white rioters who showed no remorse for their actions, Walling became convinced that the race war that had been confined to the South could spread to the North. Some national organization was needed to fight racial oppression. Walling began to correspond with other white liberals such as Mary White Ovington, who was completing a study titled *Half a Man: The Status of the Negro in New York* (1911), and Oswald Garrison Villard, an influential journalist and the grandson of abolitionist William Lloyd Garrison, concerning his idea for a new civil rights organization. Ultimately, it was Villard who drafted a call for like-minded individuals of both races to hold a national conference to discuss ways in which African American political and civil equality might be obtained. Issued in 1909, on the 100th anniversary of Lincoln's birth, the petition included the signatures of 60 activists. At the first meeting, held May 31 through June 1, 1909, some 300 men and women gathered to make plans for a permanent organization (one that would essentially absorb the Niagara Movement) that would become known as the National Association for the Advancement of Colored People (NAACP). The organizers also accepted a program of action, agreeing to work for equal education, black enfranchisement, enforcement of the Fourteenth and Fifteenth Amendments, and an end to all forced segregation.

One other important early decision taken by the organizers of the NAACP was to appoint Du Bois to be the director of publicity and research. In effect, Du Bois became the editor of *The Crisis*, the official magazine of the NAACP. For the next 20 years, he articulated the aims of the organization—condemning racial prejudice, segregation, disenfranchisement, lynching, and the denial of educational and economic opportunity for blacks—in a style laced with vituperation and sarcasm. *The Crisis* quickly made a connection with African Americans. Circulation of the magazine grew to 10,000 a month during the first year and climbed to 20,000 a month in the second. By 1913 there were 30,000 subscribers when the membership of the NAACP was only 3,000. Circulation reached 100,000 a month in 1918. About 80 percent of the readership was African American. By the time of America's entry into World War I, *The Crisis* was helping to generate a feeling of black pride and unity.

While African American leaders continued to attack white racism, they also began to celebrate the superior qualities of the black race. William Ferris, a black educator, wrote that blacks possessed "poetic imagination" and "a lovable nature, a spiritual earnestness and a musical genius." The Reverend Reverdy Ransom spoke about "the deep emotional nature" of blacks that underscored their innate religiosity. James Weldon Johnson described blacks as being "warmed by the poetic blood of Africa," which gave then "extreme rhythm, color, warmth, abandon, and movement." A black woman, said Johnson, with her "her rich coloring, her gaiety, her laughter and song" was more alluring than her "sallow, songless, lipless, hipless, tired-looking, tired moving white sister." Kelly Miller, a black college professor, wrote that the "Negro possesses patience, meekness, [and] forgiveness and spirit which surpasses that yet manifested by other races." As Southern has noted, the "belief in the saving grace of blackness led many blacks to the messianic conviction that African Americans had a mission to save America and the world from aggressive and grasping whites."[19]

The Birth of a Nation

The NAACP showed significant growth during the Progressive Era, expanding its membership to 6,000 in 1914 with 50 branches. After the appointment of James Weldon Johnson as field organizer in 1916, many new chapters of the NAACP were organized in the South and on the West Coast. By the end of World War I (aided by the appearance of the New Negro and increased black self-confidence), the association would grow to more than 80,000 members in 300 branches. Helping to boost membership in the NAACP was the controversy surrounding the release of *The Birth of a Nation* in 1915. The idea for the film came from Dixon's novel and stage melodrama *The Clansman*. The novel, as previously noted, glorified the Ku Klux Klan and ridiculed Black Reconstruction and the notion that blacks should be guaranteed political rights. The plot of the movie is wrapped in racism and the fear of sexual relations between blacks and whites. The epic silent film (it was completed in twelve reels, cost a staggering $110,000 to produce, and ran for two-and-one-half hours of screen time) focuses on the plight of a white southern family in South Carolina continuously victimized by black rapine: black soldiers loot their home, their daughter leaps to her death as she resists the advances of a black man, and the father is taken into custody by black troops for harboring a Klansman. Just as the family is about to be wiped out by blacks, they are rescued by the Klan (a moment in the film when white audiences cheered). Few white viewers could resist responding to the plight of this white family continually beset and threatened by cruel and lustful blacks. The film would gross over $18 million.

The release of the film provoked a variety of emotional responses from both blacks and whites. Du Bois editorialized in *The Crisis* that in the film, "the Negro [was] represented either as an ignorant fool, a vicious rapist, a venal or unscrupulous politician or a faithful but doddering idiot."[20] The NAACP was so outraged by the film that it sought to stop it from being distributed. At Boston's Tremont Theater, a crowd of black demonstrators led by *Boston Guardian* editor Monroe Trotter managed to get inside and pelt the screen with eggs. Trotter and 11 other blacks were arrested. The state of Ohio banned the film, as did Pasadena, California, and Wilmington, Delaware. Black protests over the film occurred in Atlantic City, Chicago, Milwaukee, Pittsburgh, Spokane, and Portland, Oregon. Even the moderate Booker T. Washington fought the film before his death that same year. Although the NAACP was able to bring about some minor cuts of objectionable scenes, the public's overwhelming enthusiasm for the film smothered most criticism. Ironically, the protest campaign led by the NAACP probably drew more viewers to the film. Black protest did, however, raise black consciousness, and NAACP membership increased sharply.

Some white reaction to *The Birth of a Nation* was extreme. An infuriated white man in Lafayette, Indiana, killed a young black man after watching the film. In Houston, Texas, viewers shouted "Lynch him!" during a scene in which a black man pursues the film's star, Lillian Gish. One white viewer stated upon leaving the theater, "It makes me want to go out and kill the first Negro I see." Southern audiences "wept, yelled, whooped, cheered" and on one occasion actually shot at the screen in an attempt to save Little Sister from Gus the rapist. At the film's premier in Spartanburg, South Carolina, audiences were "almost hysterical."[21] In St. Louis, white real estate agents stood in front of the theater to hand out circulars calling for residential segregation.

The Revival of the Ku Klux Klan

The premier of *The Birth of a Nation* in 1915 was not the only sensational event that summer that had an impact on race relations. The other was the brutal lynching of Leo M. Frank, who had been tried and convicted of murdering a 14-year-old girl named Mary Phagan in 1913. Frank had grown up in Brooklyn, New York. After graduating from Cornell University as a mechanical engineer, he moved to Atlanta in 1907 to become the manager of a factory owned by the northern-based National Pencil Company. He had quickly become a respected member of the Jewish community in that city. Phagan was a worker at the factory. Although Frank was convicted and given the death sentence, evidence strongly suggested that another worker at the factory, not Frank, had committed the crime. In 1915 Governor John Slaton, a former lawyer who was deeply troubled by the inconsistent evidence presented at the trial, decided to reduce Frank's sentence from death to life in prison. When his action became known to the public, 25 men who called themselves the Knights of Mary Phagan took Frank out of the penitentiary and hanged him.

During the trial, Atlanta newspapers printed fabricated stories about Frank's alleged sexual perversions and treated the trial more like an interracial rape than a white-on-white murder. Historian Joel Williamson has suggested that Frank was murdered at a time when southerners had come to fear new threats to their social order that he defined as "hidden blackness, the blackness within seeming whiteness." He argued that southerners "began to look with great suspicion upon mulattoes who looked white, white people who behaved as black, and a whole congeries of aliens [Jews, Catholics, labor organizers] insidious in their midst who would destroy their...moral universe." Frank fit the new profile. "He stood for the alien menace to the South, and the alien menace stood for blacks."

As a result, Frank was "killed as a surrogate for the black beast rapist."[22] Fascinated by the public response to *The Birth of a Nation* and engrossed in the Frank case and the "exploits" of the Knights of Mary Phagan was William J. Simmons, a lay preacher, salesman, and promoter of fraternal orders. Seeking to recapture the allure of heroic fraternal associations, he appointed himself the imperial wizard of a resurrected Ku Klux Klan in 1915. The second Klan, like the first, stressed the idea of white brotherhood and utilized regalia, rituals, and exotic titles as part of its appeal. But unlike the Reconstruction era organization, the modern, twentieth-century Klan was now rabidly antiforeign, anti-Catholic, and anti-Semitic as well as anti-black. It also reached deep into the Midwest and West with its message of imminent foreign dangers and the need to stand against the corruption of morality that supposedly came with immigration and any effort to promote or protect blacks and other nonwhites.

Despite the virulent racism that seemed to be prevalent in mainstream white society, the NAACP was able to achieve some small but encouraging successes during its first decade. It conducted a persistent crusade against lynching, and started to gain the support of many whites for a federal anti-lynching law (as noted previously, an NAACP-backed anti-lynching bill passed the House in the early 1920s only to be defeated in the Senate). In 1917 Du Bois and James Weldon Johnson led a silent march down Fifth Avenue in New York City to protest the East St. Louis Race Riot. In addition, the organization's ongoing investigation of lynching led to the publication of a significant historical document, *Thirty Years of Lynching, 1889–1918* (1919). *The Crisis* also exposed the horrors of numerous race riots that occurred during and immediately after World War I. The NAACP, through its Legal Redress Committee, also won victories in two civil rights cases before the U.S. Supreme Court. The first, *Guinn v. United States* (1915), declared unconstitutional a grandfather clause in the Oklahoma state constitution; and the second, *Buchanan v. Warley* (1917) invalidated a Louisville ordinance requiring racial segregation in residential areas. Although the victories were small, they did offer hope that legal action through the courts might become an effective weapon in the fight for full citizenship.

Marcus Garvey: Black Nationalism and Black Separatism

Although the NAACP had recorded significant growth in its membership and *The Crisis* had gained an impressive readership by 1920, the organization had failed to enlist the masses. Many blacks at the lower socioeconomic level seemed inclined to regard the NAACP as an agency controlled by upper-class blacks and liberal whites. It was this very feeling that made possible the rise of Marcus Garvey. Garvey, a native of Jamaica, seemed to undergo a life-changing experience after reading Booker T. Washington's autobiography, *Up From Slavery* (1901). He especially liked Washington's practicality, his emphasis on self-help, and his interest in encouraging black business. After founding the Universal Negro Improvement Association (UNIA) in Jamaica in 1914, Garvey moved to New York City in 1916 and established a chapter of his organization there a year later. Arriving at a time of increased anti-black rioting and the influx of large numbers of working-class blacks to urban ghettos such as Harlem, Garvey promised to transform racial segregation to the benefit of black people. He did this by stressing two ideas— black nationalism and black separatism.

To promote black nationalism, Garvey encouraged blacks who were suffering from frustration and despair to develop a positive self-image, and offered them encouragement: "Up, you mighty race, you can accomplish what you will!"[23] To foster a feeling of racial pride and individual self-worth, Garvey exalted everything black, which he asserted stood for strength and beauty, not inferiority. He told blacks that they had a noble past and should be proud of their ancestry. Garvey's UNIA established the *Negro World*, which would become the most widely read black newspaper in America, and established its own church (African Orthodox), its own women's group (Black Cross nurses), its own marching society, and its own labor union. It operated its own businesses (a chain of cooperative grocery stores, a steam laundry, a tailor and dressmaking shop, a printing plant, and a restaurant) and industries (a factory that produced uniforms, hats, and shirts for UNIA members, and another that manufactured black dolls). The UNIA claimed to employ over 1,000 black people. UNIA members paid monthly dues of 35 cents. In return, they received modest sickness and death benefits, and the satisfaction of promoting racial solidarity.

The second part of Garvey's credo was black separatism. In his mind, plans for interracial cooperation were a waste of time. Because racial prejudice was so embedded in the dominant white culture, blacks would never achieve any true sense of equality or justice in American society. To Garvey, blacks and whites simply had separate destinies. As a result, he believed that blacks could achieve power and dignity only if they left the United States and relocated to Africa to build their own country. Central to the realization of that dream was the Black Star shipping company, created by the UNIA through the sale of stocks at $5 a share. In 1919 the company purchased its first ship, with which it intended to commercially link the three parts of the black world—the United States, the West Indies, and Africa—and transport black people to new homes in Africa. Garvey even offered his followers a three-colored flag—red ("the color of the blood men must shed for their liberty"), black ("the color of the noble race to which we belong"), and green ("for the luxuriant vegetation of our Motherland"). One young black man remembered watching a UNIA parade in the early 1920s. "They came with much shouting and blare of bugles and a forest of flags—a black star centered in a red field. They made speeches in the vacant lot where carnivals used to spread their tents. They had a huge, colorful parade, and young women, tensely sober of mien and plain even in their uniforms, distributed millions of streamers bearing the slogan 'Back to Africa.'"[24]

Eventually, attacks by the more educated black establishment and harassment by the federal government (J. Edgar Hoover and the FBI considered Garvey a dangerous unifier of urban, working-class blacks and a threat to the racial status quo) led to Garvey's downfall in 1922. He was indicted on mail fraud, sent to prison, and eventually deported. But the effect that Garvey's program had on uneducated blacks and rural migrants recently arrived in the big city was magnetic. The UNIA claimed to have a million members by 1920, and even Garvey's harshest critics conceded that his organization had at least half that number. Garvey's real importance, however, was the way he galvanized the black masses behind a program of hope in the midst of despair. He encouraged blacks to join together in a common cause and told them that they should feel pride in their heritage. He also offered blacks the hope—or illusion—that their daily lives could change for the better.

THE SEARCH FOR BLACK AUTONOMY

The Church

Historian John Hope Franklin has commented that it was "more important for Negroes to maintain a separate existence socially and culturally than it was for them to do so economically" during the late nineteenth and early twentieth century.[25] As whites in the South, and to a considerable degree in the North, distanced themselves from the everyday lives of blacks, black Americans had to create their own agencies to cope with oppression. One of these was the church, which offered a way to maintain group solidarity and served as a means for self-help. Ever since emancipation blacks had established their own congregations and denominations, and their manner of worshipping increasingly took on a style that blended their African and American heritage. Most African Americans attended small southern rural churches, and most churches could not afford to pay for a full-time preacher. But it was, as one observer noted in 1913, "the only institution which the Negro may call his own."

A new Church may be built, a new pastor installed, new members received and all the machinery of the church set in motion without even consulting any white person. In a word, the church is the Negro's own institution, developing according to his own standards, and more nearly than anything else represents the real life of the race.[26]

Worshippers in these rural churches adopted an emotional style of prayer, and the preachers who presided over those kinds of services were very popular. Although many black intellectuals criticized the poor educational backgrounds and lack of professionalism exhibited by much of the black clergy, most African Americans seemed unconcerned. As one observer of black churches in rural Georgia noted in 1903, "The church which does not have its shouting, the church which does not measure the abilities of a preacher by the 'rousement' of his sermons, and indeed does not tacitly demand of its minister the shout-producing discourse, is an exception to the rule."[27] Even when many African Americans migrated to northern cities, they often rejected the more formal black churches and sought worship in the more intimate Pentecostal and Holiness services. Many chose to attend revival meetings. The evidence seems to support the conclusion that blacks, like many white Pentecostals, continued to worship in an emotional style that they found most satisfying.

Mutual Aid Societies

African Americans also supported a number of social organizations and mutual aid societies that contributed to their sense of group autonomy. In the state of Georgia, the Masons had more than 10,000 black male members prior to World War I, the Colored Knights of Pythias had 15,000, and the Grand Order of Odd Fellows had 33,000. The Odd Fellows occupied a large office building in Atlanta with its own auditorium and maintained a $300,000 revolving loan fund to help members start a business or buy a home. Lodges and fraternal orders were just as important to the black population in the North. In New York City in 1909, 35 percent of black families claimed some fraternal affiliation. Similar organizations for black women included the Order of the Eastern Star and the Sisters of Calanthe. Other societies—such as the International Order of Good Samaritans, the Grand United Order of True Reformers, and the Independent Order of St. Luke—offered insurance against sickness and death, assisted widows, and provided further opportunities for social interaction.

These various African American lodges supplied a small measure of economic security to black people, many of whom were struggling just to get by. Orphanages, homes for the elderly, hospitals, and sanitariums were also established in many communities and maintained solely by blacks. The Tennessee Orphanage and Industrial School at Nashville, the Carrie Steele Orphanage at Atlanta, and the Pickford Tuberculosis Sanitarium at Southern Pines, North Carolina, were all supported in whole or in large part from funds raised among blacks. Denied common schools by state governments in the South, blacks built their own, and they often supported those schools with little or no state money. In 1915 Georgia's county school boards owned 208 school buildings for black students, but African Americans in the state owned 1,544. In addition, black YMCAs and YWCAs (Young Men's [and Women's] Christian Association) sponsored recreational programs for black youths, and black-owned newspapers offered community news that was excluded from the white press and served as a forum for the discussion of racially charged issues. Taken as a whole, black institutions fostered group self-reliance and enabled black people to contest white supremacy.

Music: The Blues

Another means to confront experiences common in the lives of many working men and women was to embrace a new form of music—the blues. Blues musician W. C. Handy said that he had first heard the blues as a musical form around 1903 in the Delta region of Mississippi, but others who understood the blues as a state of mind dismissed the idea that anyone created the blues at a specific point in time. One New Orleans blues fiddler commented, "The blues? Ain't no first blues! The blues always been."[28] The roots of the blues can be found in the religious music and work songs of African Americans that drew from a common store of expression and feelings. But the blues were deeper, more immediate, more gripping, and more painful. As Ishman Bracey, who grew up in Hinds County, Mississippi, sang, "I've been down so long, Lawd, down don't worry me."[29] In the early twentieth century, the blues (distinguished by its three-line verse with an AAB rhyme scheme) could be heard on street corners and in cafés; at house parties, country dances and fish fries; and in turpentine and lumber work camps.

Those who played for money traveled the circuit of "joints," roadhouses, dance halls, cabarets, and honky-tonks that dotted the southern landscape. Most of the men and women who played and sang the blues were poor, without property, and illiterate. Constantly on the move, they had a strong desire to enjoy freedom of movement and freedom of expression. As historian Leon Litwack has noted, they valued being "free of a labor system that tied others (including their families) to the land through violence, coercion, and the law." Those who sang or played the blues stirred things up. Some found the new music frightening, threatening, and subversive. Many middle-class blacks resented the primitive stereotypes that the blues seemed to reinforce. Many churchgoers found the blues blasphemous and called it the devil's music. Others, however, embraced the new genre. The blues examined the daily occurrences that preoccupied many southern blacks, and did so on a very personalized level. Everyone could relate to the subject matter of the songs—the pain of loneliness, dislocation, or loss; being unfaithful in love; the indignity of underpaid labor; the ruination that might accompany natural disasters such as boll weevils and floods; poverty; escape through drink and drugs; legal inequities; and the constant threat of violence and death. The musicians, as they reflected and philosophized, connected with their audiences through shared experiences. As one Texas bluesman sang in 1915, "There's lots of trouble here, and more on down the road. You will always find trouble, no matter where you go."[30]

There was a racial dimension to blues music as well. Blues performers could express themselves lyrically with a directness that whites would not tolerate in public. Those who sang the blues "had a way of using humor and wit, images and metaphors, to unmask the society around them, to explore forbidden subjects, to subvert prevailing values and faiths, and to suggest ways of working out difficulties. The best of them had a liberating effect on their audiences, if only because they echoed shared concerns, questions, and sensibilities." Occasionally, a song might confront segregation or white duplicity directly. In one song a blues singer turns segregation on its head.

> Well, I'm goin' to buy me a little railroad of my own;
>   Ain't goin' to let nobody ride but the chocolate to the bone.
> Well, I goin' to buy me a hotel of my own;
>   Ain't goin' to let nobody eat but the chocolate to the bone."

In another song, a blues singer expresses his frustration at being cheated by his white employer.

> I asked that boss-man for to gimme my time;
>   Sez he, 'Ole Nigger, you're a day behin'.'
> I asked him once, I asked him twaist;
>   Ef I ask him again, I'll take his life.

Such tunes allowed black southerners to confront accumulated frustrations and betrayed expectations. As Litwack aptly put it, to listen to the blues is to feel "the despair, the thoughts, the passions, the aspirations, the anxieties, the deferred dreams, the frightening honesty of a new generation of black Southerners and their efforts to grapple with day-to-day life, to make it somehow more bearable, perhaps even transcend it."[31]

Race Pride: The Triumph of Jack Johnson

One major event in the popular culture of the early twentieth century that enabled tens of thousands of black Americans to vicariously experience triumph over whites and, for just a moment, to exorcise the frustration and bitterness that surrounded a lifetime of insults was the triumph of boxer Jack Johnson over Jim Jeffries in 1910. Born in Galveston, Texas, in 1878, Johnson became a professional boxer in 1897. Between 1902 and 1907, he won 57 bouts against both white and black fighters. In 1908 he defeated white heavyweight champion Tommy Burns, a Canadian, in a match in Australia. Many white fight fans immediately began looking for a "great white hope" to defeat Johnson. They thought they had found their man in Jeffries, a former champion, who they coaxed out of retirement to fight Johnson in Reno, Nevada, on July 4, 1910. Billed as "the fight of the century," the Johnson-Jeffries bout attracted national attention, and its implications in a racially conscious America were obvious. "That portion of the white race that has been looking to me to defend its athletic superiority," said Jeffries, "may feel assured that I am fit to do my very best." Equally

Boxer Jack Johnson looking dapper in
bowler hat and vested suit, 1909. (Courtesy of the Library of Congress)

cognizant of the moment, Johnson remarked, "[I]t was my own
honor, and in a degree the honor of my race."[32] The outdoor match,
fought before 20,000 spectators in blistering afternoon heat ended
in the 15th round when Johnson knocked out Jeffries.

Blacks celebrated. In Chicago, Johnson's home town, people
poured into the streets in Chicago's black neighborhoods, bang-
ing on pots and pans, blowing horns, and chanting the champion's
name. Hundreds of revelers pinned the front page of the Chicago
American to their clothing with the headline "JOHNSON WINS"
spelled out in big red letters above the fighter's picture. Blacks living in the poor southern Illinois coal mining town of Du Quoin
heard the news "from a group of running, shouting men" who had
been waiting for the results of the fight at the local newspaper office.
"The Negroes were jubilant," remembered a black woman who had
been a young girl at the time. "Everybody wanted to buy someone
else a dinner, a glass of beer, or a shot of whiskey.... The older people
laughed and cried, and the children danced around and knocked
each other about in good fun. Grandma Thompson...raised her
quivering voice in song. We all joined in. 'Hallelujah, hallelujah,

the storm is passing over, hallelujah!'" Poet William Waring Cuney recalled how his family felt when they got the news in his poem "My Lord What a Morning."

> O, My Lord
> What a morning,
> O My lord,
> What a feeling,
> When Jack Johnson
> Turned Jim Jeffries'
> Snow-White Face,
> to the Ceiling.[33]

One black woman was seen carefully removing her hat before boarding a train in Reno. Asked why, she responded, "Cause I wants everybody to know that I'm a nigger, that's why, and I'm proud of it."[34] A black newspaper in Richmond, Virginia, headlined the event in bold type and then editorially commented that "no event in forty years has given more genuine satisfaction to the colored people of this country."[35] Back in Chicago, hundreds of policemen were kept on call in case of trouble. They were not needed. "It's their night," said the officer in charge, "Let them have their fun."[36] It was a rare triumph in an era of crushing and often humiliating defeats.

In other sections of the country, however, there was trouble. To many whites, Johnson symbolized the uppity, lustful, menacing black man that their culture had taught them to fear. A Richmond, Virginia, newspaper advised that anyone who imagined himself Jack Johnson would get an awful beating. Word of Johnson's victory set off race riots. There were racial confrontations in Chattanooga, Columbus, Los Angeles, Norfolk, New York, Pittsburgh, Philadelphia, St. Louis, and Washington, D.C., to name only a few. In Clarksburg, West Virginia, a mob of more than 1,000 whites raged through black neighborhoods. In Houston a white man slit a black man's throat just because he had cheered for Johnson. In Wheeling, West Virginia, when a white mob came upon a black man driving a fancy automobile, as Johnson was known for doing, the man was dragged out of the driver's seat and lynched. There was one story that when a young black man entered a diner in Evansville, Indiana, and ordered "a cup of coffee as strong as Jack Johnson and a steak beat up like Jeffries," the white owner shot him five times.[37] On Canal Street in New Orleans, a 10-year-old boy named Louis Armstrong was told to run for his life. At least 11 and perhaps as many as 26 black people would die before violent emotions finally died down.

There were, however, further repercussions from the fight. Congress banned the showing of films of the Reno match. Two years after the championship fight, the New York State Boxing Commission outlawed bouts between black and white fighters. Jack Johnson's personal actions did not help. He continued to spend his money on big, fast cars and openly flaunted his freewheeling lifestyle. He then did what was unforgiveable to many white people: he divorced his black wife and married a white woman in 1911. Several months later, apparently overcome by social ostracism and unceasing public attention, she committed suicide. After Johnson married a second white woman, there was an outcry for laws prohibiting interracial marriages. Looking to discredit Johnson as they had Garvey, the intelligence division of the federal government searched for incriminating evidence to be used against him. In 1913 an all-white jury convicted Johnson of violating the Mann Act, the federal statute that made it illegal to transport women across state lines for immoral purposes. Although there was no evidence of abduction, Johnson was sentenced to a year in jail and fined $1,000. Rather than serve the term, Johnson fled to Canada and then to Europe. At the end of 1914, Johnson agreed to a title fight the next year in Havana, Cuba, against the new "white hope," Jess Willard. Johnson lost the match in the 26th round in a fight that many thought that Johnson threw. He returned to the United States in 1920 and served a 10-month prison sentence. Despite all the scandal, Johnson never stopped being adored by many black people as the hero of his race.

Black Reform Organizations

African Americans united in still other ways. Although whites generally excluded them from the Progressive movement, blacks routinely created their own reform agencies. When many white leaders in the National American Woman Suffrage Association stressed expediency as a tactic and showed a willingness to accept segregation in the South to obtain broader support for woman suffrage, black activists such as Ida Wells (now Wells-Barnett) took offense. Suffrage achieved by condoning segregation, she believed, would leave black women as disenfranchised as black men. Unwilling to participate in an organization that adhered to a double standard, Wells-Barnett founded the Alpha Suffrage Club in Chicago in 1913, the first African American woman suffrage association in Illinois. In addition to her ongoing crusade against lynching,

Wells-Barnett organized the Negro Fellowship League (NFL) in 1910 and encouraged members to actively engage themselves in social service. The NFL established an African American settlement house in the Chicago ghetto. One of the center's functions was to serve as an employment bureau to assist the increasing number of black migrants from the South in finding work. After accepting a patronage position as a probation officer for the Chicago Municipal Court, Wells-Barnett used her appointment to draw attention to racial abuses in the criminal justice system. Concerned about the treatment of black prisoners, the NFL appointed "jail visitors" who would meet with inmates at the various correctional facilities.

Two other organizations concerned about urban conditions were the National Urban League established in 1910 and the YMCA/ YWCA. The Urban League worked to help rural black migrants adjust to living in an urban environment and to find jobs for them, improve housing and medical care, and establish recreational facilities for black residents living in segregated sections of the city. It also assisted young people who were having trouble with the law by creating the Big Brother and Big Sister programs. Operating primarily in large northern cities, the Urban League established 27 chapters by 1918. Forced to create their own separate YMCAs, blacks used the organizations to teach young men how to lead healthy and moral lives and to help them develop leadership and organizational skills. The YMCAs also duplicated many of the functions of settlement houses and cooperated with black churches in social work activities. The YWCAs followed a similar path and were often led by women who were leaders in the black women's club movement.

Black women played a major role in social reform work. As mentioned previously, black club women, who were by-and-large excluded from white women's clubs, founded the NACW in 1896. Although the NACW's initial focus was on improving the "image" of black women, it broadened its agenda in the early twentieth century to address the "structures of oppression" that impacted all blacks.[38] The association campaigned for woman suffrage, public health, day care for working women, prison reform, the adoption of a juvenile court system, better schools and better pay for black teachers, playgrounds for children, improved working conditions, and an end to both the convict leasing system and lynching. By 1916 the NACW could claim more than 100,000 members in its numerous state and local affiliates. Similar activity took place in the South. One excellent example was the work of Lugenia Burns

Hope, who founded the Neighborhood Union in Atlanta in 1908. The Neighborhood Union worked to improve health and operated an anti-tuberculosis clinic. It also established kindergartens, playgrounds, day-care centers, and outreach programs for young women, and it mobilized assistance for the sick and the elderly. Hope led a crusade against overcrowded black public schools, and joined white reformers in trying to close saloons and houses of prostitution along Decatur Street in Atlanta. Under Hope's direction, the Neighborhood Union became an organizational model for other black communities.

The Great Migration

A crucial event in American history was the migration of more than 500,000 blacks from the South to the North in the years surrounding World War I. Although there had been an ongoing out-migration of blacks from the South to the North ever since the end of Reconstruction (200,000 blacks moved north between 1890 and 1900), that process accelerated after 1914 (roughly 250,000 black southerners moved north between 1915 and mid-1917) and eventually became what historians have called the Great Migration. It was a process that would begin to shift the majority of the black population out of the South and make race relations a truly national problem. When the outbreak of World War I effectively ended European immigration, the demand for workers increased. As word spread that there were jobs to be had in the cities of the North, blacks moved to enter an industrial labor market from which they had been largely excluded. By 1920 there would be over 900,000 black industrial workers, nearly double the 1910 total. Although the black population in the North was becoming widely dispersed in a number of towns and cities in Illinois, Ohio, Pennsylvania, New York, and Michigan, the largest numbers went to Chicago (65,000—an increase of 150%), Detroit (35,000—an increase of over 600%), Cleveland (26,000—an increase of over 300%), and Akron (where the increase was almost 750%). Pushed out of the South by poverty, discrimination, and persistent racial violence, and pulled to the North by the promise of greater economic opportunity, better education, and more freedom, blacks increasingly decided to make the move. For some, it involved a question of dignity as well. As one migrant wrote, "I should have been here twenty years ago. I just begin to feel like a man.... My children are going to the same school with the whites and I don't have to humble to no one. I have registered. Will vote in the next election and there isn't any yes Sir and no Sir. It's all yes and no, Sam and Bill."[39]

Many white southerners assumed that blacks were contented and that they were leaving only because of unscrupulous labor agents and radical agitators. Labor recruiters from northern industries did assist the process by offering free railroad passes, guaranteed jobs, and the promise of good wages. Henry Ford even sent special trains to bring black workers to Detroit. "Radical" northern newspapers such as the *Chicago Defender* encouraged blacks to migrate, and black railroad porters distributed thousands of copies of the newspaper throughout the South. But the real key to migration north was spontaneity. Contemporary observers especially took note of the lack of support for the idea from southern black leaders. "The movement," noted one individual, "is without organization or opportunities. The Negroes just quietly move away without taking their recognized leaders into their confidence any more than they do the white people about them." An article that appeared in the *Dallas Express* underscored the same point. "The strangest thing, the real mystery about the exodus," noted the writer, "is that in all the southland there has not been a single meeting or promoter to start the migration. Just simultaneously all over the South about a year ago, the Negro began to cross the Mason-Dixon line."[40] As Alain Locke noted in the preface to *The New Negro* (1925), the new black migrants, primarily young men and women, brought with them "a new vision of opportunity, of social and economic freedom."[41]

The Hope of Racial Progress

For many blacks, however, the hope of finding security and acceptance proved disappointing. What awaited many migrants were segregated urban slums, restricted employment opportunities, low-paying jobs, discrimination, and white resentment. The influx of poor, uneducated sharecroppers and tenant farmers caused the black populations of numerous northern cities to double almost at once, heightening social tensions in the process. Soon, newspapers such as the *New York Times* were featuring articles with titles including "Harmful Rush of Negro Workers to the North," and making a case that the migration was creating a labor shortage in the South, generating unwanted labor competition in the North, and contributing to residential overcrowding and racial tension. As one historian noted, "Even under the best of circumstances, the surge of southern immigrants would have strained the resources and social

cohesion of any city."[42] Worried about the effects of the black migration, the governor of Minnesota expressed his own apprehension
and stated, "The government must stop the movement of Negros
[sic] into this section at once. I shudder to think of the consequences
if this is not done."[43] The fear of racial violence implicit in the governor's comment was soon validated. The first in a series of major
race riots occurred in East St. Louis in July of 1917 for reasons
related to overcrowding, job competition, and threats to labor standards (unionization). Officially, at least 39 blacks and 8 whites died
in the rioting that was especially violent, but the number of deaths
was probably much higher. Smaller race riots broke out in Chester,
Pennsylvania, and in Philadelphia later that same month. Outraged
by the violence, the NAACP staged a march down Fifth Avenue
in New York City in which 8,000 black people wearing black arm-
bands marched in silent protest.

When the United States entered World War I in the spring of
1917 and President Wilson proclaimed that it would be a crusade
to "make the world safe for democracy," many black leaders, like
many white progressives, imagined the positive results that might
occur. There was a feeling among some black leaders that the war
might raise American consciousness about the denial of democracy
at home and be a catalyst for racial change. Even a racial skeptic such
as Du Bois took the optimistic position that the war could advance
the cause of civil rights for African Americans. "Out of this war will
rise," he stated, "an American Negro with a right to vote and a right
to work and a right to live without insult."[44] In a famous editorial
that appeared in *The Crisis* in July 1918 titled "Close Ranks," Du
Bois advised blacks to forget their grievances and join with whites
in a common undertaking.

The treatment of black soldiers during the war quickly belied the
hopes for racial progress. Draft boards inducted blacks at higher
rates than whites and offered them fewer exemptions. The navy
accepted only 5,000 blacks as sailors and immediately put them
to work at menial jobs. The marines refused to accept any blacks.
The army segregated black soldiers in training camps, provided
them with inferior facilities, training, and equipment, and offered
them few of the new social services available to whites. White men
refused to salute black officers, and black officers were denied
admission to officer's clubs. Military authorities did not intend to
use blacks in combat, planning instead to use them in labor squads,
as stevedores, on road construction projects, and as cooks and
dishwashers. Only after pressure from organizations such as the
NAACP did military authorities relent and assign black soldiers

a combat role (of the more than 380,000 black men who served in World War I, only 42,000 saw action in combat in the main theater of the war in Europe). The army told black soldiers not to fraternize with French women, and advised the French people not to treat blacks as equals. Black military units were not allowed to partici-pate in the Allied victory parade in Paris, and black troops returned home on segregated ships.

Similar treatment confronted black soldiers who remained in the United States during the war. Black soldiers of the Third Battalion, 24th Infantry assigned to guard a training camp under construction near Houston, Texas, in the summer of 1917 found that wearing a uniform offered them no protection against racial discrimination. Harassed by local police, constantly insulted by local white and Hispanic residents who made them the targets of racial epithets, and indignant at the city's rigid segregation policy, a number of the seasoned black soldiers soon reached the limit of their patience. After a rumor spread that a black soldier from their battalion had been killed by police (he had actually been beaten but not seriously injured) while trying to visit another soldier who had been arrested for trying to stop a police officer from beating a black woman, some black soldiers decided to retaliate. After stealing ammunition from a supply tent, about 100 black soldiers then marched into town, where they exchanged gunfire with police and local residents. At the end of the three-hour riot, 16 white and Hispanic residents, along with 4 black soldiers and 2 black civilians, were dead. Court martial proceedings soon followed. The army tried 156 black sol-diers for disobeying orders, aggravated assault, mutiny, and mur-der, and sentenced 13 to death and 41 to lengthy prison sentences. The 13 soldiers were hanged in December 1917 before they had an opportunity to appeal their death sentences.

The Houston Race Riot reminded many black people of a similar incident that had taken place in Brownsville, Texas, in 1906, when a group of black soldiers, frustrated and angry at the verbal abuse shown them by local residents, engaged in a riot in which one white man was killed and two others were wounded. Although the cause of the riot was not clearly determined (black soldiers refused to testify against other members of their unit), President Theodore Roosevelt ordered that all 167 members of three companies be dis-honorably discharged. It seemed to blacks an unjust punishment for a crime that had been adjudicated primarily as a violation of the South's racial code (and 66 years later, the secretary general of the U.S. Army would grant honorable discharges to the men). Many African Americans saw the Houston soldiers as martyrs, and regarded the swiftness of the military trial and the speed of the executions as another example of Jim Crow justice. The incident seemed to make a sham of all talk of democracy and improved race relations.

The end of the war brought an increased incidence of racial violence in the form of lynchings and race riots. Sixty-two blacks died at the hands of lynch mobs in 1918. One year later, 83 lynchings took place, the highest number recorded since 1903. At least 10 of the victims were black soldiers, some still in uniform, only recently returned from the war. Twenty-five major race riots broke out in 1919. The largest race riot in a year that James Weldon Johnson called the Red Summer (because of all the African American blood that was shed in anti-black, urban riots) took place in Chicago. The city was a microcosm of racial tensions. The recent surge in the number of black residents had created a severe shortage of residential housing. As ghetto-trapped blacks looked for better housing in white neighborhoods, whites formed neighborhood associations and vowed to keep them out. Job competition intensified racial animosities. Roughly 90 percent of white workers in the city were unionized, whereas 75 percent of black workers were not. Some two dozen bombings of black homes had occurred between 1917 and 1919, and there had been a number of racial gang fights and shootings prior to the riot.

The riot started on Sunday, July 27, 1919, ironically one day after black troops were welcomed home with a parade down Michigan Avenue. Five black boys on a homemade raft had inadvertently floated past an invisible boundary that separated white and black bathing areas. When white bathers saw the black swimmers, they threw stones at them, and one boy drowned. A false rumor then spread that an Irish policeman had prevented anyone from attempting to rescue the injured youth. The incident touched off a week of violence in which 23 blacks and 15 whites were killed. More than 500 people were injured, and nearly 1,000 families, mostly black, were left homeless. What many people noticed about the Chicago Race Riot, however, was that blacks fought back. Poet Claude McKay tried to capture what he thought was a new black spirit in a hymn "to besieged black manhood" titled "If We Must Die."

> If we must die, let it not be like hogs
> Hunted and penned in an inglorious spot....
> Like men we'll face the murderous, cowardly pack,
> Pressed to the wall, dying, but fighting back![45]

By the end of the war, black leaders who had supported American entry into the conflict had become deeply embittered by the overall treatment of African Americans. Looking back on his earlier statements from the vantage point of 1930, Du Bois confessed that he was too zealous and naïve in supporting America's entry into World War I and for encouraging black people to "close ranks."

I was swept off my feet during the world war by the emotional response of America to what seemed to be a great call to duty. The thing that I did not understand is how easy and inevitable it is for an appeal to blood and force to smash to utter negation any ideal for which it is used. Instead of a war to end war, or a war to save democracy, we found ourselves during and after the war descending to the meanest and most sordid of selfish actions.[46]

Du Bois could see that black loyalty and sacrifice during the war had not lessened white racism. In May 1919, he wrote a strident editorial in *The Crisis* in which he characterized the United States as a "shameful land" because "It *lynches*. . . . It *disfranchises* its own citizens. . . . It encourages *ignorance*. . . . It *steals* from us. . . . It *insults* us. . . ." Concluding his editorial, Du Bois defiantly announced, "We *return*. We *return from fighting*. We *return fighting*. Make way for Democracy! We saved it in France, and by the Great Jehovah, we will save it in the U.S.A., or know the reason why."[47]

The New Negro

Numerous historians have argued that the international experience gained by African American soldiers broadened their horizons. Although badly treated in the American army, black soldiers were warmly received by the French. That experience taught them that there were limits to American racism. Black soldiers also encountered people of African descent, either serving in colonial armies or as civilians living in France or Great Britain. Conversations with Africans and West Indians broadened their conceptions of race. Like other white soldiers, they had the sense that they were participating in a moral crusade to make political justice and democracy a reality around the world. They had made their contribution as soldiers, they had served their country despite the obstacles placed in their way, and now they felt entitled to be treated like full citizens. Even black leaders who did not support the war believed that black participation militarily had earned the race some legitimacy in American society. In a real sense, the war had both enlightened the black soldier and given him a sense of self-worth.

This new feeling was evident in New York City and to the nation at large when New York's 15th Infantry regiment returned from Europe. Starting as an organization of black volunteers, the unit had been called into service in July 1917. After suffering the usual indignities accorded black soldiers and the army's reluctance to utilize black troops for combat, the unit was attached to the French Army as the 369th regiment. During the course of the war, the regiment established an outstanding record of valor in combat, serving in the trenches for 191 days. The entire unit was awarded the Croix de Guerre for its action in battle, and 171 men were awarded the Legion of Honor for exceptional bravery. Their victory parade in New York City on February 17, 1919, symbolized something more than just the return of soldiers from the war. It was a proud day for the soldiers, but also for the thousands of black New Yorkers who came out to cheer them. Led by Lt. James Reece Europe's marching band, which had made itself and American jazz music famous in France, they marched up Fifth Avenue under banners proclaiming their heroism. As the parade made its way up to Harlem, the crowds went wild. Caught up in the enthusiasm, it would have been possible to think that this martial and manly spirit would last, that white Americans would no longer be able to treat them as less than men and full citizens. As Nathan Irvin Huggins has commented, "The irony was considerable. Among other things, the post-war years saw a spectacular revival of racism; the new Ku Klux Klan found white support throughout the country, and violence against Negroes increased. Apparently, white Americans believed in the New Negro as much as black Americans did; he was a threat to one as much as a hope to the other."[48]

After the end of World War I, African American "radicals" such as Du Bois, who edited *The Crisis*; A. Philip Randolph and Chandler Owen, who published the socialist *Messenger*; and Garvey, who used the *Negro World* as the voice of the UNIA, became increasingly outspoken that a "new style" Negro was emerging. He was self-assertive. He would no longer accept an insult or turn the other cheek. When confronted with violence, he would, as he would demonstrate in Chicago in 1919, fight back. Sensing this new spirit, Garvey boasted in a 1920 speech that "the Negro of yesterday has disappeared from the scene of human activities and his place taken by a new Negro who stands erect, conscious of his manhood rights and fully determined to preserve them at all costs."[49] Helping to develop this new race consciousness were the black newspapers—such as the

New York *Crusader*, the Pittsburgh *Courier*, the *Cleveland Gazette*, the *Chicago Defender*, the Washington *Colored American*, the Indianapolis *Freeman*, and the *Boston Guardian*—that had become beacons to the black populations in northern cities. *The Crisis*, which reached a circulation of 100,000 at this time, and *Opportunity*, published by the National Urban League, were also very influential and would be key in promoting the development of the Harlem Renaissance of the 1920s. The spirit of the New Negro, and the developing racial consciousness, also led to the rapid expansion of the NAACP, which would grow to 300 branches (155 in the South) and more than 80,000 members in 1919. As one historian noted, "[A]cross the nation, even in the Deep South, African Americans now anticipated a day when it would not be counterproductive or lethal to voice their growing grievances and resentments. The seeds of far-reaching racial change had been planted."[50]

NOTES

1. David W. Southern, *The Progressive Era and Race: Reaction and Reform, 1900–1917* (Wheeling, IL: Harlan Davidson, 2005), 4, 47.

2. Darlene Clark Hine, et al., *The African-American Odyssey* (Upper Saddle River, NJ: Prentice Hall, 2000), 315.

3. Alfreda M. Duster, ed., *Crusade for Justice: The Autobiography of Ida B. Wells* (Chicago: University of Chicago Press, 1970), 64.

4. Steven L. Piott, *American Reformers, 1870–1920: Progressives in Word and Deed* (Lanham, MD: Rowman and Littlefield, 2006), 64, 66.

5. Southern, *Progressive Era and Race*, 40.

6. Hine, *African-American Odyssey*, 324.

7. Ibid.

8. Southern, *Progressive Era and Race*, 81.

9. Ibid., 39.

10. Hine, *African-American* Odyssey, 365.

11. Southern, *Progressive Era and Race*, 39.

12. Hine, *African-American Odyssey*, 363.

13. W.E.B. Du Bois, *The Souls of Black Folk*, ed. with an intro. by David W. Blight and Robert Gooding-Williams (Boston: Bedford/St. Martin's, 1997), 67, 68.

14. Hine, *African-American Odyssey*, 367.

15. Southern, *Progressive Era and Race*, 161.

16. Nell Irvin Painter, *Standing at Armageddon: The United States, 1877–1919* (New York: W. W. Norton, 1987), 221.

17. Southern, *Progressive Era and Race*, 98.

18. Painter, *Standing at Armageddon*, 222.

19. Southern, *Progressive Era and Race*, 168–169.

20. Hine, *African-American Odyssey*, 395.

21. Wyn Craig Wade, *The Fiery Cross: The Ku Klux Klan in America* (New York: Oxford University Press, 1987), 138, 139.

22. Joel Williamson, *The Crucible of Race: Black-White Relations in the American South Since Emancipation* (New York: Oxford University Press, 1984), 465, 471.

23. E. David Cronon, *Black Moses: The Story of Marcus Garvey and the Universal Negro Improvement Association* (Madison: University of Wisconsin Press, 1969), 70.

24. Michael E. Parrish, *Anxious Decades: America in Prosperity and Depression, 1920–1941* (New York: W. W. Norton, 1992), 124.

25. John Hope Franklin, *From Slavery to Freedom: A History of Negro Americans* (New York: Alfred A. Knopf, 1980), 287.

26. Steven J. Diner, *A Very Different Age: Americans of the Progressive Era* (New York: Hill and Wang, 1998), 141.

27. Ibid., 143.

28. Nell Irvin Painter, *Creating Black Americans: African-American History and Its Meanings, 1619 to the Present* (New York: Oxford University Press, 2006), 159.

29. Leon F. Litwack, *Trouble in Mind: Black Southerners in the Age of Jim Crow* (New York: Alfred A. Knopf, 1998), 453.

30. Ibid., 452, 454.

31. Ibid., 454–455, 456, 457.

32. Ibid., 440.

33. Geoffrey C. Ward, *Unforgivable Blackness: The Rise and Fall of Jack Johnson* (New York: Vintage Books, 2004), 214–215.

34. Ibid., 215.

35. Litwack, *Trouble in Mind*, 440.

36. Ward, *Unforgivable Blackness*, 213.

37. Southern, *Progressive Era and Race*, 69.

38. Ibid., 176.

39. Painter, *Creating Black Americans*, 177.

40. Diner, *Very Different Age*, 152.

41. Alain Locke, ed., *The New Negro: An Interpretation* (New York: Arno Press, 1968), 6. (Originally published in 1925.)

42. Southern, *Progressive Era and Race*, 184.

43. Neil A. Wynn, *From Progressivism to Prosperity: World War I and American Society* (New York: Holmes and Meier, 1986), 185.

44. Southern, *Progressive Era and Race*, 183.

45. Painter, *Creating Black Americans*, 185.

46. Hine, *African-American Odyssey*, 378.

47. Southern, *Progressive Era and Race*, 190.

48. Nathan Irvin Huggins, *Harlem Renaissance* (New York: Oxford University Press, 1971), 56.

49. Cronon, *Black Moses*, 71.

50. Southern, *Progressive Era and Race*, 181.

6

The First World War and
American Society

Neutrality

World War I broke out in Europe in the summer of 1914, but the United States did not formally get involved until the spring of 1917. During that time before U.S. involvement, the stated policy of the Wilson administration was neutrality, and the president asked that Americans be "impartial" in their thoughts as well as their actions. For many, that proved difficult. Roughly 13 percent of the population were people of German birth or descent, and a considerable number beyond that were comprised of nationalities represented in the Austro-Hungarian Empire. In addition, there were several hundred thousand Russian Jews who despised anti-Semitic, czarist Russia, and nearly 5 million Irish Americans who harbored similar feelings against the British government. Just as ethnicity divided Americans on the war issue, so too did geography. The eastern section of the country seemed far more willing to become engaged in the conflict than did those who lived in the South or West, who had historically regarded Britain with some suspicion as a center of international moneyed interests. There were also ideological divisions among preparedness advocates (those favoring either universal military training or a stronger army and navy) and pacifists (those who opposed war on principle). Although the divisions in American society were numerous and deeply felt, Mark Sullivan, a contemporary of events then, noted that there was a larger group that did not seem affected. "The people in this group," said Sullivan, "were comparatively detached about the war; they either mildly favored the Allies or took neither side; so far as they reflected at all upon what we should do, their instinct said we should stay out of it, the war was none of our business."[1]

Submarine Warfare

As the European conflict deepened, both sides competed for support from the American public. In this battle, the British had the advantage. Dominating transatlantic communication channels, they bombarded the media with reports of German atrocities and stereotyped Germans as "Huns." Only years later was it learned that many of the British charges had been based on unsubstantiated rumor and secondhand accounts. The Germans, for their part, emphasized British violations of international law, their seizure of neutral ships, and the blocking of food shipments to Germany. Actual events, however, soon relegated propaganda to secondary importance and caused the American public to increasingly view Germany as the aggressor. The German dismissal of Belgium's neutrality and the brutal conquest of that country alienated many Americans. Even more damning in the eyes of many was the German decision to use submarines (U-boats) to interdict enemy merchant ships. Ignoring the established rules of warfare—requiring submarines to stop their prey, examine the manifest and cargo list, and allow crew and passengers to escape in lifeboats before sinking the vessel—Germany announced that within the war zone, they would torpedo any enemy vessel without warning. Ironically, British officials had actually encouraged this policy by asking merchant ships to install deck guns and attempt to ram surfaced submarines.

The Sinking of the *Lusitania*

The German decision soon had tragic consequences. On May 7, 1915, a German U-boat sank the *Lusitania*, a British luxury liner en route from New York City to Southampton, England. Nearly 1,200 men, women, and children went down with the ship, which sank in just 18 minutes. Included in the list of casualties were 128 Americans, more than one-half of the 209 Americans who would die as a result of German submarine attacks while traveling on ships of nations at war with Germany. Before the ship sailed, the German counsel had published warnings in New York newspapers that the German government considered the ship subject to attack because it had carried munitions on previous voyages (the ship manifest, released 50 years later, confirmed that the *Lusitania* carried shrapnel, fuses, and 4.2 million rounds of ammunition). Despite the warning of the German government, the disaster shocked Americans. President Woodrow Wilson insisted that Germany repudiate its submarine policy, and for a time it did. The German government also eventually issued an apology for the deaths of Americans traveling on the *Lusitania* and paid an indemnity. In the spring of 1916, a German U-boat commander mistakenly targeted an unarmed British steamer, the *Sussex,* which he believed to be a mine layer, and torpedoed the ship as it ferried passengers and freight across the English Channel. In response, Wilson gave Germany an ultimatum—if Germany did not stop sinking nonmilitary vessels without warning, the United States would sever diplomatic relations. Germany agreed to Wilson's demand and issued the *Sussex* pledge in May of 1916 suspending its aggressive submarine policy.

The Declaration of War

Germany honored its pledge until January 31, 1917, when the German government announced that it would resume unrestricted submarine warfare. On February 3, 1917, Wilson severed diplomatic relations. Because most neutral shipping was now reluctant to venture out into the Atlantic, goods began to pile up in eastern ports. Three weeks later Wilson asked Congress for authority to install weapons and naval gun crews on American merchant ships. When a group of ardent noninterventionists in the Senate staged a filibuster to block his request, the president waited until Congress adjourned, and armed the ships by executive order. After German U-boats sank five American ships in March of 1917, Wilson asked Congress for a full declaration of war. After a vigorous debate in which antiwar politicians from the South and Midwest charged that America would be entering the war to protect the investments of American bankers and the profits of munitions manufacturers, the war resolution passed by a vote of 82 to 6 in the Senate, and 373 to 50 in the House of Representatives. The United States formally entered the war on April 6, 1917. Although the vote was overwhelmingly in favor of going to war, the Wilson administration would worry about how many millions of Americans were represented by the 56 senators and representatives who had voted no. It would have an effect on how the government conducted the war effort at home.

Immediately after the declaration of war, the Wilson administration began a sloganeering campaign to whip up American patriotism. Idealistic slogans such as the "war to end all wars," "peace without victory," and "make the world safe for democracy" were designed to awaken patriotic fervor and create a sense of national purpose. They could also be seen as attempts to tap into the already vibrant reform spirit that characterized the era, and to link the progressive crusade at home to a war for progressive aims abroad. As a result, the war became a great moral undertaking. Selective service (the draft), preparedness campaigns and bond drives, and the "grow more food" efforts and meatless and wheatless days were all part of the campaign. "Slacker" became the great smear word as the war effort created an environment in which the government monitored the loyalty of its citizens and individuals gauged the patriotism of their neighbors.

PREPAREDNESS

Selective Service

One of the first tasks facing the administration was the recruitment of an army. Although thousands of young men rushed to enlist, the government needed millions. Raising an all-volunteer army was not practical; some form of conscription would be necessary. Draft administrators, however, were aware that the Union Army's experiment with the draft during the Civil War had proved a disaster—characterized by an inequitable system of exemptions (a wealthy individual could hire a substitute and avoid the draft), draft riots, and violence directed at the uniformed officials who tried to administer it. As a result, selective service administrator Provost Marshal Gen. Enoch H. Crowder devised a plan to minimize draft resistance by entrusting the administration of the process to civilians at the local level. The Conscription Law passed in May of 1917 required that every male between the ages of 21 and 30 (age limits were extended to 18 and 45 in August of 1918) register at one of 5,000 local draft boards scattered around the country. On June 5, 1917, the first day of the program, roughly 12,000 board members, assisted by 125,000 clerical personnel, registered just under 10 million men. Each potential recruit received a small green card certifying his registration. By entrusting local officials to carry out the process, the government was able to maintain the appearance that it was their neighbors who were drafting these men and not the government.

The young men who registered could claim an exemption from military service on the grounds of physical disability, occupational requirement, or dependency. Local boards determined the validity of the requests, but there were significant differences in how the law was interpreted. Some boards granted deferments to virtually all married men. Other boards were much more thorough and examined a wife's means of support, her chances for employment, help that might be available from relatives, and a family's assets. Such probing inquiries seemed like prying into one's personal affairs and provoked a great deal of resentment. Many young men did what they legally could to avoid service. Approximately 60 to 70 percent of all registrants applied for draft exemptions, and the government estimated that an average of 69 men in every local draft board married to avoid service before the government ended the exemption in May of 1918. Another problem involving exemptions developed from the quota system that was part of the original legislation. Under this program, draft calls at the state level were to be proportional based on total population. But that provision of the law failed to subtract the 2½ million "nondeclared" alien males (men without preliminary citizenship papers) who were automatically exempted from military service. "Native" residents in areas with large immigrant populations felt victimized by yet another inequity in the draft selection process.

The awarding of draft deferments by local boards also exhibited a racial bias. Of black registrants, 36 percent were deemed eligible for service, but only 25 percent of whites. Part of the difference can be explained by the prohibition against black volunteering, which left the black pool of able-bodied men undepleted by voluntary enlistments. Another reason was economic. Generally restricted as a race in their access to the skilled trades, blacks were hard pressed to claim deferments based on the essential nature of their jobs. And in a cruel twist of fate, many black family men were too poor to claim the usual exemptions for husbands and fathers. The modest army pay and compulsory family allotment (perhaps $50 a month to an enlisted man's wife and children) would actually increase their earnings and disqualify them from claiming a deferment on the grounds of economic need. Although the recorded examples of overt racism are few, members of one draft board in Fulton County, Georgia, were so blatantly discriminatory that they granted exemptions to 65 percent of whites in the county but to only 3 percent of blacks. The members were removed from the board.

The Draft Lottery

The process of actually choosing who would go and who would stay home began on July 20, 1917, with a lottery in Washington, D.C. On that day a group of officials, senators, congressmen, and army officers convened in the hearing room of the Senate Office Building and gathered around a large glass bowl that contained 10,500 black capsules with numbered slips inside. Shortly before 10:00 A.M., Secretary of War Newton D. Baker, blindfolded, drew out the first capsule (number 258). That number was quickly sent by telegraph and telephone to waiting newspaper presses all over the country, to stock tickers, and to draft offices, where it was posted on bulletin boards before waiting crowds. The lottery continued until after 2:00 A.M. the following day—a blindfolded man selecting capsules, three tellers verifying the numbers chosen, and six tallymen recoding the numbers on a list and then posting them on a large blackboard, which was photographed and sent to newspapers everywhere. As journalist Sullivan remembered the event, "That day there was more excitement throughout the country than on the day of declaring war, for the lottery told each registrant how close he was to battle. War in general had become war personally."[2]

Conscientious Objectors

Although the draft seemed to operate efficiently, it was not without its coercive aspects. A number of men resisted conscription for reasons of conscience, and the Selective Service Act allowed for religious exemptions. But, as in other circumstances, local boards often acted arbitrarily based on what they deemed to be the sincerity of a claimant's conscience. Another problem resulted from the government's failure to adequately plan for what type of alternative service might be substituted for combat duty. As a result, some 20,000 conscientious objectors were inducted into the army, sent to training camps, and held there in limbo until their futures could be determined. Although the U.S. Department of War instructed camp commanders to segregate the conscientious objectors and treat them humanely, they were very often hazed, jeered, and humiliated.

Draft Resistance

With draft boards located in local communities, it was difficult for any young man to avoid the scrutiny of local vigilantes, the police, or representatives of the state council of defense. Although it will never be known how many men dodged the draft, the provost marshall general estimated that 337,000 men did so (roughly 12% of the men inducted). About one-half of those who resisted the draft were eventually apprehended, and the government resigned itself to publishing the names of the remainder. State and federal officers were given the power to arrest draft evaders and offered a $50 bounty for every one brought in. The U.S. Department of Justice's Bureau of Investigation was very active in this regard. By mid-1918, the Justice Department had prosecuted 10,000 individuals for failing to register for the draft. Law enforcement agents, aided by supportive local groups such as the American Protective League and assisted by armed soldiers and sailors, conducted periodic "slacker" raids, in which young men were stopped on the street (sometimes at bayonet point) and required to produce draft registration cards. Police in St. Louis conducted house-to-house searches during the summer of 1917 looking for draft dodgers. Draft resisters would have to give serious thought before deciding to oppose the government's program.

Despite its apparently efficient operation, the draft functioned amid an undercurrent of resistance. Christopher C. Gibbs has found examples of antidraft uprisings in Texas, Montana, North Carolina, Georgia, West Virginia, Utah, Virginia, Arizona, and Arkansas. Eastern Oklahoma witnessed what was called the Green Corn Rebellion, in which 400 to 500 draft-protesting sharecroppers and tenant farmers gathered to march on Washington, D.C., only to be arrested by a local posse before they could even get started. In August 1917, the Springfield, Missouri, draft board started to receive threatening phone calls. Members of the board were called murderers and given death threats unless they resigned. By late September the local board had received so many threats that it stopped reporting them to federal agents. One draft board member in Dallas County, Missouri, angered so many people with his apparently uncompromising decisions that his barber shop was painted yellow. For some, conscription represented the militarization of society and the loss of individual freedom, and for others, the process seemed to threaten family unity. For more than a few, and echoing the sentiments of many in Congress who had voted against the war, conscription seemed to symbolize a war waged more for profits than for principle—a rich man's war, but a poor man's fight. As one man reportedly shouted at a member of his local draft board, "Is Pierpont Morgan paying you for this kind of work?"[3]

Training Camps

In September the first men began leaving home for training camp. Lacking facilities and equipment at first, recruits had to deal with overcrowding, an insufficient supply of weapons to train with, and a shortage of uniforms. They also had to adjust to army routine and boredom. To deal with the latter problem, the Commission on Training Camp Activities (CTCA) was set up to provide recreation. It constructed 34 Liberty Theaters, each with a capacity of from 2,000 to 10,000 men, and showed current movies every night. The commission also sponsored plays, vaudeville performances, and amateur theatricals. It assigned 44 athletic directors, 30 boxing instructors, and 53 song leaders to the various camps. Army officials promoted singing as a morale booster, and numerous songs from the era underscore how important singing was to both the soldier and the civilian. Songs adopted from the British, such as "Pack Up Your Troubles in Your Old Kit Bag, and Smile, Smile, Smile" and "It's a Long Way to Tipperary," were very popular. So too were "Mademoiselle from Armentières," the folk song of the army; "The Long, Long Trail," which offered the romantic allure of distant adventure; and George M. Cohan's "Over There," a quick-stepping song with a simple bugle melody.

> Over there, over there. Send the word, send the word over there,
> That the Yanks are coming, the Yanks are coming, the drums
>   rum-tumming everywhere.
> So prepare, say a pray'r. Send the word, send the word to beware,
> We'll be over, were coming over, and we won't come back till it's
>   over over there.[4]

Supporting the efforts of the CTCA were a number of benevolent and charitable associations. The Red Cross built club houses, put on vaudeville shows, and staged Christmas parties. The Young Men's Christian Association (YMCA) constructed buildings for the soldiers, each with a fireplace, a piano, a phonograph, athletic equipment, books, magazines, hometown newspapers, easy chairs, and writing desks. The Knights of Columbus and the Jewish Welfare Board made similar facilities available, as did the Salvation Army and the YWCA.

Moral Reformers

Soldiers also had to contend with moral reformers. Temperance crusaders descended on the camps hoping to stop the debauchery that would accompany army life. The influence of the Anti-Saloon League (a powerful political lobby) and the rising support for prohibition nationally (there were 26 prohibition states in the Union by April of 1917, and 21 of those had passed prohibition laws after 1906) convinced the War Department to ban the sale of liquor in the vicinity of training camps and to prohibit any soldier in uniform from buying a drink. Actually, it was the war that gave the prohibitionist argument greater urgency, for it underscored both a desire for military efficiency and a need to preserve grain. Although it was estimated that the loss of foodstuffs due to the manufacture of intoxicating liquors was less than 2 percent of the nation's annual cereal production, that amount was more than enough, supporters argued, to offset world shortages. To help conserve grain, Congress, in August 1917, forbade the use of foodstuffs in the production of distilled spirits for the duration of the war. A few months later, at the insistence of U.S. Food Administrator Herbert Hoover, Wilson issued a proclamation that expanded the idea to include the manufacture of beer by reducing the amount of foodstuffs that could be used in the production of that beverage by 30 percent. Although a national prohibition amendment would not be passed until November 21, 1918, the magnitude of that action (it would become a focal point of political, social, and cultural conflict that would resonate through society for the next 15 years), and the speed by which it finally came about, owed a great deal to the patriotic argument made for it and the spirit of sacrifice on the part of the general population at that time.

Joining the temperance advocates were the crusaders against sexual vice. Following the lead of the American Social Hygiene Association, the army, aided by a number of civilian service organizations, launched a concerted offensive against venereal disease. Pamphlets, films, and lectures urged sexual purity in the name of patriotism, a campaign that continued when the doughboys landed in France. One notable example of this crusade was the film *Fit to Fight*, which was shown to almost every serviceman. This hour-long drama followed the lives of five recruits. Four of them wound up associating with the wrong crowd and caught venereal disease. In suggesting that more intelligent choices could have been made, the film made a point to glorify athletics as a substitute for sex. The main point of the film, however, was to emphasize the importance of patriotism and purity for America's soldiers. It was perhaps the first concerted effort at sex education conducted in a frank and open manner to take place in a society that had been shockingly reticent on the subject. As David Kennedy noted, "In its own blunt way, the Army contributed to the demythologizing of erotic life by bringing sexual matters into the arena of public discourse, which was to become a characteristic feature of twentieth-century American culture."[5]

The Army took part in one other social experiment in the training camps—intelligence testing and the classification of recruits by mental ability. When America entered the war, the American Psychological Association pressed the War Department to design tests to classify all new recruits on the basis of their intelligence. After some reluctance, the army assigned professional examiners to all the training camps. After testing, recruits were designated "superior," "average," and "inferior." The results allowed the military to cull out potential officer trainees, but also revealed the surprising level of illiteracy (approximately 25% of those tested) and the generally low level of education among the draftees. Most enlisted men had dropped out of school between grades five and seven. The median years of education ranged from 6.9 years for native whites and 4.7 years for immigrants to 2.6 for southern blacks. Although the psychologists denied that their examinations were biased toward educational or cultural backgrounds, an analysis of the test questions has revealed that to be the case. As one historian summed up the overall training camp experience, "Forewarned about disease, tested and labeled, introduced to the manual of arms, trained to drill, drill, drill, fitted out with a new-fangled safety razor,...and saddled with packs, the doughboys marched out of the camps and up the ramps of the ships of the 'Atlantic Ferry.'"[6] They were off to war.

Financing the War

The financial cost of World War I was enormous. The cost of fighting the war for the United States was more than $24 billion plus another $11 billion that had been extended as loans to the Allies. The national debt, which totaled $1 billion in 1915, grew to $20 billion by 1920. Americans got their first real look at large-scale government spending. Wilson and Secretary of the Treasury William Gibbs McAdoo had initially planned to pay for at least half of the cost of the war through taxation, and had hoped that the emphasis would be placed on excess profits, corporate earnings, large inheritances, and those with higher incomes. The resulting Revenue Acts of 1917 and 1918 did, in fact, levy the first substantial taxes on the earnings of businesses and individuals in American history. As a result, the number of individuals paying income taxes increased from 437,000 in 1916 to 4,425,000 in 1918. In the process, the government shifted the main source of government revenue away from tariff duties and excise taxes to taxes on profits and incomes.

As war-related expenses grew exponentially, the government realized that tax revenues (which eventually totaled just under $9 billion, or a little more than one-third of the cost) would not be enough. The remainder would have to come from borrowing, either through short-term, large Treasury issues to big investors and financiers or through long-term, small-denomination bond sales to average citizens. In the end, the government used both methods. There were five bond drives during the war. The first four were called Liberty Loan drives, and the fifth (which took place after the war was over) the Victory Bond drive. The U.S. Department of the Treasury set interest rates at 3½, 4, and 4½ percent with 30-year maturities. To make the bonds more attractive to purchasers, however, the government exempted earnings from all federal income taxes and allowed bonds to be convertible to any future issue that might carry a higher interest rate. The generous exemption lured businesses and wealthy individuals who purchased bonds in large numbers. As a result, the government lost tax revenues. The Federal Reserve also allowed banks that purchased the bonds to count them as assets, which increased the amount of notes they could issue (thereby expanding the money supply about 75% between 1916 and 1920). In the end, all the various methods of borrowing contributed to severe inflation and a spike in the cost of living for the average consumer. The consumer price index nearly doubled between 1916 and 1920, reducing consumer purchasing power to essentially one-half of what it had been before the war. Wages rose as well, but they could not keep pace with inflation. The American consumer felt the pinch. Some grocery stores froze charge accounts and ended home delivery. Laundries refused to accept credit. Physicians raised fees to cover the increased cost of drugs.

Bond Drives and Patriotic Rallies

Despite the negative consequences related to borrowing, the bond drives provided a positive psychological boost to the government's preparedness campaign. In literally "selling" the war to the American people, the government used the latest advertising and public relations techniques. Posters showed a young, attractive goddess of liberty urging citizens to buy bonds. Advertisements in newspapers and magazines promoted the drives with visual images that showed spiked clubs ostensibly used by the Germans, and encouraged Americans to save civilization from such barbarians. Films such as *The Kaiser, The Beast of Berlin* played in movie theaters. Wounded soldiers who had recently returned from the front gave speeches and sold war bonds. Caught up in the hype, school children learned the following song:

> What are you going to do for Uncle Sammy?
> What are you going to do to help the boys?
> If you mean to stay at home
> While they're fighting o'er the foam,
> The least you can do is buy a Liberty Bond or two.
>
> If you're going to be a sympathetic miser
> You're no better than one who loves the Kaiser.
> It makes no difference who you are
> Or whence you came or how,
> Your Uncle Sammy helped you then, and you must help him now.[7]

The bond drives offered opportunities to stage huge patriotic rallies. Every major city conducted mass gatherings, and millions of people turned out. With government prodding, businesses even gave employees time off to attend. Famous actors and sports figures added to the excitement. The list of Four-Minute Men, celebrities who regularly participated as part of the national preparedness campaign and were so designated because of the length of their talks, included movie actors Douglas Fairbanks and Mary Pickford, comedian Charlie Chaplin, and singers Al Jolson and Enrico Caruso. Sports idols such as Ty Cobb and Babe Ruth were also regular participants. These popular appearances were often recorded as newsreel productions or captured as newspaper photographs for circulation to an even broader mass audience.

Supporting the preparedness campaign were charitable organizations such as the Salvation Army, the YMCA, and the Red Cross. In 1918 the Red Cross claimed 30 million members as active supporters in the war effort at home, and women assumed most of the volunteer work. Each chapter received a production quota, and each chapter met its quota. The chapters produced millions of sweaters, blankets, and socks. When the U.S. Food Administration announced that pits from fruit were needed to make carbon for gas masks, Red Cross chapters across the country collected thousands of tons of fruit pits. They collected so many fruit pits that they were finally told to stop. As a former resident of Lincoln, Illinois, recalled, "[M]other would go down to roll bandages for the soldiers. She put something like a dish towel on her head with a red cross on the front and wore white, and in school we saved prune pits which were supposed to be turned into gas masks so that the town was aware of the war effort.... At all events there was an active sense of taking part in the war."[8]

Like the draft, the campaign to sell war bonds was not without its coercive aspects. Businesses of all types competed with each other to see whose employees would buy the most bonds, and put a great deal of pressure on their workers in the process. Helpful employers offered to have bond payments deducted from a worker's paycheck. "Flying squads" visited schools with subscription blanks and encouraged students to take them home to their parents. Rural delivery carriers in the country and letter carriers in the urban areas carried purchase forms. Farmers were often obligated to accept both money and bonds when they sold their grain to local millers. Groups and clubs holding raffles often awarded bonds as prizes. Companies gave bonds as Christmas bonuses. Boy Scouts and Campfire Girls stopped people on the streets and asked them to buy bonds, and in some locales Home Guardsmen went door-to-door selling bonds. Preachers gave sermons on topics such as "A Liberty Bond in Every Home" on Liberty Bond Sunday. Police stopping speeders in St. Louis let them off if they subscribed to a war bond on the spot. Early in 1918 the press in Missouri reported that the federal government was actually asking for information on every American's financial contribution to the war. In the "Show Me" state, the Boone County Council of Defense sent out letters to teachers, editors, and prominent individuals asking for information on bond slackers.

Despite all the fanfare, propaganda, and not-so-subtle attempts at coercion, the bond sales (all of which were oversubscribed) failed to exhibit broad support in a population where the average citizen had little money to spare. Only 4 percent of the population bought bonds during the first Liberty Loan drive, 10 percent did so in the second, 18 percent in the third, and 21 percent in the fourth. Eleven percent of the population purchased a Victory Bond. So who did the heavy buying? The evidence seems to suggest that most of the purchases were made by individuals in middle- to upper-income brackets, local philanthropists, and businesses and financial institutions with ready cash to subscribe or the atypical inclination to invest. In the end, the various Liberty Loan drives collected over 60 million subscriptions, but they also encouraged patriotic conformity and helped set the tone of much of the popular sentiment.

Food Production and Food Conservation

While the federal government took steps to mobilize men and money, it quickly became evident that the ability to maintain food production would be crucial to the war effort as well. In order to feed both the soldiers and the civilians, the government would have to take steps to increase food production and encourage food conservation. The agency that was created to meet this goal was the Food Administration headed by Herbert Hoover. Hoover, operating through a system of state and county food administrators and an army of 75,000 volunteers, sought to mobilize people as producers and consumers. To do so, food administrators appealed to a spirit of self-sacrifice, linked increased production and reduced consumption to support for the war, and implied that anyone who did not take part was a slacker. Farmers were encouraged to expand acreage under cultivation and to use improved farming techniques, such as increasing the use of fertilizers to intensify yields and more carefully plowing the land.

At the same time, consumers were asked to eat less. To encourage food conservation, the Food Administration asked Americans to engage in gardening and canning, refrain from hoarding, and pledge to consume less. Libraries listed books on gardening, and local newspapers offered instructions on the best way to grow vegetables and the optimum methods of preservation. Working through the various agricultural colleges, the Food Administration published information on growing and preserving foods and sent out home demonstration agents. These agents, usually young women from college home economics departments or middle-class housewives from the suburbs, were engaged to teach proper methods of homemaking in the same way that county agents or college experts would teach farmers how to farm more efficiently and scientifically. Instead of mandatory food rationing, the Food Administration asked people to voluntarily observe meatless and wheatless days. Of 21 possible meals during a week, Americans were asked to go without wheat and meat at 11 of them—no wheat at all on Mondays, no meat on Tuesdays, and no pork on Thursdays and Saturdays. Hoover's agency also undertook a national advertising campaign for food conservation, and pressured grocers to display posters commanding people to conserve. Hotels and restaurants were encouraged to demonstrate their patriotism by reducing food portions and removing sugar bowls from the tables.

Food Pledge Drives

Hoover's campaign of "voluntarism" reached a peak with the food pledge drives. During the summer of 1917, the federal government attempted to get housewives to sign a pledge promising to try to conserve food for the war effort. In Missouri teachers were instructed to enroll all female students over the age of 16. Women set up registration booths in rural towns on market day and traveled

U.S. Food Administration poster imploring citizens to conserve food. (Courtesy of the Library of Congress)

the countryside in search of signatures. In urban areas in the state, middle-class women accompanied by policemen went into ethnic and racially segregated neighborhoods looking to enlist Italian, Polish, and African American women. Pushing the pledge drive to the limit, the Food Administration launched a massive advertising campaign designed to impact people at every turn. Food pledge workers showed films and cartoons; the agency produced 43,000 posters that were mounted on any available outside surface, and issued 2,000 press releases urging people to save food and use substitutes for scarce commodities. One press release focusing on the need to conserve wheat flour provided recipes for different breads, such as buckwheat bread, potato bread, and corn bread. The Food Administration sent out hundreds of speakers and increased its legion of home demonstrators. In Missouri, with the help of education groups and the support of the state's school superintendent, school children were given instruction on community life and told how to conserve food by signing the pledge and helping their mothers at home. Nine thousand teachers in the state enrolled students in their classes. Some 7,500 clergymen in the state received preformatted sermon outlines to use on Sunday. Half a million food workers went door-to-door to hand housewives pledge cards that enlisted their patriotic cooperation. They even gave pledge cards to city policemen, who stopped people on the street and asked them to sign.

As one historian noted, the Food Administration "literally reached into every kitchen in America, and its measures no doubt accomplished much by encouraging food conservation. But its techniques also intensified the same patriotic fevers on which the Treasury relied to finance the war."[9] As another summed it up, "everywhere people turned they were confronted with someone asking them to sign up to support the war. And the issue was put in precisely those terms, with various threats, implied or stated, often lying behind them." Many people refused to sign the food pledge because they thought the government-directed campaign made unfair demands on consumers. Prices were high, food was scarce, and newspapers constantly printed stories of food profiteers. Many embittered consumers resented being asked to tighten their belts another notch. One pledge worker complained that it was a "nasty, thankless job trying to get poor people to save with teaspoons." Others undoubtedly resented the coercion. In Savannah, Missouri, Wirt Ball refused to sign the food pledge because "she don't think this is a free country any more."[10]

Wartime Propaganda

Selling the war to the American public became the mission of the Committee on Public Information (CPI), headed by Denver newspaperman George Creel. The CPI recruited artists, movie directors, journalists, psychologists, and scholars to help publicize the war effort. The committee distributed more than 100 million pieces of literature in the form of leaflets, articles, and pamphlets. The CPI also produced photographs, newspaper and magazine advertising, and a barrage of posters. Some of the posters portrayed the enemy as an uncivilized beast that burned cathedrals and committed atrocities, and, in one instance, depicted the Kaiser as a crazed ape (wielding a club labeled "cultur") carrying off a half-naked female captive. Others were effective without the hyperbole. James Montgomery

U.S. Navy recruiting poster drawn by Howard Chandler Christy, 1917. (Courtesy of the Library of Congress)

Flagg encouraged young men to volunteer with his famous finger-pointing poster of Uncle Sam with the caption "I Want *You* for the U.S. Army." Howard Chandler Christy used Lady Liberty to urge citizens to buy Liberty Bonds. And Charles Dana Gibson glorified dedicated workers in a poster with the caption "Together you [soldiers and workers] will win!" Perhaps the committee's most effective device was the enlistment of public orators, organizing 75,000 speakers (the Four-Minute Men mentioned earlier) to deliver short speeches with texts prepared by the CPI at any public gathering that promised a sizable audience. The agency generated new speeches every 10 days. Creel claimed that his army of orators delivered over 7½ million speeches to more than 300 million listeners. Although his figures were probably inflated, the CPI did bring the war into the everyday lives of a vast number of Americans.

In selling the war to Americans, the CPI pitched its propaganda in terms of good versus evil. The Allies were portrayed as Christian, decent, and democratic—the defenders of liberty—whereas Germany and the other Central Powers were portrayed as depraved, cruel, and autocratic—the destroyers of freedom. The German was commonly referred to as the "Hun" to suggest his barbarism, and was usually portrayed in political cartoons in military uniform with high leather boots and a spiked helmet to emphasize his militaristic proclivities. In promoting the war the way businesses hawked their products, the CPI whipped war spirit to a peak. City and county school boards banned the teaching of the German language, and some localities prohibited the playing of music by German composers. Some community libraries even removed books by German authors. In the silliness that ensued, frankfurters became referred to as "liberty sausage," German measles became "liberty measles," and sauerkraut found new identification as "liberty cabbage."

In promoting the war effort, the CPI contributed to a climate of intimidation and fear. The intensity of the propaganda, the inflammatory statements, and the zealous activities of voluntary, ultranationalistic groups such as the American Protective League fanned ethnic animosities to near-hysterical levels. Examples of vigilante activity could be found anywhere. German Americans, or anyone suspected of disloyalty, were stopped on the street and forced by angry crowds to kiss the American flag, recite the Pledge of Allegiance, or buy war bonds. In Cincinnati, Ohio, Reverend Herbert S. Bigelow, a pacifist clergyman, was spirited out of town by an angry mob and horsewhipped. In April 1918, in Collinsville, Illinois, an anti-German mob of nearly 500 seized Robert Praeger, a naturalized American citizen, draped him in an American flag, and then lynched him. The American Civil Liberties Union (ACLU) recorded 164 cases of mob violence during the war, but that figure is certainly underestimated. Feeling the sting of social disapproval, many Germans stopped speaking their native language, and many others anglicized their names in the hope of avoiding censure or harm.

Restrictions on Free Speech

Further contributing to the reactive domestic environment were four laws enacted in 1917 and 1918 that restricted the free exercise of speech and opinion. The Espionage Act prohibited spying and sabotage, but it also outlawed public criticism that could be construed as being detrimental to the military, for example by obstructing recruitment or causing insubordination or disloyalty. Penalties included fines up to $10,000 and harsh prison sentences that could reach up to 20 years for those convicted. To enforce the Espionage Act, the government had to increase its law enforcement and surveillance capability. One by-product of this was the creation of a federal loyalty program that enabled heads of departments to fire any employee deemed to be a risk because of actions, sympathies, or statements. As a result, some 2,600 individuals were questioned.

The Trading with the Enemy Act outlawed commerce with Germany, but it also granted the postmaster the authority to open mail and suspend the mailing privileges of publications he found to be treasonable. The Alien Act gave the commissioner of immigration the power to deport any non-naturalized person suspected of radical beliefs or possible violent actions. The Sedition Act invoked a sweeping ban on speaking, writing, or publishing any disloyal remarks against the government or the military, and included penalties identical with the Espionage Act. Roughly 2,200 individuals were prosecuted under the Espionage Act, and approximately one-half that number were convicted under the Sedition Act. Reacting to the federal government's broad-based, wartime powers to restrict freedom of expression, Roger Baldwin, himself a conscientious objector who was later convicted for refusing to register for the draft, created the National Civil Liberties Bureau in 1917, which became the ACLU in 1920.

INDUSTRIAL MOBILIZATION

The rapid increase in war orders after the declaration of hostilities greatly intensified the demand for workers. Complicating this new demand for workers was the concurrent reduction in the number of new immigrants, which fell from 1.2 million in 1914 to just 110,000 in 1918, and the constant mobilization of 4.8 million men (roughly 16% of the labor force) into military service. In an attempt to deal with the shortages, the government granted deferments to workers in essential industries such as arsenals and shipyards, and lowered the draft classifications of over half a million agricultural workers. As the desperation to find workers increased, some states passed "anti-loafing" laws. In May 1918, the federal government issued a "Work or Fight" order and amended the Selective Service Act to require workers in nonessential jobs to find other employment or be drafted. In an attempt to free agricultural workers for deployment in other sectors, the U.S. Employment Service recruited unskilled workers from Mexico. Although the Immigration Act of 1917 had banned the importation of such contract workers, those provisions were suspended for the duration of the war. As a result, some 35,000 Mexicans entered the country under an agreement between the two countries. It has been estimated that twice that many Mexican workers actually entered the United States between 1917 and 1921 seeking employment. In addition to the number of imported agricultural workers from Mexico, approximately 110,000 Puerto Rican workers were brought into the country to help build army camps.

Americanization Programs

The difficulty in finding an adequate number of workers to "man" the factories in a shrinking labor market convinced a number of employers that Americanization programs might be a way to increase the efficiency, cooperation, and productivity of the existing workforce. The Detroit Board of Commerce pointed the way in this regard in 1915 when it started a civic campaign to draw non-English-speaking immigrants into night schools. Henry Ford established his own Ford English School and required his foreign employees to attend it two days a week. Ford believed that immigrant workers needed to be taught the values associated with consumerism and family life, but he also felt that workers' lack of English language skills impeded production at the plant. Their reluctance to be assimilated into the mainstream of American society affected their ability to accept the tenets of modern industrial society, which included a willingness to become a disciplined labor force. As a result, Ford sought to Americanize workers as a way to instill work discipline and enhance the company's control over the production process. By late 1916 the Ford English School had 2,700 students. The school followed the instructional lead of Peter Roberts, a YMCA teacher, and had sessions on topics such as "Beginning the Day's Work" and other work-related tasks. In a broader sense, however, the lessons sought to inculcate middle-class values of hard work, sobriety, and punctuality.

The Americanization efforts of Ford before America's entry into World War I soon caught the attention of others. Both the National Association of Manufacturers and the United States Chamber of Commerce urged their members to adopt industrial education programs for their immigrant workforce, and classes in English were started in at least 27 industries. Businessmen created their own factory classes and even subsidized evening classes in the public schools. The Immigration Committee of the Chamber of Commerce distributed approximately 300,000 sets of Americanization leaflets to employers for insertion in workers' pay envelopes. The belief was that these civics lessons would increase productivity and enhance worker morale. With America's entry into the war, Americanization programs intensified and merged with Liberty Bond campaigns, food conservation efforts, Red Cross work, and detecting disloyalty as patriotic campaigns. Many factory owners adopted a policy of promoting only citizens or those in the process of becoming naturalized. Others offered economic incentives (wage increases) for those who enrolled in English classes.

Caught up in the fervor of militant Americanization during the war, the National Americanization Committee led by Frances Kellor established a Man-Power Engineering Service to advise employers on how best to utilize alien enemies in their plants, and how to guard against sabotage. To advocates such as Kellor, industrial Americanization held "the greatest hope for the prevention of labor troubles, for the stabilizing of the labor market, for increased production through securing the cooperation of foreign-language groups, for enabling our industries to stand the strain of the economic changes of the war."[11] In such an environment, it was only a short step for conservative capitalists imbued with the spirit of 100 percent Americanism to dismiss even legitimate labor demands with the charge of disloyalty.

Women Workers

The most important source of new workers, however, came from the ranks of women and blacks. In rural and urban America, women actively engaged in the effort at home to win the war. In doing so, many women accepted work in various nontraditional jobs. In the rural countryside, women replaced men in the harvesting of crops. In the cities, women directed rush-hour traffic, worked as streetcar conductors or ticket agents, delivered the daily mail, cut men's hair and shaved men's beards in barbershops, and delivered blocks of ice to urban homes and restaurants. In the industrial sector, women crossed previously gender-segregated lines of work to operate cranes and produce bombs, grenades, firearms, and ammunition in the iron and steel industry. They manufactured cartridge belts, pistol holsters, canteen covers, tents, and barrack bags. They operated drills, turret lathes, bolt-threading machines, and pneumatic hammers. Often clad in uniforms known as "womanalls," females worked with welding torches and oxyacetylene cutters. In airplane factories women performed semiskilled jobs as milling machine

World War I poster encouraging women to join the labor force and support the war effort. (Courtesy of the Library of Congress)

operators as well as the more skilled work of assembling airplane motors. According to one government survey, women comprised 20 percent or more of all workers manufacturing electrical machinery, airplanes, and leather goods.

As new avenues for female labor opened up and as better-paying jobs became available, the pace of occupational change that had begun before the war quickened. Between 1910 and 1920, the number of female domestic servants dropped by 20 percent, the number of dressmakers fell by 47 percent, and the number of laundresses declined by 25 percent. The growth areas for women were in clerical work (an increase of 344,000 or 288%), semiskilled manufacturing work (an increase of 319,000 or 33%), and employment as stenographers and typists (an increase of 171,000 or 92%). Most of the gains during the period were in war-related industries. Of the nearly 9.5 million war workers, 2.25 million were women and 1.25 million of those were engaged in manufacturing work. One hundred thousand women worked in munitions plants, and in one grenade factory, 19 out of every 20 workers were women. More than one-half of the workers in industrial plants manufacturing shells were women, and in one gas mask factory 8,500 out of a workforce of 12,000 were women. According to a survey done by the Women's Bureau, women, who comprised only 3 percent of the total work force in iron and steel in 1914, accounted for 6.1 percent of that workforce in February 1918 and 9.5 percent by the following October.

Gender Discrimination on the Job

The new employment opportunities that opened up for women during the war were not without accompanying problems. Many women experienced discrimination in pay. Although women earned higher wages than they had before the war, their average earnings were still only one-half those of men. Milling companies in Cincinnati paid men $15 to $20 per week, but paid women between $6 and $10. In Grand Rapids, Michigan, the average daily wage for 23 men was $3.16, but for 5,000 women workers, only $1.98. In 1918 in Atlanta, Georgia, where over 2,700 women were employed in war work, the average wage was between $10 and $15 per week. At the same time, 25 percent of those women earned less than $15 and 30 percent made less than $10.

Many women found living accommodations scarce and discovered that rising prices quickly cancelled out any wage gains.

In addition, gender segregation continued to define the nature of women's employment. Sexual harassment was a fact of life in railroad clerical work and reinforced women's subordinate position. Bosses and male co-workers often contested women's right to higher-paying, skilled jobs. In railroad yards, protective labor regulations were ironically used to force many women from well-paying jobs, and sexism and racism on the part of railroad carmen often denied white and black women union membership. For many women there was also the stress of knowing that one's job was temporary or at least viewed that way by most people. At the end of the war, women were expected to give up their jobs despite the feeling of economic independence, heightened consciousness, and increased self-fulfillment that many mothers of latter-day Rosie the Riveters must have felt. By 1920 women actually made up a smaller percentage of the workforce than they had in 1910.

Racial Segregation in the Workforce

New employment opportunities, however, were not open equally to all women. Racial segregation of the workforce was just as prevalent as gender segregation. For the most part, compared to white women, black women continued to be concentrated in more traditional forms of employment. Initially, black women comprised only a small percentage of women working in manufacturing, and the majority of those workers were concentrated in tobacco and cigar-making establishments as common laborers or machine tenders. Restrictions followed black women into other areas as well. In retail houses they continued to work as custodial personnel. Black telephone operators, secretaries, and receptionists continued to find employment only in black-owned businesses in black neighborhoods. Yet as white women increasingly found employment in war industries, black women took their former jobs—although many of these were as domestic servants in northern cities. Eventually, jobs in factories began to become available for black women. In addition to work in the tobacco and food processing industries, black women gained entry into the leather, metal, paper products, clothing, and textile industries. One side benefit of the new jobs was that they offered regular hours and free evenings, which domestic service did not. As one former black servant stated, "I'll never work in nobody's kitchen but my own any more. No, indeed! That's the one thing that makes me stick to this job [in a paper box factory]. You...have some time to call your own."[12]

New Economic Opportunities for Black Workers

In terms of advancement and wages, black women found their best wartime opportunities in the garment trades, government arsenals, and the railroad industry. In the garment trade, black women cut, embroidered, finished, pressed, and trimmed garments. Because the clothing trades had a large proportion of unionized workers, some black women were able to take advantage of pay increases. In government arsenals black women made and inspected garments. As government employees, they earned a weekly wage of from $15 to $20, which was roughly twice the wage of most black female workers in the industry. Best of all, perhaps, at providing decent working conditions, steady employment, and high wages was the railroad industry (under government control during the war). Here black women mopped floors, washed windows, and polished metal parts. A small number of black female workers wiped engines, and a few even operated electric lift trucks at freight transfer depots. Some black women collected and distributed linens in Pullman cars (formerly a male prerogative), and others performed the more arduous work of moving forgings and castings by wheelbarrow. Earning even more than arsenal workers, black female railroad employees took home more than $20 a week. Even when jobs were dirty and physically demanding, many women could share the sentiment of one black woman streetcar-track cleaner who stated that the "'almighty dollar' made the work worth the physical effort."[13]

Although there had been an out-migration of blacks from the South to the North in the prewar period, that process accelerated after 1914 and eventually swelled into the Great Migration. As word spread that there were jobs to be had in the cities of the North, blacks began to embrace the prospect of entering an industrial labor market from which they had been largely excluded. By 1920 there would be over 900,000 black industrial workers, nearly double the 1910 total. During the war period, roughly half a million blacks moved to booming industrial centers in the North. Pushed out of the South by poverty, inequality, and persistent racial violence, and pulled to the North by the promise of greater economic opportunity, better education, and more freedom, blacks increasingly decided to make the move. Assisting the migration process were labor agents from northern industries who offered free transportation and good wages. Although many would be disappointed after their arrival, most of the new arrivals were able to find employment.

It was not, however, just the number of jobs that had opened up for black workers that was significant, but the range and quality of those jobs as well. In Chicago in 1910, over 50 percent of black workers had been engaged in some form of domestic service, and the figure for blacks in Cleveland had stood at roughly 33 percent. By 1920 those numbers had been reduced to 28 percent and 12 percent, respectively. In cities such as Detroit, where many blacks had worked as porters and elevator operators, they were now auto workers and crane operators. Companies such as Westinghouse that had employed only 25 black workers in 1916 employed 1,500 two years later. The number of black shipyard workers grew from roughly 37,000 to over 100,000, and black men began to enter some skilled and semiskilled occupations in that industry. Black women made similar advances. Over 40 percent moved from domestic work to factory occupations and often replaced white women in the textile, food, clothing, and tobacco industries. The number of black women in manufacturing rose from approximately 67,000 in 1910 to almost 105,000 in 1920. Letters from black migrants offer a glimpse of the improved economic circumstances that many blacks realized. Correspondence mentions wages of from $6 to $8 a day in the North, which were often the equivalent of a week's earnings in the South. In Chicago the average rate of pay was $0.50 an hour, which could be compared to $0.75 a day in the South. Such improvements led the *Chicago Defender,* a leading black newspaper, to proclaim, "The opportunity we have longed for is here; it is ours now to grasp it. The war has given us a place upon which to stand."[14]

Racial Discrimination on the Job

Despite the gains, the reality of black employment during World War I also included lower wage rates and wage discrimination, unequal employment opportunities, and substandard living conditions. Like women, black workers were usually drawn into the lower-paid jobs and were often discriminated against in rates of pay so that they were paid less for doing the same work as whites. Even government agencies, such as the U.S. Shipping Labor Adjustment Board, approved wage rates that were $0.10 to $0.20 lower for black workers than for whites. Many of the economic gains for black workers were in unskilled jobs and concentrated in a few industries such as iron, steel, meat packing, and automobiles. In 1910 blacks had accounted for 6.4 percent of unskilled steel workers. By 1920 that number had increased to 17 percent. As increased technological change in the automobile industry reduced the proportion of skilled work from 75 to 10 percent, black employment increased. In the process, a new stereotype began to appear of the unskilled black worker doing the most arduous labor. Compounding problems for black workers was the shortage of housing and the racial prejudice that confined them to existing black areas. As a result, the black ghetto increasingly became part of urban life for a rising number of black workers and their families. Although the causal factors are more complex, the rapid increase in the black population in concentrated urban areas, the competition for scarce housing, and the growing perception on the part of white workers that the influx of so many black migrants threatened to undermine existing labor standards and reduce labor's bargaining power all contributed to the increase in race riots that seemed to mark the wartime years.

Race Riots

The increased tension between whites and black migrants over available housing, jobs, and wages came to a tragic climax in East St. Louis, Illinois, in the summer of 1917 and served as a portent of escalating racial violence in 1918 and 1919. As northern employers began to import southern blacks to fill the sudden demand for industrial workers, white workers became alarmed. Because employers hired black workers at lower wage rates (to blacks, the rates were high by southern standards), white workers feared that their own wage standards were in jeopardy. To protect their economic position, white workers organized a union, affiliated with the American Federation of Labor (AFL), and began to demand higher wages. When they did so, employers threatened to replace them with black workers. Because of the existing racially prejudiced environment (a great deal of racial bitterness had resulted from prior political campaigns in which race had been an issue), no genuine effort was made to incorporate black workers into the union. In April, white union workers at an aluminum plant in the city went out on strike. When they did so, the company blamed the strike on radicals, then hired strikebreakers, and got the courts to issue an injunction against the union. After losing the strike, union members directed their anger at black workers, some of whom had accepted jobs as scab labor at the plant.

Exacerbating the racial situation in East St. Louis were rumors that local manufacturers planned to add an additional 15,000 blacks to the existing labor force (trade unionists regarded this as a deliberate attempt to diminish their bargaining power by creating a surplus labor market). As tensions mounted, the Central Trades and Labor Union (a federation of AFL craft unions) sent a letter to city officials stating that over the previous eight months 10,000 "undesirable" black workers had entered the city and were being used by capitalists and real estate owners "to the detriment of our white citizens." The union demanded that city officials take action to halt this "growing menace," and "devise a way to get rid of a certain portion of those who are already there." It warned that "violence" would result if no immediate action was taken.[15] Fearing mob violence, frightened blacks began to arm themselves in self-defense.

On the night of July 1, 1917, a carload of whites drove through a black neighborhood firing gunshots into houses. The police were called and responded in an unmarked patrol car. Mistakenly thinking that the police were, in fact, the returning vigilantes, black residents fired at the automobile and killed two officers. When news of the shootings spread throughout the city the following day, mobs of enraged white residents went on a rampage and began indiscriminately shooting and lynching black men, women, and children. The riot continued for two days. Although local officials recorded that there had been 47 deaths from the rioting (8 whites and 39 blacks), other accounts suggested that as many as 200 to 400 may have been killed. The riot left 240 buildings destroyed, and estimates of property damage ran as high as $1.4 million. As one black woman worker wrote, "It was awful. We lost everything but what we had on and that was very little."[16] Although the East St. Louis Race Riot underscored the racial tensions that occurred as a result of overcrowding and job competition, racial violence was not just a by-product of wartime production and black migration. As black author James Weldon Johnson was to write in 1919, "An increased hatred of race was an integral part of wartime intolerance."[17]

Increased Strike Activity

Generalizations about wages and earning power are difficult to make during the war period. For some, such as garment workers in New York City, average annual incomes nearly tripled between 1914 and 1918. Average real wages (purchasing power adjusted for price inflation) for manual laborers, who were in great demand in industries such as shipbuilding, steel, textiles, and munitions, increased by nearly 20 percent during the same period. For others, increased wages barely kept them ahead of rising prices. Many of these economic gains, however, did not come without a struggle. Looking to improve their economic position in a time of increasing labor scarcity, workers struck. Strike figures throughout the war period were on the rise. There were 979 strikes in 1914, almost 1,500 in 1915, and over 3,600 in 1916. In 1917 there were over 4,500 strikes involving more than 1 million workers. By 1917 prices were already up 60 percent compared to prewar levels. Rumors of war profiteering among businessmen only added to worker discontent.

Gains for Organized Labor

In response to the alarming increase in strike activity by independent locals of the AFL (Samuel Gompers, head of the union, supported the war and agreed to a no-strike pledge for the duration of the conflict) and radical unions primarily connected to the Industrial Workers of the World (IWW), the Wilson administration created the National War Labor Board (NWLB) in 1918. In return for no-strike promises, the board recognized the right of workers to organize, to bargain collectively, and to form trade unions. Further, the board recognized the eight-hour day, the principle of equal pay for equal work by women, and the right of a worker to a living wage. In granting the eight-hour day in 151 cases that came before it, the NWLB encouraged the acceptance of the idea as a standard workday. By 1919 almost 49 percent of American workers were employed on that basis. In encouraging collective bargaining and trade union membership, the board contributed significantly to the addition of 1 million new union members (membership for all unions rose from 2.7 million in 1914 to over 5 million in 1920). To define what constituted a living wage, the NWLB created a Cost of Living Section (CLS) within the U.S. Department of Labor. The CLS determined that for a family of five to subsist in New York City, it needed an annual income of around $1,500 in 1918. To achieve that level, the minimum hourly rate of pay would have to be $0.55. When employers complained that the rate was too high, the NWLB agreed to a compromise by which it applied a figure of $0.40 an hour for unskilled labor (a figure that rose to $0.45 cents by the end of the war).

POSTWAR PROBLEMS

The war, or at least the nation's direct commitment to it, ended sooner than many had anticipated. Without any formal plan for postwar economic reconversion, policymakers confronted a period of economic chaos. One problem was rampant inflation. Throughout most of 1919 and 1920, prices rose by a rate of more than 15 percent a year. With inflation spiking in 1919, many workers began to see their modest wage gains disappear. Others worried about job security as veterans returned looking to rejoin the workforce. Employers added to the stress by using the end of the war as a reason to discontinue concessions that they had been forced to make to workers during the war. As war orders stopped and government protection was curtailed, employers resumed their old hostility toward unions. As a result, the year 1919 brought a wave of strikes that ultimately involved more than 4 million workers.

As mentioned earlier, the suppression of dissent during the war contributed to a repressive environment where patriotism (defined as pro-war) and Americanism (increasingly defined as anti-radicalism) had become sharply contested ideals. Exacerbating circumstances was the Bolshevik Revolution that occurred in October 1917, an event that overthrew the Russian czar and established the world's first socialist state. Although wartime repression had crippled the IWW and reduced the Socialist Party to fewer than 30,000 members, the Bolshevik triumph threw a scare into many American government officials and businessmen. Although these leaders talked a good deal in public about the potential for revolution in this country, their real fear was the threat of industrial unionization. In a sense, the Bolshevik Revolution and the recent confrontation with American dissenters and radicals gave American businessmen a convenient justification to crush any uprising of American industrial workers. The efforts of labor organizers could be discredited in the eyes of an extremely tense and nervous American public by labeling the organizers as Communists, or more commonly for the time, Bolsheviks.

1919: Year of Unrest

The year of unrest began shortly after the armistice in November 1918, when 60,000 clothing workers struck for three months and won a 40-four hour workweek and a 15 percent pay raise. In early 1919 high prices and housing shortages led 35,000 Seattle, Washington, shipyard workers to walk off their jobs. On February 6 the Seattle Central Labor Council called for a general strike in support of the shipyard workers, and 60,000 laborers left their jobs. Although the labor council made sure that essential services—electrical power, garbage collection, and food and fuel deliveries—were maintained, the action paralyzed the city for four days. Important for later events was the news that many of the leaders of the Seattle strike were socialists and former members of the IWW who compounded the fears of many by referring to the body of striking unions as a "soviet." One newspaper headline proclaimed, "Reds Directing Seattle Strike—To Test Chance for Revolution."[18] Despite the legitimate economic grievances, Seattle mayor Ole Hanson, who requested federal troops during the strike, denounced the strikers as revolutionaries who were attempting to "duplicate the anarchy of Russia."[19] On April 28 a bomb arrived in the mail at Mayor Hanson's office. On the alert, mail inspectors quickly intercepted three dozen additional bomb packages intended for high-ranking government officials and high-profile businessmen. On May 1, 1919, rallies called by radicals in Boston, Cleveland, and New York were broken up by "patriotic" mobs. On June 2 bomb explosions occurred in eight cities and killed two people.

The upsurge in strike activity continued into the fall. In September, three-fourths of Boston's 1,500 policemen, who were forbidden from forming a union, went out on strike. The police were upset over low wages (they had not had a pay increase since 1913), the fatigue that came with working 80 hours a week, and the economic hardship that accompanied the rising cost of living. Reported as the first police strike in American history, it was ill-received by the public, especially after two nights of looting, rioting, and vandalism. Order was finally restored after the governor sent in state militiamen. In reporting on the events, Boston's newspapers referred to the striking policemen as "agents of Lenin" and characterized the city as being trapped in a "Bolshevist nightmare."[20] That same fall 450,000 coal miners went out on strike demanding a 60 percent wage increase, a six-hour day, and a five-day work week. Mine owners refused to negotiate, claiming that the strike was ordered by Russian leaders (Lenin and Trotsky) and financed by Moscow. When the union (the United Mine Workers) refused to acknowledge a court order instructing its members to return to work, the Wilson administration invoked the wartime controls it exercised over the coal industry to force them back to the mines. Although the union accepted the action, many miners stayed out. With much of the press portraying the strike action as contributing to soaring inflation, the miners garnered little public sympathy. When coal shortages forced schools and factories to close, negative public reaction intensified.

The Great Influenza Pandemic

Contributing to the general climate of unease and paranoia that seemed to intensify during 1918 and 1919 was the great influenza pandemic. Evidence points to the United States as the source of the influenza outbreak in early 1918, and to isolated Haskell County, Kansas, in particular. There, in late January, Dr. Loring Miner, a local physician, began to encounter an unusual outbreak of severe cases of influenza. But by mid-March, the disease seemed to have disappeared. Children returned to school, and men and women went back to work. Local newspapers had worried about the outbreak hurting morale during wartime and said little about the event or the deaths that had occurred as a result.

The virus that had infected Haskell County might have died and failed to spread any further except that it was wartime. Evidence suggests that one or more young soldiers from the area had come home on leave from Camp Funston, located within the Fort Riley military installation roughly 300 miles to the east. Camp Funston was the second largest cantonment in the country and housed approximately 56,000 troops. The winter of 1917–1918 was bitter cold, and barracks and tents were crowded and inadequately heated. As a result, the men were crammed into frigid living quarters that forced them to huddle together around stoves for warmth. Men inducted into the army from Haskell County trained at Camp Funston, and there was a constant stream of soldiers moving between the two locations. On March 4 a private at Funston reported ill with influenza. Within three weeks there were 1,100 soldiers sick enough to be admitted to the military hospital and thousands more being treated at infirmaries on the base. Although pneumonia developed in 237 cases, only 38 men died (a higher rate than normal but not high enough to trigger alarm). Someone had brought a mild form of the influenza virus to the base. But influenza viruses mutate constantly, and this form of the virus had the capacity to mutate into lethal forms.

The problem, however, was larger than the crowding at Camp Funston. As the nation mobilized for war, men inducted into the army were increasingly jammed into hastily constructed barracks that were designed for a much smaller numbers. As the enlistment of troops mushroomed, the number of recruits entering training camps increased from tens of thousands to millions in just a few short months. In response to this surge in numbers, the army constructed huge cantonments, each capable of holding 50,000 men.

The process not only brought large numbers of young men into close proximity, but also mixed farm boys and city boys, each with different disease immunities and vulnerabilities.

Two weeks after the first outbreak at Camp Funston in March 1918, influenza cases began to mount at camps in Georgia, where roughly 10 percent of the soldiers reported sick. Soon, 24 of the 36 largest army camps in the country experienced influenza outbreaks undoubtedly caused by military personnel being transferred between the camps. During April, 30 of the 50 largest cities in the nation, many lying close to contaminated military facilities, showed a marked increase in influenza cases. At the same moment, the first outbreaks of the disease surfaced in Brest, France, where American troops disembarked for the front. Influenza there spread to the French army and the British army. When British troops returned home, they brought the influenza virus to England. Cases of influenza also began to appear in Spain, Portugal, Greece, and, after spreading to naval personnel, in Algeria, Egypt, Tunisia, India, and China. Many got sick, but the cases were still mild and there were relatively few deaths. Then, in early August, the epidemic seemed to be over. But as one historian noted, "[T]he virus had not disappeared. It had only gone underground, like a forest fire left burning in the roots, swarming and mutating, adapting…waiting to burst into flame."[21]

In the fall of 1918, the epidemic entered its lethal stage and began to spread around the country and the world. In September influenza struck soldiers at Camp Devens, about 35 miles northwest of Boston. By the end of the month, the base hospital, which had been originally designed to accommodate 1,200 patients, held over 6,000. Officials in major cities began to ban public meetings, businesses and schools closed, and quarantines descended on military bases. It was the Great War, however, that allowed the crisis to become a pandemic. As nations mobilized soldiers in large numbers, housed them in close quarters, and then transported them to the Western front, the disease spread. Ship transport brought infection to sailors and dockworkers, who transmitted the virus to workers on other ships bound for distant ports. Compounding the crisis was the propaganda campaign that fueled the war effort. To preserve morale, officials were reluctant to make honest statements that might alarm people. Alarm, it was feared, would generate insularity and withdrawal, and would impede the war effort. President Wilson made no public reference to the disease, and the thrust of the government's war effort was never diverted. As a result, warnings and precautions that might have been taken to save lives were ignored for a "greater good."

The worst example of the refusal of public officials to deviate from their perceived role during wartime occurred in Philadelphia, where the director of city's Department of Public Health, a political appointee who did the mayor's bidding, refused to cancel a Liberty Loan parade scheduled for September 28 despite being warned that such a large gathering would spread the disease and raise the death rate. None of the city's newspapers was willing to break the silence and issue a warning on its own. Within 10 days after the parade, the epidemic exploded from a few hundred cases and one or two deaths a day to hundreds of thousands of cases and hundreds of deaths each day. During the week of October 16, 4,597 Philadelphians died from influenza or pneumonia. Despite the numbers, city authorities and the press continued to minimize the danger. Eventually, public reassurances could no longer calm public fears. Terrified, people avoided each other on the sidewalk, ceased conversation, wore masks, stayed home from work, and became isolated. Everything grew quiet. As one North Carolina resident recalled,

We were actually almost afraid to breathe, the theaters were closed down so you didn't get into any crowds.... You felt like you were walking on eggshells, you were afraid even to go out. You couldn't play with your playmates, your classmates, your neighbors, you had to stay home and just be careful. The fear was so great people were actually afraid to leave their homes. People were actually afraid to talk to one another.... You never knew from day to day who was going to be next on the death list.... That was the horrible part, people just died so quickly.[22]

People began to refer to the epidemic as the plague or the Black Death. It was common practice to hang a piece of crepe on the front door to mark a death in a home. There was crepe everywhere— white crepe to designate the loss of a young family member, black crepe for someone middle-aged, and gray crepe for the elderly.

By the time the epidemic had run its course in 1919, it had sickened tens of millions of people in the United States and hundreds of millions worldwide. In many American cities, more than 50 percent of families had at least one family member sick with influenza. Investigators today believe the epidemic caused a death toll in the United States in excess of 675,000 (roughly 0.65% of the total population that was approximately one-third the size it is today). Worldwide death estimates have been placed at over 50 million. During the epidemic, 47 percent of all deaths in the United States from all

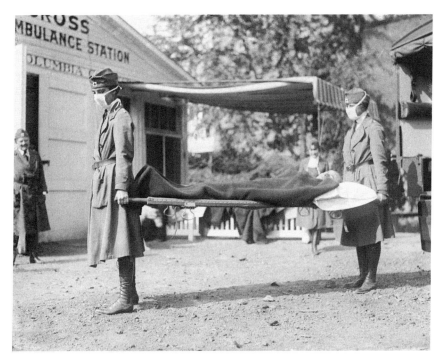

Demonstration at a Red Cross emergency station during the influenza
epidemic of 1918. (Courtesy of the Library of Congress)

causes resulted from influenza. The disease killed enough people
to lower the average life expectancy in the Unites States by more
than 10 years. John M. Barry has suggested that although slighted
as a topic in most history texts, the influenza epidemic contributed
to the "sense of bewilderment and betrayal and loss and nihilism
of the 1920s."[23]

The Red Scare

In response to the labor actions and bomb plots that followed on
the heels of the influenza epidemic, Attorney General A. Mitchell
Palmer created a new anti-radical unit in the Justice Department
called the General Intelligence Division (GID), headed by J. Edgar
Hoover. With a hefty appropriation from Congress, the new division quickly instituted a campaign to root out suspected revolutionaries. On November 7, 1919, the GID conducted raids against
radical workers in a dozen cities. After netting several hundred
alien radicals, the Justice Department saw 249 of them deported to

Russia in late December. Even more massive raids against similar suspects in 33 cities on January 2, 1920, ensnared more than 4,000 suspected subversives. Many of the break-ins and arrests were conducted without warrants, and those arrested were badly mistreated. Palmer focused on aliens rather than citizens because the wartime Alien Act (unlike the Espionage and Sedition Acts) did not require formal indictments and lengthy trials. Instead, individuals who were members of any organization that advocated the violent overthrow of the government were susceptible to immediate deportation.

Among Palmer's many supporters were various employer associations, such as the National Association of Manufacturers. For these groups, the surging fear of radicalism that came to be known as the Red Scare offered a golden opportunity to associate the entire labor movement with Bolshevism. In this reinvigorated anti-union environment, the closed shop (where union membership would be a precondition for hiring) was referred to as "sovietism in disguise," unionism as "nothing less than bolshevism [Soviet collectivism]," and strikes as "plots to establish communism."[24] Conversely, the open shop (where employers would have the freedom to hire any worker) became tied to patriotism and was commonly referred to by employers as the American Plan. Anti-unionization became linked to the long-cherished American virtue of individualism. No other single event more clearly demonstrates the effectiveness of the "open shop" campaign than the Great Steel Strike of 1919.

The Great Steel Strike

During the Progressive Era, the steel industry in the United States was dominated by the United States Steel Corporation. Together with a handful of smaller independent companies, it controlled the production of steel in the nation. Headed by Elbert H. Gary, the corporation adhered to the open shop; Gary believed that low production costs were incompatible with labor organization and that unions should be strongly resisted. Steelworkers saw things differently. During wartime, they increasingly regarded themselves as patriotic producers and expected to be rewarded for their hard work. Instead, they found themselves bound to 12-hour workdays and 6-day workweeks. Increases in the cost of living during the war pushed many workers below the minimum level of subsistence and intensified their dissatisfaction. But, as one historian noted, "[T]he dispute was not over wages, hours or conditions, but over unionism itself. Organized labor was demanding the right to represent and bargain for the steelworkers. The industry could not surrender on that point without surrendering managerial prerogatives."[25] When the government, in 1918, began to establish wartime labor-management programs, and allowed workers the right to organize into trade unions and to bargain with management (through shop committees, not union representatives), steelworkers felt they were about to realize long-denied rights and benefits. But the war had stirred up a class consciousness on the part of both labor and capital. As one observer noted, "The theoretic status of each may have been very little altered, but the intensity of the beliefs of each class has deepened."[26] The industry stood poised for an epic contest.

Hoping to take advantage of the wartime demand for workers and the sympathetic ear of government was William Z. Foster. A successful organizer for the AFL, Foster hoped to press for the immediate organization of nearly half a million steelworkers. With AFL approval, a National Committee for Organizing Iron and Steel Workers was created in August 1918, with Foster as the unofficial chief organizer. Foster began his organization drive in the region around Chicago, Illinois, and Gary, Indiana, under the banner of "eight hours and a union." As his organizational efforts gained momentum, he moved his headquarters to Pittsburgh, Pennsylvania, the country's steel manufacturing center. Organizers soon began to fan out through the steel towns of western Pennsylvania, eastern Ohio, and West Virginia. But there were problems. The influenza epidemic forced the cancelation of meetings during October and November, and the formal end of the war in November raised concerns about the future of the federal government's labor relations program.

Foster's biggest problems, however, were the difficulties organizers encountered in the steel regions. Officials passed ordinances requiring permits for labor meetings or refused to allow organizing meetings to take place. Individuals who rented halls to organizers were pressured to cancel the leases. Pro-labor speakers were arrested as outside agitators and held in jail. Such actions were violations of the rights of free speech and assembly, but taking legal action to fight them meant costly delays for the organizing campaign. Foster tried to respond to the restrictions by sending "flying squadrons" of organizers to specific areas, but they were repeatedly arrested and their meetings disrupted by the police. The steel companies kept blacklists of union agitators, discharged union sympathizers, hired detectives to infiltrate the organizing campaign, and exerted pressure on the press, police, local officials, and church leaders to impede labor's efforts. Despite the setbacks, organizers made progress. Meetings were held in vacant lots outside town limits, workers boycotted unsupportive local businesses, and organizers refused to be intimidated. During the late summer of 1919, the organizing committee presented Gary with a list of demands that included the right of collective bargaining, the eight-hour day, the reinstatement of workers discharged for their unionizing activities, and wage increases as a structure for negotiation. Gary refused to listen to them. When President Wilson rejected requests to intervene, 350,000 steelworkers voted to go on strike starting on September 22, 1919.

Foster soon found other problems to contend with. The public's reaction to the Red Scare and the persistent level of strike activity nationally allowed steel company owners to connect the organizing drive to Bolshevism, and to paint Foster as a "Red." Newspaper accounts portrayed steel districts as seedbeds of revolution. Owners heightened paranoia with their own propaganda, which charged that steelworkers were predominately immigrant radicals. The Justice Department, already on the lookout for radicals, shifted its attention to the steel centers. Excerpts were taken from Foster's earlier writings (he had formerly been a member of the IWW before joining the AFL) and reprinted to charge that he was really a syndicalist who advocated the overthrow of capitalism. Foster's refusal to disavow all of his earlier statements before a special Senate committee investigating the strike in October 1919 cost him a great deal of support and weakened the strike.

With the strike call, the anti-union campaign became increasingly repressive. Police continued to arrest organizers, forced protesters off the streets and clubbed those who resisted, broke up meetings and rallies, invaded homes, and even robbed strikers. Foster produced hundreds of sworn statements charging the police with criminal behavior, but no one was prosecuted. The sheriff of Allegheny County (Pittsburgh) deputized loyal employees of the steel companies for strike duty, prohibited the gathering of three or more people, and required that all indoor meetings be conducted in English. When strike leaders lodged complaints with the Department of Justice charging terrorism and violation of their civil liberties, Attorney General Palmer refused to intercede in what he considered a local matter. The public outside the steel districts seemed unsympathetic. Finally, after months of intimidation and harassment, an effective anti-union propaganda campaign, and refusal by the owners to accept any sort of compromise, organizers acknowledged defeat and called off the strike on January 8, 1920.

The Fight over the Peace Treaty

In the summer of 1919, in the midst of mail bombs, continued labor unrest, and escalating racial violence (race riots would break out in 25 cities and towns that summer), Wilson returned from Paris with the Treaty of Versailles. He officially presented the treaty to the Senate (which was constitutionally required to ratify the treaty before it could take effect) for deliberation on July 10. Despite many criticisms, the majority of Americans seemed to be willing to accept membership in Wilson's coveted League of Nations. Editorial opinion, polling data, and resolutions passed by 32 state legislatures, labor unions, women's organizations, farm associations, and professional societies suggested that there was a groundswell of support for the treaty.

But among those who would have a direct say in deciding the issue, there were points of contention. Liberal critics berated Wilson for having abandoned his idealistic principles (the original Fourteen Points) and for allowing the European powers to impose a harsh, vindictive peace on Germany. They also castigated Wilson for allowing European powers to reconstruct imperialistic balances of power that they believed could trigger future wars. Conservative opponents blanched at the collective security commitment under the League of Nations Covenant (Article X) and demanded greater safeguards for American independence. When politicians, both Democrats and Republicans, insisted that reservations be added to the treaty document, and Wilson just as insistently refused to accept them, the treaty languished in the Senate. By late August it became plain to the president that he was losing the fight for ratification. There were signs that the public's interest in the league was waning as well. Journalist Ray Stannard Baker remarked that the "domestic crisis [inflation, unemployment, and labor unrest] appeared to many observers even more threatening than the problems of international relationships."[27] One midwestern congressman underscored that point when he stated that he wanted to tell the president "in all good faith that now where there is one man in a thousand who cares a rap about the League of Nations, there are nine hundred and ninety-nine who are vitally and distressingly concerned about the high cost of living."[28]

Looking to break the deadlock, Wilson decided to take the issue to the people in the hope that they might pressure the Senate to ratify the treaty without amendments. To do this, he agreed to a three-week speaking tour of western states during which he would travel 10,000 miles by train. During the tour, Wilson delivered nearly 40 major addresses to enthusiastic crowds of 20 to 30 thousand and gave numerous impromptu speeches from the platform of his train. He spent hours at parades and rallies and in shaking hands with well-wishers, all in a vain attempt to save the treaty. The grueling pace of the speaking tour exhausted the 62-year-old president, who had not been in good health previously (it has been suggested that Wilson suffered from a disease of the carotid arteries that restricted blood flow to the brain, and from hypertension that aggravated the condition). On September 25, in Pueblo, Colorado, Wilson seemed close to collapse. That night he complained of blinding headaches and numbness on his left side. On the advice of his physician, the rest of the tour was cancelled, and the president's train returned immediately to Washington. Back at the White House, on October 2, 1919, the president suffered a massive stroke that almost killed him. As a result of the attack, Wilson suffered permanent partial paralysis of his left side, some loss of vision, diminished ability to concentrate, and weakened emotional control. He never recovered and remained a semi-invalid for the remainder of his term in office. The immediate consequence of the stroke was to produce a permanent stalemate over the question of America's membership in the League of Nations. On November 19, 1919, the Senate took two votes on the Treaty of Versailles (one with reservations and another without reservations) and rejected it each time. As one historian commented, "That the American people failed to protest the defeat of the grand vision of the League was a symptom of the reactionary, repressive political climate of 1919 and 1920."[29]

NOTES

1. Mark Sullivan, *Our Times: America at the Birth of the Twentieth Century*, ed. Dan Rather (New York: Scribner, 1996), 478.

2. Ibid., 521.

3. Christopher C. Gibbs, *The Great Silent Majority: Missouri's Resistance to World War I* (Columbia: University of Missouri Press, 1988), 104.

4. Sullivan, *Our Times*, 538.

5. David M. Kennedy, *Over Here: The First World War and American Society* (New York: Oxford University Press, 1980), 187.

6. Ibid., 189.

7. Gibbs, *Great Silent Majority,* 86.

8. John M. Barry, *The Great Influenza: The Story of the Deadliest Pandemic in History* (New York: Penguin Books, 2005), 130.

9. Kennedy, *Over Here,* 118.

10. Gibbs, *Great Silent Majority,* 129–130.

11. John F. McClymer, *War and Welfare: Social Engineering in America, 1890–1925* (Westport, CT: Greenwood Press, 1980), 119.

12. Maurine Weiner Greenwald, *Women, War, and Work: The Impact of World War I on Women Workers in the United States* (Westport, CT: Greenwood Press, 1980), 24.

13. Ibid., 32.

14. Neil A. Wynn, *From Progressivism to Prosperity: World War I and American Society* (New York: Holmes and Meier, 1986), 183.

15. Philip S. Foner, *History of the Labor Movement in the United States,* vol. VII, *Labor and World War I, 1914–1918* (New York: International Publishers, 1987), 225.

16. Ibid.

17. Wynn, *From Progressivism to Prosperity,* 186.

18. John Whiteclay Chambers II, *The Tyranny of Change: America in the Progressive Era, 1890–1920* (New York: St. Martin's Press, 1992), 269.

19. Kennedy, *Over Here,* 288.

20. John Milton Cooper Jr., *Pivotal Decades: The United States, 1900–1920* (New York: W. W. Norton, 1990), 324.

21. Barry, *Great Influenza,* 175.

22. Ibid., 346.

23. Ibid., 398.

24. Kennedy, *Over Here,* 291.

25. Ibid., 272.

26. Ibid., 271.

27. Page Smith, *America Enters the World: A People's History of the Progressive Era and World War I* (New York: Penguin Books, 1985), 729.

28. Nell Irvin Painter, *Standing at Armageddon: The United States, 1877–1920* (New York: W. W. Norton, 1987), 367.

29. Chambers, *Tyranny of Change,* 268.

Epilogue

For most Americans the end of the war meant the opportunity to return to everyday life as they remembered it. Historian Robert K. Murray has argued that this longing was actually the search for a life that was devoid of political and social responsibility. "As a result," he concluded, "the nation in 1919 soon found itself frustrated, not because its hopes were awry, but because it sought to fulfill them by moving backward." By refusing to look forward and confront either their new international responsibilities or the complex postwar domestic problems that confronted them, Americans "gradually sank into despair and irresponsibility." Events helped this process along. The abrupt end of the war surprised government officials, who failed to develop a formal reconversion plan. The demobilization of the military was completed as rapidly as possible, again, without effective direction from Washington, D.C. Many of the returning doughboys, eager to get home, quickly found themselves caught up in a saturated labor market, and soon became disillusioned about the hoped-for benefits of peacetime. As a result, the ex-soldier was "prone to search for scapegoats in order to rationalize his predicament."[1]

The general public felt trapped in a cycle of escalating prices. By 1919 the purchasing power of the dollar had shrunk to less than one-half of what it had been in 1913. The price of food had increased by 84 percent and clothing by 115 percent. For the average family, the cost of living was roughly 100 percent higher than it had been just five years before. This spike in inflation contributed to much of the postwar instability and unrest. The government seemed to have no desire to directly confront the problem. When organized labor saw the abandonment of wartime agreements with management, and watched as postwar price increases quickly eroded prior wage gains, they went on the offensive—demanding higher wages, union recognition, and the right to collective bargaining. Employers, unwilling to concede to unionism and collective bargaining, fought back. Taking advantage of the confusion and reaction that seemed so prevalent, they sought to destroy labor's position by linking unionism with radicalism and un-Americanism.

Contributing to the national malaise that seemed to grip America at the end of 1919 was the refusal of the Senate to accept the League of Nations. Political partisanship killed it. Meanwhile, the American people, who had embraced the reform spirit of progressivism with great enthusiasm, and then allowed themselves to be drawn into the lofty idealism of war, had become weary of any further experimentation with reform on either the domestic or international fronts. President Woodrow Wilson's stroke left the country essentially leaderless. Other individuals, such as Attorney General A. Mitchell Palmer, sought to fill the vacuum and direct a population at drift. It was in the midst of this chaotic atmosphere that the Red Scare occurred. In the intolerant year of 1919, people had become conditioned to the danger of sabotage and violence. General strikes, riots, and bomb plots had convinced many that the country was under siege by radicals. One British journalist remarked, "No one who was in the United States as I chanced to be, in the autumn of 1919, will forget the feverish condition of the public mind at that time. It was hag-ridden by the spectre of Bolshevism." Shocked by events, unnerved by the dire warnings of business groups and employer associations, and brainwashed by domestic propaganda, "the national mind ultimately succumbed to hysteria."[2] In the end, the forces of reaction won out. Civil liberties were violated, the labor movement was routed and placed on the defensive, the spirit of reform was largely abandoned, and Americans were left struggling with an overwhelming sense of disillusionment.

Despite the negative impact that the war had on the general optimistic mood that had preceded it, there is much about the Progressive Era that endured. The development of American industry would continue to impact daily life as society moved into a new decade of increasing mass consumption. The further introduction of new technologies to improve large-scale factory production, and the resultant displacement of workers, the trend toward corporate consolidation, the growing acceptance of welfare capitalism as a labor management device, and the increase in the number of white-collar and professional workers would continue. Although workers lost most of their wartime gains during the 1920s, the trend toward the eight-hour workday, the elimination of child labor, and the number of women working outside the home would persist. And though the coherence of the women's movement seemed to disappear after having won the vote, the popularized notion of the New Woman of the 1920s suggested that women continued to contest cultural boundaries based on gender. The overall pace of cultural change toward the modern that had begun during the Progressive Era quickened.

The Progressive Era's emphasis on expertise and science would continue as well. As U.S. secretary of commerce, Herbert Hoover was able to advance his political career and enhance his reputation as the architect of the new economic order through his reliance on experts and specialists to design and implement public policy. Under Hoover's direction, the Department of Commerce gathered and distributed statistics on prices, costs, volume of production, and markets. Companies were encouraged to form trade associations and share information about their business so that the entire industry rather than just their own operation could be rationalized. Investigating economic problems and pointing the way to solutions that were useful to businessmen was the mission of economists in the Bureau of Foreign and Domestic Commerce. Likewise, the Bureau of Standards under Hoover became an important scientific research institution particularly concerned with engineering standardization. The next decade would also be a time when the growing emphasis on science would publicly challenge an earlier emphasis on Scripture as the ultimate authority.

In 1920 the United States became classed as predominately urban for the first time, and although limitations on immigration would characterize the decade, the migration of black Americans from the South to the North would maintain its momentum. Though class, ethnic, and racial tensions persisted, the pattern of race relations that had shown signs of change during the war would continue along similar lines in the next decade. The increased ghettoization of the black population in the North exacerbated racial tensions and intensified economic problems, but it helped further the sense

of black community and identity. A developing black consciousness could be seen in the increase in newspaper circulation among
the black middle class, the growth of organizations such as the
NAACP, the Urban League, and the Universal Negro Improvement
Association, and the significant outpouring of black culture known
as the Harlem Renaissance. Talk of the New Negro was more com-
monplace than ever.

One other legacy of the Progressive Era was the change in the
nature of governance and the assumptions that supported that
change. The government and the courts shifted the nature of the
political debate, and in doing so established a political agenda for
a good deal of twentieth-century liberalism. A passive government gave way to an active one, more willing to assume a greater
responsibility for the welfare of the citizenry. This shift could be
seen in the passage of protective labor legislation relating to hours,
health, safety, and child labor. Similarly, the change was evident in
consumer protection—the Pure Food and Drug Act and the Federal Meat Inspection Act—and in attempts to safeguard opportunity and competition through the creation of a powerful regulatory
state that began to take form as the Federal Trade Commission, the
Tariff Commission, the Food and Drug Administration, and the
Federal Reserve Board. These new agencies seemed to invite politically active pressure groups, who now rushed to influence public
policy. Ironically, many progressives failed to anticipate that these
new regulatory commissions could become dominated by the very
powerful interest groups they were designed to control. Similar
lasting change took place in the field of law. With the decision in
Munn v. Oregon (1908), the court broke new ground by accepting
the idea of sociological jurisprudence and acknowledging that the
law would have to evolve in relation to social need.

Such institutional changes suggested that a shift in attitude
had occurred as well. Progressives generally believed that intelli-
gently directed efforts could effect changes in the environment for
the improvement of society. This new attitude inspired countless
Americans to undertake some form of citizen activism. There was a
widespread belief that the cure for the ills of democracy was more
democracy. As a result, progressives sought to empower voters by
creating new political mechanisms that would increase citizen participation in politics. The direct election of U.S. senators; the direct
primary; woman suffrage; and the initiative, referendum, and recall
were all Progressive Era creations. Here again, progressives failed to
anticipate that ballot reforms such as the initiative and referendum

could be used to advance the interests of well-organized and well-financed special interest groups with conservative or reactionary agendas.

The legacy of progressivism was a conflicted one, both in international affairs and at home. Policymakers began to chart an interventionist role in foreign policy but, with the failure to ratify the peace treaty at the end of World War I, could not achieve agreement over the nation's proper role in the world. Although the nation took many precedent-setting steps to lessen the harsh effects of unregulated industrial capitalism, it also sought to impose cultural views that reflected primarily white, Anglo-Saxon Protestant attitudes and values, and it became more openly intolerant in the process. Progressives championed social justice, but at the same time acquiesced in disregarding civil liberties. The Progressive Era was pivotal in shaping modern America with both its achievements and its failures.

NOTES

1. Robert K. Murray, *Red Scare: A Study in National Hysteria, 1919–1920* (New York: McGraw-Hill, 1964), 4, 7.

2. Ibid., 17, 16.

Glossary

Blacklist—a list of individuals who have been targeted because of unacceptable activities or behavior. A means of targeting union organizers who would be fired from a job and then denied employment elsewhere.

Board and batten—a siding for houses consisting of sheets of wide boards set vertically with smaller strips of wood used to cover the joints between the boards.

Bolshevik Revolution—the series of events in Russia in 1917 orchestrated by Vladimir Lenin that led to the overthrow of the czarist regime and the seizure of power by the Bolshevik Party.

Colliery—a coal mine and all the buildings and equipment connected to its operation.

Company town—a town in which residents are dependent on one company for employment, housing, and supplies.

Conspicuous consumption—a term made popular by Thorstein Veblen in his book *The Theory of the Leisure Class* (1899) to describe the public enjoyment of things that are known to be extravagant so that one's ability to make such purchases (wealth) is flaunted.

Cradle—a frame of wood with a row of long curved teeth used to lay wheat and other grains in bunches as they are cut.

Crop-lien system—the process by which a tenant farmer or sharecropper gave a lien (claim) on the crop to the merchant as collateral for credit granted at the country store. A term generally used to describe southern farming during the late nineteenth and early twentieth century. Such farmers often became trapped in a cycle of debt from which they never escaped (debt peonage).

Direct legislation—the power given to voters to govern for themselves using the initiative (to create law), referendum (to veto existing law), or recall (to remove an elected official from office). Such questions are placed on the ballot by petition and must be approved by the voters at the polls.

Exposé—a public exposure of wrongdoing. A term used to describe the type of article written by early twentieth-century investigative journalists known as muckrakers.

Feminist—someone who advocates social, political, and economic rights and opportunities for women.

Furnishing merchant—the owner of the country store who, under the crop-lien system, supplied goods to farmers on credit at highly inflated prices. The furnishing merchant not only controlled interest rates and prices, but also determined the type of crop to be planted and dictated the marketing of the mortgaged crop.

Graft—the act of acquiring money or gain by dishonest or illegal means, especially through the use of one's influence or position in politics.

Great Migration—the process by which nearly half a million blacks migrated from the rural South to northern cities in the period before, during, and after World War I. It transformed the racial demographic of the nation.

Harrow—an agricultural implement with spiked teeth or disks used to break up clods of dirt or level plowed land.

Jim Crow laws—laws that either restrict the franchise or segregate public facilities by race.

Laissez-faire—the idea that the government should intervene as little as possible in the conduct of the economic system.

Literary naturalism—a literary style that projects a deterministic view of human actions and life. Characters exist in a mechanical world and are victimized by outer forces or by inner impulses or instincts. Some have called the style pessimistic realism.

Muckrakers—crusading journalists who began to direct public attention toward social, political, and economic injustices. Often seen as investigative reporters, they wrote in a manner that was moralistic and sensationalistic yet, at the same time, rooted in factual accuracy.

Nativism—hostility shown toward immigrants because of perceptions that immigrants' appearance in this country undermined the existing system of values and threatened the American way of life.

Neutrality—the policy of the U.S. government to deal with belligerents on equal terms and not get involved in war. In 1914 President Wilson called on American citizens to act as neutrals as well, and to remain "impartial in thought as well as deed."

New Negro—the title of a 1925 book by Alain Locke in which he suggested that the recently transplanted African American migrant from the South possessed a new vision of hope that he or she could obtain social and economic freedom. The term was also used during World War I and immediately after to describe a more self-assertive black person.

Patronage—the political power to grant appointments, jobs in city government or police, or favors in exchange for political support. Commonly used by political machines.

Prohibition—the outlawing of the sale and manufacture of alcoholic beverages.

Scab—a worker who refuses to participate in a union strike or who agrees to take a striking worker's place on a job.

Scientific management—a system devised by engineers to improve the performance of the workforce. The most famous of the proponents of this idea was Frederick W. Taylor, who used time-and-motion studies to refashion human actions to eliminate wasted motions and advance production on the assembly line.

Scrip—a certificate given to workers in place of cash that could only be exchanged for goods at a company-run store. It allowed companies to sell goods at inflated prices and essentially made workers dependent on the company.

Scythe—a tool consisting of a long, curved blade fastened at an angle to a wooden handle for cutting grass, light grain, or hay by hand.

Segregation—the process of separating people on the basis of race or ethnicity. Usually a policy aimed at denying groups full civil rights or access to public accommodations.

Slacker—a person who demonstrated insufficient patriotism during World War I by refusing to buy war bonds, attempting to avoid the draft, or simply showing a lack of enthusiasm in support of the war effort.

Sweatshop—a workshop where a contractor might supply tables and sewing machines and then hire women to work turning cloth into finished garments for piecework wages. Driven to work fast and pressured not to make mistakes, workers would often be worn out by the exhausting labor after only a few years.

Tenement—an overcrowded apartment building of six or seven stories that was often poorly ventilated and had little or no plumbing or heating. A housing type vividly described in Jacob Riis's *How the Other Half Lives* (1890).

Tenure—holding or possessing property in return for services to be rendered. A term commonly applied to sharecropping or tenant farming.

Tipple—a structure where coal from a mine is cleaned and then loaded into railroad cars.

Trust—a term that was synonymous with monopoly and came to represent any big business. Gradually farmers, workers, small businessmen, and consumers came to use the term as a label for any large corporation that exploited workers, destroyed competition, or controlled prices or services.

WASP—a white Anglo-Saxon Protestant.

Welfare capitalism—a paternalistic program whereby employers would offer workers benefits such as higher wages, a shorter workweek, improved working conditions, pensions, health and accident insurance, paid vacations, or profit sharing in return for promises not to join a union.

Yellow Press—a term used in the 1890s to describe the newspapers of William Randolph Hearst and Joseph Pulitzer. In competing against each other for circulation, each ran sensationalistic stories to stir up public support for the Cuban rebels in their efforts to win independence from Spain. Similar to tabloid journalism today, the accounts were often exaggerated and lacked factual accuracy.

Bibliography

Argersinger, Jo Ann E. *The Triangle Fire: A Brief History with Documents*. Boston: Bedford/St. Martin's, 2009.

Asinof, Eliot. *1919: America's Loss of Innocence*. New York: Donald I. Fine, 1990.

Babson, Steve. *The Unfinished Struggle: Turning Points in American Labor, 1877–Present*. Lanham, MD: Rowman and Littlefield, 1999.

Baker, Ray Stannard. *American Chronicle: The Autobiography of Ray Stannard Baker*. New York: Charles Scribner's Sons, 1945.

Barrett, James R. *Work and Community in the Jungle: Chicago's Packinghouse Workers, 1894–1922*. Urbana: University of Illinois Press, 1987.

Barry, John M. *The Great Influenza: The Story of the Deadliest Pandemic in History*. New York: Penguin Books, 2005.

Belasco, Warren James. *Americans on the Road: From Autocamp to Motel, 1910–1945*. Cambridge, MA: MIT Press, 1979.

Bell, Thomas. *Out of This Furnace: A Novel of Immigrant Labor in America*. Pittsburgh: University of Pittsburgh Press, 1976.

Benson, Susan Porter. *Counter Cultures: Saleswomen, Managers, and Customers in American Department Stores, 1890–1940*. Urbana: University of Illinois Press, 1988.

Berger, Michael L. *The Devil Wagon in God's Country: The Automobile and Social Change in Rural America, 1893–1929*. Hamden, CT: Archon Books, 1979.

Bowers, William L. *The Country Life Movement in America, 1900–1920*. Port Washington, NY: Kennikat Press, 1974.

Brinkley, Alan. *The Unfinished Nation: A Concise History of the American People*. Vol. 2. New York: McGraw-Hill, 2010.

Brody, David. *Labor in Crisis: The Steel Strike of 1919*. Philadelphia: J. B. Lippincott, 1965.

Brody, David. *Steelworkers in America: The Nonunion Era*. Cambridge, MA: Harvard University Press, 1960.

Brody, David. *Workers in Industrial America: Essays on the Twentieth Century Struggle*. New York: Oxford University Press, 1993.

Brody, David, ed. *Industrial America in the Twentieth Century*. New York: Thomas Y. Crowell Co., 1967.

Brown, Carol. *America through the Eyes of Its People: A Collection of Primary Sources*. New York: HarperCollins, 1993.

Brown, Carrie. *Rosie's Mom: Forgotten Women Workers of the First World War*. Boston: Northeastern University Press, 2002.

Brown, Milton W. "The Ash Can School." *American Quarterly* 1 (1949): 127–134.

Cashman, Sean Dennis. *America Ascendant: From Theodore Roosevelt to FDR in the Century of American Power, 1901–1945*. New York: New York University Press, 1998.

Catt, Carrie Chapman, and Nettie Rogers Shuler. *Woman Suffrage and Politics: The Inner Story of the Suffrage Movement*. Seattle: University of Washington Press, 1970.

Chambers, John Whiteclay II. *The Tyranny of Change: America in the Progressive Era, 1890–1920*. New York: St. Martin's Press, 1992.

Cooper, John Milton Jr. *Pivotal Decades: The United States, 1900–1920*. New York: W. W. Norton, 1990.

Corn, Joseph J. *The Winged Gospel: America's Romance with Aviation, 1900–1950*. New York: Oxford University Press, 1983.

Cott, Nancy F., ed. *No Small Courage: A History of Women in the United States*. New York: Oxford University Press, 2000.

Cripps, Thomas. *Slow Fade to Black: The Negro in American Film, 1900–1942*. New York: Oxford University Press, 1977.

Cronon, E. David. *Black Moses: The Story of Marcus Garvey and the Universal Negro Improvement Association*. Madison: University of Wisconsin Press, 1969.

Crosby, Alfred W. *America's Forgotten Pandemic: The Influenza of 1918*. New York: Cambridge University Press, 2003.

Crunden, Robert M. *Ministers of Reform: The Progressives' Achievement in American Civilization, 1889–1920*. Urbana: University of Illinois Press, 1984.

Curtis, Susan. *Dancing to the Black Man's Tune: A Life of Scott Joplin*. Columbia: University of Missouri Press, 1994.

Danbom, David B. *Born in the Country: A History of Rural America*. Baltimore: Johns Hopkins University Press, 2006.

Danbom, David B. *The Resisted Revolution: Urban America and the Industrialization of Agriculture, 1900–1930*. Ames: Iowa State University Press, 1979.

Daniel, Pete. *Breaking the Land: The Transformation of Cotton, Tobacco, and Rice Cultures since 1880*. Urbana: University of Illinois Press, 1985.

Daniel, Pete. *Standing at the Crossroads: Southern Life since 1900*. New York: Hill and Wang, 1986.

Davis, Allen F. *American Heroine: The Life and Legend of Jane Addams*. Chicago: Ivan R. Dee, 2000.

Dawley, Alan. *Changing the World: American Progressives in War and Revolution*. Princeton, NJ: Princeton University Press, 2003.

Dawley, Alan. *Struggles for Justice: Social Responsibility and the Liberal State*. Cambridge, MA: Harvard University Press, 1991.

Diner, Steven J. *A Very Different Age: Americans of the Progressive Era*. New York: Hill and Wang, 1998.

Doezema, Marianne. "The Real New York." In *The Paintings of George Bellows*, edited by Michael Quick, Jane Myers, Marianne Doezema, and Franklin Kelly, 97–133. New York: Harry N. Abrams, 1992.

Dubofsky, Melvin, and Foster Rhea Dulles. *Labor in America: A History*. Wheeling, IL: Harlan Davidson, 2004.

Dubois, Ellen Carol, and Lynn Dumenil. *Through Women's Eyes: An American History*. Boston: Bedford/St. Martin's, 2009.

Du Bois, W.E.B. *The Souls of Black Folk*. Edited with an introduction by David W. Blight and Robert Gooding-Williams. Boston: Bedford/St. Martin's, 1997.

Dulles, Foster Rhea. *A History of Recreation: America Learns to Play*. New York: Appleton-Century-Crofts, 1965.

Dunne, Finley Peter. *Mr. Dooley on Ivrything and Ivrybody*. Edited by Robert Hutchinson. New York: Dover Publications, 1963.

Duster, Alfreda M., ed. *Crusade for Justice: The Autobiography of Ida B. Wells*. Chicago: University of Chicago Press, 1970.

Edwards, Rebecca. *New Spirits: Americans in the Gilded Age, 1865–1905*. New York: Oxford University Press, 2006.

Eller, Ronald D. *Miners, Millhands, and Mountaineers: Industrialization of the Appalachian South, 1880–1930*. Knoxville: University of Tennessee Press, 1982.

Elshtain, Jean Bethke. *Jane Addams and the Dream of American Democracy: A Life*. New York: Basic Books, 2002.

Ewen, David. *All the Years of American Popular Music*. Englewood Cliffs, NJ: Prentice Hall, 1977.

Filippelli, Ronald L. *Labor in the USA: A History*. New York: Alfred A. Knopf, 1984.

Filler, Louis. *Crusaders for American Liberalism*. Yellow Springs, OH: Antioch Press, 1964.

Fite, Gilbert C. *Cotton Fields No More: Southern Agriculture, 1865–1980.* Lexington: University Press of Kentucky, 1984.

Fitzpatrick, Ellen F. *Muckraking: Three Landmark Articles.* Boston: Bedford Books, 1994.

Flanagan, Maureen A. *America Reformed: Progressives and Progressivisms, 1890s-1920s.* New York: Oxford University Press, 2007.

Flower, B. O. "Frederick Opper: A Cartoonist of Democracy," *Arena* 33, June 1905, 583–593.

Foner, Philip S. *History of the Labor Movement in the United States.* Vol. III, *The Policies and Practices of the American Federation of Labor, 1900–1909.* New York: International Publishers, 1964.

Foner, Philip S. *History of the Labor Movement in the United States.* Vol. V, *The A.F.L. in the Progressive Era, 1910–1915.* New York: International Publishers, 1980.

Foner, Philip S. *History of the Labor Movement in the United States.* Vol. VII, *Labor and World War I, 1914–1918.* New York: International Publishers, 1987.

Foster, William Z. *The Great Steel Strike and Its Lessons.* New York: Da Capo Press, 1971.

Franklin, John Hope. *From Slavery to Freedom: A History of Negro Americans.* New York: Alfred A. Knopf, 1980.

Freeman, Joshua, Nelson Lichtenstein, et al. *Who Built America? Working People and the Nation's Economy, Politics, Culture and Society.* Vol. II. New York: Pantheon Books, 1992.

Fuller, Wayne E. *The Old Country School: The Story of Rural Education in the Middle West* Chicago: University of Chicago Press, 1982.

Gibbs, Christopher C. *The Great Silent Majority: Missouri's Resistance to World War I.* Columbia: University of Missouri Press, 1988.

Gilman, Charlotte Perkins. *Women and Economics.* New York: Harper and Row, 1966.

Goldman, Eric F. *Rendezvous with Destiny: A History of American Reform.* Chicago: Ivan R. Dee, 2001.

Goodwin, Lorine Swainston. *The Pure Food, Drink, and Drug Crusaders, 1879–1914.* Jefferson, NC: McFarland and Co., 1999.

Gorn, Elliott and Warren Goldstein. *A Brief History of American Sports.* New York: Hill and Wang, 1993.

Greenwald, Maurine Weiner. *Women, War, and Work: The Impact of World War I on Women Workers in the United States.* Westport, CT: Greenwood Press, 1980.

Gregory, Ross. *Modern America, 1914 to 1945.* New York: Facts on File, 1995.

Hartmann, Edward George. *The Movement to Americanize the Immigrant.* New York: AMS Press, 1967.

Henri, Florette. *Black Migration: Movement North, 1900–1920.* Garden City, NY: Anchor Press, 1975.

Higham, John. *Strangers in the Land: Patterns of American Nativism, 1860–1925*. New York: Atheneum, 1969.

Higham, John. *Writing American History: Essays on Modern Scholarship*. Bloomington: University of Indiana Press, 1970.

Hine, Darlene Clark, et al. *The African-American Odyssey*. Upper Saddle River, NJ: Prentice Hall, 2000.

Hounshell, David A. *From the American System to Mass Production, 1800–1932: The Development of Manufacturing Technology in the United States*. Baltimore: Johns Hopkins University Press, 1984.

Huggins, Nathan Irvin. *Harlem Renaissance*. New York: Oxford University Press, 1971.

Jacobs, Lewis. *The Rise of the American Film: A Critical History*. New York: Teachers College Press, 1969.

Jakle, John A., and Keith A. Sculle. *Motoring: The Highway Experience in America*. Athens: University of Georgia Press, 2008.

Johnson, Julia E. *Selected Articles on Child Labor*. New York: H. W. Wilson Co., 1925.

Kasson, John F. *Amusing the Million: Coney Island at the Turn of the Century*. New York: Hill and Wang, 1978.

Kennedy, David M. *Over Here: The First World War and American Society*. New York: Oxford University Press, 1980.

Korman, Gerd. *Industrialization, Immigrants and Americanizers: The View from Milwaukee, 1866–1921*. Madison: State Historical Society of Wisconsin, 1967.

Lauck, W. Jett, and Edgar Sydenstricker. *Conditions of Labor in American Industries*. New York: Funk and Wagnalls, 1917.

Leach, William. *Land of Desire: Merchants, Power, and the Rise of a New American Culture*. New York: Vintage Books, 1993.

Lens, Sidney. *The Labor Wars: From the Molly Maguires to the Sitdowns*. Garden City, NY: Doubleday, 1973.

Lescohier, Don D., and Elizabeth Brandeis. *History of Labor in the United States, 1896–1932*. Vol. III. New York: Augustus M. Kelley, 1966.

Litwack, Leon F. *Trouble in Mind: Black Southerners in the Age of Jim Crow*. New York: Alfred A. Knopf, 1998.

Locke, Alain, ed. *The New Negro: An Interpretation*. New York: Arno Press, 1968.

Lunardini, Christine A. *From Equal Suffrage to Equal Rights: Alice Paul and the National Woman's Party, 1910–1928*. New York: New York University Press, 1986.

Marcus, Robert D., and David Burner, eds. *America Firsthand: From Reconstruction to the Present*. Vol. II. New York: St. Martin's Press, 1995.

Martin, Tony. *Race First: The Ideological and Organizational Struggles of Marcus Garvey and the Universal Negro Improvement Association*. Westport, CT.: Greenwood Press, 1976.

McClymer, John F. *War and Welfare: Social Engineering in America, 1890–1925.* Westport, CT: Greenwood Press, 1980.

McGerr, Michael. *A Fierce Discontent: The Rise and Fall of the Progressive Movement in America.* New York: Oxford University Press, 2005.

McMurry, Linda O. *To Keep the Waters Troubled: The Life of Ida B. Wells.* New York: Oxford University Press, 1998.

Montgomery, David. "Workers' Control of Machine Production in the Nineteenth Century." *Labor History* 17 (1976): 485–509.

Mintz, Steven, and Randy Roberts, eds. *Hollywood's America: United States History through Its Films.* St. James, NY: Brandywine Press, 1993.

Murray, Robert K. *Red Scare: A Study of National Hysteria, 1919–1920.* New York: McGraw-Hill, 1964.

Nash, Gary B., Julie Roy Jeffrey, et al. *The American People: Creating a Nation and Society.* New York: HarperCollins, 1994.

Nash, Roderick. *Wilderness and the American Mind.* New Haven, CT: Yale University Press, 1982.

Neth, Mary. *Preserving the Family Farm: Women, Community, and the Foundations of Agribusiness in the Midwest, 1900–1940.* Baltimore: Johns Hopkins University Press, 1995.

Painter, Nell Irvin. *Creating Black Americans: African-American History and Its Meanings, 1619 to the Present.* New York: Oxford University Press, 2006.

Painter, Nell Irvin. *Standing at Armageddon: The United States, 1877–1920.* New York: W. W. Norton, 1987.

Parrington, Vernon Louis. *The Beginnings of Critical Realism in America, 1860–1920.* New York: Harcourt, Brace and World, 1958.

Parrish, Michael E. *Anxious Decades: America in Prosperity and Depression, 1920–1941.* New York: W. W. Norton, 1992.

Paul, Rodman W. *The Far West and the Great Plains in Transition, 1859–1900.* New York: Harper and Row, 1988.

Payne, Darwin. *Owen Wister: Chronicler of the West, Gentleman of the East.* Dallas: Southern Methodist University Press, 1985.

Peiss, Kathy. *Cheap Amusements: Working Women and Leisure in Turn-of-the-Century New York.* Philadelphia: Temple University Press, 1986.

Piott, Steven L. *American Reformers, 1870–1920: Progressives in Word and Deed.* Lanham, MD: Rowman and Littlefield, 2006.

Piott, Steven L. *The Anti-Monopoly Persuasion: Popular Resistance to the Rise of Big Business in the Midwest.* Westport, CT: Greenwood Press, 1985.

Piott, Steven L. "B. O. Flower and the Muckraking Cartoonists." *Journal of American Culture* 10 (1987): 53–58.

Piott, Steven L. *Giving Voters a Voice: The Origins of the Initiative and Referendum in America.* Columbia: University of Missouri Press, 2003.

Rader, Benjamin G. *American Sports: From the Age of Folk Games to the Age of Spectators.* Englewood Cliffs, NJ: Prentice-Hall, 1983.

Reef, Catherine. *Working in America*. New York: Facts on File, 2000.

Riess, Steven A. *Sport in Industrial America, 1850–1920*. Wheeling, IL: Harlan Davidson, 1995.

Riess, Steven A. *Touching Base: Professional Baseball and American Culture in the Progressive Era*. Westport, CT: Greenwood Press, 1980.

Rosengarten, Theodore. *All God's Dangers: The Life of Nate Shaw*. New York: Avon Books, 1974.

Rosenzweig, Roy. *Eight Hours for What We Will: Workers and Leisure in an Industrial City, 1870–1920*. Cambridge: Cambridge University Press, 1983.

Schechter, Patricia A. *Ida Wells-Barnett and American Reform, 1880–1930*. Chapel Hill: University of North Carolina Press, 2001.

Schlereth, Thomas J. *Victorian America: Transformations in Everyday Life, 1876–1915*. New York: HarperCollins, 1991.

Schwantes, Carlos A. *Radical Heritage: Labor, Socialism, and Reform in Washington and British Columbia, 1885–1917*. Seattle: University of Washington Press, 1979.

Scott, Roy V. *The Reluctant Farmer: The Rise of Agricultural Extension to 1914*. Urbana: University of Illinois Press, 1970.

Shi, David E. *Facing Facts: Realism in American Thought and Culture, 1850–1920*. New York: Oxford University Press, 1995.

Shifflett, Crandall. *Victorian America, 1976–1913*. New York: Facts on File, 1996.

Sinclair, Upton. *The Jungle*. New York: New American Library, 1960.

Sklar, Robert. *Movie-Made America: A Cultural History of American Movies*. New York: Random House, 1975.

Smith, Page. *America Enters the World: A People's History of the Progressive Era and World War I*. New York: Penguin Books, 1985.

Southern, David W. *The Progressive Era and Race: Reaction and Reform, 1900–1917*. Wheeling, IL.: Harlan Davidson, 2005.

Starr, Kevin. *Inventing the Dream: California through the Progressive Era*. New York: Oxford University Press, 1985.

Starr, Larry, and Christopher Waterman. *American Popular Music: From Minstrelsy to MP3*. New York: Oxford University Press, 2010.

Stein, Leon. *The Triangle Fire*. New York: Carroll and Graf, 1962.

Stevens, Doris. *Jailed for Freedom: American Women Win the Vote*. Troutdale, OR: New Sage Press, 1995.

Sullivan, Mark. *Our Times: America at the Birth of the Twentieth Century*. Edited by Dan Rather. New York: Scribner, 1996.

Tax, Meredith. *The Rising of the Women: Feminist Solidarity and Class Conflict, 1880–1917*. New York: Monthly Review Press, 1980.

Tentler, Leslie Woodcock. *Wage-Earning Women: Industrial Work and Family Life in the United States, 1900–1930*. New York: Oxford University Press, 1979.

Thelen, David P. *The New Citizenship: Origins of Progressivism in Wisconsin, 1885–1900*. Columbia: University of Missouri Press, 1972.

Thelen, David P. "Progressivism as a Radical Movement." In *Main Problems in American History,* edited by Howard H. Quint, Milton Cantor, and Dean Albertson. Vol. 2, 149–173. Homewood, IL: Dorsey Press, 1972.

Thelen, David P. "Social Tensions and the Origins of Progressivism." *Journal of American History* 56 (1969): 323–341.

Thomas, Brook. *Plessy v. Ferguson: A Brief History with Documents.* Boston: Bedford Books, 1997.

Timberlake, James H. *Prohibition and the Progressive Movement, 1900–1920.* New York: Atheneum, 1970.

Tindall, George Brown. *America: A Narrative History.* New York: W. W. Norton, 1984.

Traxel, David. *Crusader Nation: The United States in Peace and the Great War, 1898–1920.* New York: Vintage Books, 2007.

Van Voris, Jacqueline. *Carrie Chapman Catt: A Public Life.* New York: Feminist Press, 1987.

Wade, Wyn Craig. *The Fiery Cross: The Ku Klux Klan in America.* New York: Oxford University Press, 1987.

Ward, Geoffrey C. *Unforgivable Blackness: The Rise and Fall of Jack Johnson.* New York: Vintage Books, 2004.

Watts, Steven. *The People's Tycoon: Henry Ford and the American Century.* New York: Vintage Books, 2005.

Williamson, Joel. *The Crucible of Race: Black-White Relations in the American South since Emancipation.* New York: Oxford University Press, 1984.

Woloch, Nancy. *Muller v. Oregon: A Brief History with Documents.* Boston: St. Martin's Press, 1996.

Wynn, Neil A. *From Progressivism to Prosperity: World War I and American Society.* New York: Holmes and Meier, 1986.

Young, James Harvey. *Pure Food: Securing the Federal Food and Drugs Act of 1906.* Princeton, NJ: Princeton University Press, 1989.

Index

About the Author

STEVEN L. PIOTT is professor of history at Clarion University of Pennsylvania. He holds BA and MA degrees from the University of Utah and his PhD from the University of Missouri. His published works include *The Anti-Monopoly Persuasion: Popular Resistance to the Rise of Big Business* (1985); *Holy Joe: Joseph W. Folk and the Missouri Idea* (1997); *Giving Voters a Voice: The Origins of the Initiative and Referendum in America* (2003); and *American Reformers, 1870–1920: Progressives in Word and Deed* (2006). He is a former Fulbright Teaching Fellow at Massey University in New Zealand.